The Private Lives of Pictures

The Private Lives of Pictures

Art at Home in Britain, 1800–1940

Nicholas Tromans

REAKTION BOOKS

Published by
Reaktion Books Ltd
Unit 32, Waterside
44–48 Wharf Road
London N1 7UX, UK
www.reaktionbooks.co.uk

First published 2022

Supported by the Paul Mellon Centre for Studies in British Art

PAUL MELLON CENTRE
for Studies in British Art

Printed and bound in India by Replika Press Pvt. Ltd

A catalogue record for this book is available from the British Library

ISBN 978 1 78914 623 3

Contents

Introduction

This book asks what artworks got up to when out of the public eye. The artworks in question are pictures, defined here as portable flat images mounted in some way for display. These might range from scrappy prints tacked on a bedroom wall to famous masterpieces by household names displayed in purpose-built private galleries. You may have one or two on the walls of the room in which you are reading this. Maybe you don't often look at them very closely, yet what are they for if not to be looked at? That's the question I began with, wanting to know what this private life of the picture might be, a life lived in homes where the picture becomes a special kind of furniture. If the private gaze upon the picture was erratic, intermittent, glancing, then was the domestic picture simply a lesser version of its public-gallery counterpart? Or did this object offer more to the home's identity than just passive decoration – perhaps a means of articulating the spaces within and establishing connections with the world beyond?

THE TRIUMPH OF THE PICTURE

The period I focus on primarily is the nineteenth century, when public discourse turned decisively to address pictures rather than sculptures or frescoes (murals), which had previously been the more distinguished media. Today a visitor to a contemporary art space is as likely to find assemblages of recycled materials, video or sound projections as they are pictures, much richer environments in many ways than their picture-gallery ancestors, and indeed it can now perhaps seem a rather minimalist experience to visit a museum such as the National Gallery in London, where paintings are expected to transmit whatever message there may be entirely on their own. The picture-museum visitor is not invited to *do* very much, which perhaps helps explain the longevity of this format.[1] The picture is meanwhile alive and well in the upper echelons of the art market. There it has given precious little ground to conceptual or installation work, regardless of what might be drawing attention at biennales or the Turner Prize. Except on those rare days when works directly from the hands of one of a few world-famous sculptors turn up for sale, only a picture can really look as if it might realize eight figures at the rostrum.[2]

How did the materially humble rectangle of paint or ink trump the legacy of Greek and Roman sculpture, and the architectural magniloquence of the Renaissance and Baroque fresco painters?[3] Ask a European connoisseur of 1800 to name the great artist of the day and they would probably answer: Canova, the sculptor. And the finest things to travel to see? Go to Italy, of course, to view the frescoes of Raphael and his successors, and the sculpture of Michelangelo and Bernini. Ask again in 1900, and the answer might well have been George Frederic Watts, the visionary Englishman whose canvases had their own chapel-like rooms at the new Tate Gallery. As for an art tour, skip Italy for Madrid to see Velázquez, the ultimate master of oil on canvas. The triumph of the picture had many causes, among them Romanticism's challenges to the Classical tradition and the rise of exhibitions and of art journalism. For the British Arts and Crafts movement, the whole shift represented a tragic narrowing of industrialized society's feeling for individuality and beauty. Walter Crane lamented that 'the vast general public . . . have been taught to understand by the word "art" chiefly that form of portable and often speculative property – cabinet pictures in oil.'[4]

Even those who did not share the socialist critique of culture offered by William Morris and Crane saw that the hegemony of the picture came down in large part to its capacity to turn itself into a commodity, a currency that enabled the invention of what we now think of as the art world. When annual public exhibitions of new art became common during the later eighteenth century, their staple was the picture, which was conveniently transportable, stackable and hangable in tidy grid-like patterns. A picture easily became a standardized unit in a larger structure such as an exhibition, private collection or auction. It could be succinctly described in catalogues using the kind of spreadsheet Enlightenment taxonomy that we associate with Linnaeus and the natural world – in this case, *artist: subject: size*. The picture was well adapted too to propagate itself, its essential format meaning it was comfortably compatible with reproductive media such as the engraving, photographic print or (later) 35mm projection slide.

PROPERTIES OF THE PICTURE

In the period covered by this book (the nineteenth century and into the twentieth), many of those paper reproductions of paintings themselves became pictures, as defined here. That is, they were perhaps framed and covered in a thin sheet of glass and hung up just as if they were paintings. The definition of 'picture' adopted here is that of the term's usage in our time frame, a usage rarely set out explicitly, because – as I freely admit – it was scarcely deployed with scientific precision. Nevertheless, I contend that throughout the nineteenth century and well into the twentieth, a picture, when a physical object, was understood to be: (i) a facsimile in two dimensions of something that had been seen or might theoretically have been seen; (ii) portable, so not a mural, mosaic or fresco; and (iii) ready to be, or actually, placed securely somewhere (typically a wall) where it might fully achieve its purpose, which was to be looked at and appreciated as a single visual statement. Almost always, to satisfy this last criterion, a frame was assumed to be essential, a woodwork carcass that allowed the performative element of a picture's nature to be realized (illus. 1). The frame functioned, in relation to the picture, as the producer to its actor, a showy character often not as glamorous as it seemed, its raised decoration typically (from the nineteenth century) cast in brittle plaster rather than carved in wood, and, when seen from behind for what it really was, rather crude. How disagreeable, wrote a critic in the 1880s, to see pictures sitting on the ground with their backs to us, waiting to be hung:

> *Then* we see revealed pretence and shabbiness in little: the mean edgings of wood; the miserable tacks which keep the thin boarding in its place; the meagre strip of brown paper pasted round; the cheap bending rings; the bit of string; the square of loose glass; the glue – all making up a sort of 'rickety' combination.[5]

Such was the behind-the-scenes of a picture, and yet this was as necessary as in a theatre, for, as the author of a treatise on *The Science of Taste* laid down in 1879, 'There can be, in the true sense of the term, no picture without a frame.'[6] At the very bottom end of the Victorian art market, in the barrows of street vendors, pictures (we are told by Henry Mayhew in his survey of the London poor) were cried synecdochally as 'frames'.[7] The frame was not only a stage but a carrying case. The swell and cleft of the frame's section fitted reassuringly snugly into the hand, ready to work with you to transport the image easily to any new venue. Compare a small sculpture, and the worry involved in porting that about.

The great proponent of domestic sculpture Edmund Gosse made this a virtue, for the figurine had to engage with its environment, being more stuck in it, while 'A picture is self-contained. It carries its air and its distance and its foreground within the four walls of its frame.'[8]

Gosse was in tune with advanced opinion of the 1890s in concluding that a picture could never really commit to an interior, and the interior therefore in turn had no duty to find space for pictures. That gradual divorce is an overarching theme of this book. As the picture's hopeless solipsism became broadly accepted as an aesthetic given, late in the century, earlier rationales for pictures' presence in the home were forgotten. A key item on any such list of benefits of having pictures in your rooms had been that they made those rooms look larger through juxtaposition with the things shown in the pictures, which were most often represented as smaller than they actually were (or would have been had they existed).[9] The anthropologist Claude Lévi-Strauss wanted to define the artwork, universally, as 'un modèle réduit', and that indeed covers the majority of nineteenth-century European pictures, with the exception of many portraits and most still lifes, the latter traditionally having a more pronounced haptic character that invited the spectator to reach in and pick up the life-size objects on show.[10]

Pictures, in our sense, related to things in the world, and were popularly understood to provoke reactions comparable to the responses likely to be engendered by those things themselves. David Freedberg, towards the end of his ambitious *The Power of Images*, concludes that historians have overplayed the difference, in terms of response, that people made between things and representations of them.[11] Indeed a Victorian such as John Lucas Tupper, an intimate of the early Pre-Raphaelite circle, assumed that 'works of Fine Art affect the beholder in the same ratio as the *natural prototypes* of those works would affect him'.[12]

Moldings for Glass Frames and Pictures. Plate 154.

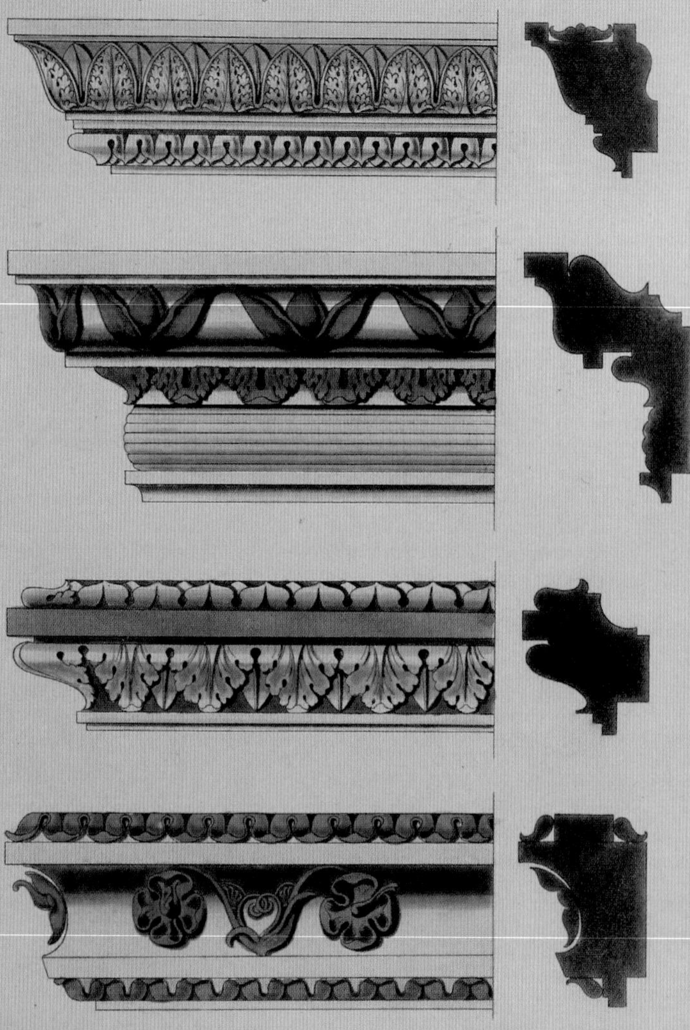

London, Published Decr. 1st. 1806, by J. Taylor, 59, High Holborn.

So through a typological understanding the world and its range of human experience could be compressed and brought home by pictures. But this book will pay very little attention to the subject-matter of pictures in the home – to the people, places and things represented therein. There already exist whole libraries of books and articles about such questions as who painted what, when and in what style. Nor is this a history of collecting: I will be referencing very few specific famous paintings. What I hope to offer here is an original contribution to the history of art by asking about the domestic picture *as such*. What exactly was it for? Where was it put? How was it used?

TIME FRAME

The Private Lives of Pictures uses examples from the later eighteenth century to the 1930s, and treats the picture in this period as homogeneous enough to establish some coherence. That claim perhaps only appears ambitious because we are so used to thinking of the history of art as a succession of styles that, in these years, moved from Joshua Reynolds to the Surrealists. But this is not a linear history; it is rather – as I shall duly explain – circular, in the form of a tour of an imaginary house.[13] On our room-by-room tour I will be bringing in examples from across this broad time frame, during which a 'picture' was – I submit – sufficiently consistent in its character to allow us to proceed meaningfully. When Virginia Woolf or D. H. Lawrence wrote

1 George Smith published his *Collection of Designs for Household Furniture and Interior Decoration* in 1808 just after Thomas Hope's book of almost the same title, borrowing much of its thoroughgoing classicism. This plate emphasizes how closely related pictures and mirrors were in terms of their roles as furniture, and how complex was the carpentry traditionally involved in creating decorative frames for them.

about the problems of the domestic picture, they were writing about a category of object not fundamentally changed since the time of William Blake. To be sure, much did change within the domestic interior over this period, from lighting technologies to wallpaper design, from plumbing to fabric patterns. But I will no more be able to retell here those narrative histories than I will be able to narrate again the headline History of Art in Britain. Again, this is not a chronological narrative but a circular one, given form by the enclosed and private spaces of the home rather than by a public museological history of art and design.

By the time that abstract painting was broadly accepted in Britain as a legitimate art form, in the 1930s, our definition of 'picture' had begun to fracture. The Modernist painting retreated yet further into its own space, decorating its own surface in pursuit of significant form, while a 'picture' was now just as often a lens-based image, a photograph, film or the flickering apparition on the television screen starting to appear in homes during that same decade. Of course, by this time the photograph had been available for getting on towards a century, and its exclusion from this book requires a word of explanation. A photographic portrait ostensibly satisfies our three criteria, but it was in practice frequently classed and located apart. Little portrait photographs were typically *placed*, not hung, even when framed, and were not generally discussed under the rubric of 'picture' in nineteenth-century texts. A framed photographic reproduction of an artwork, such as an autotype (see illus. 58), could, however, certainly be a picture because it was treated in essentially the same way as its original would have been. Again, I can hardly press this on the reader as an iron rule – there are no iron rules governing domestic interiors – and certainly one does not have to look far for examples of portrait photographs that *were* hung as pictures. But I suggest that distinct cultures and conventions surrounded the picture and the portrait photograph, sufficiently so to justify their being treated apart. To take just one example, in one of his many suggestive off-hand observations Walter Benjamin noted that portrait photograph albums were placed in emotionally cold locations such as on marble table-tops, whereas (we can add in contrast) a picture's happiest place was understood to be over the fireplace.[14]

Historians taking the long view of the picture, and of the image more generally, have seen the nineteenth century as something of an anomaly within the larger history of art. Caroline van Eck, for example, writes: 'The idea that art is made for its own sake, the notion of *l'art pour l'art,* is a 19th-century view.'[15] In earlier periods, she stresses, artworks had more openly moral and exhortatory functions. We should add to this the picture's former liturgical or ceremonial roles. It is true that what defines the picture in our period is above all the insistence that it exists to be looked at. Any further purpose was said to be inessential. In the landmark work of early British art history, *Anecdotes of Painting* (published from 1762), Horace Walpole carefully denied that pictures could any longer make a theological impact on a modern English person, however uneducated.[16] In that age of aggressive Protestant triumphalism, painting was given the green light to become the default style of performance within the new-fangled art exhibitions held, for example, at the Royal Academy from 1769. (It also gave licence to Walpole himself to indulge a catholicizing gothic taste for old pictures and much else, given that such a taste was now claimed to be harmless.) Exhibitions such as those at the Academy, and later displays at permanent collections such as the National Gallery, were, to be sure, entirely secular in their mission. Yet visits to such public displays provoked many social and psychological responses which continued older religious traditions associated with pictures.

Art historians have in recent years been stressing the capacity of social ritual and the use of texts to animate the image, not necessarily to the point of a conviction that it had actually come

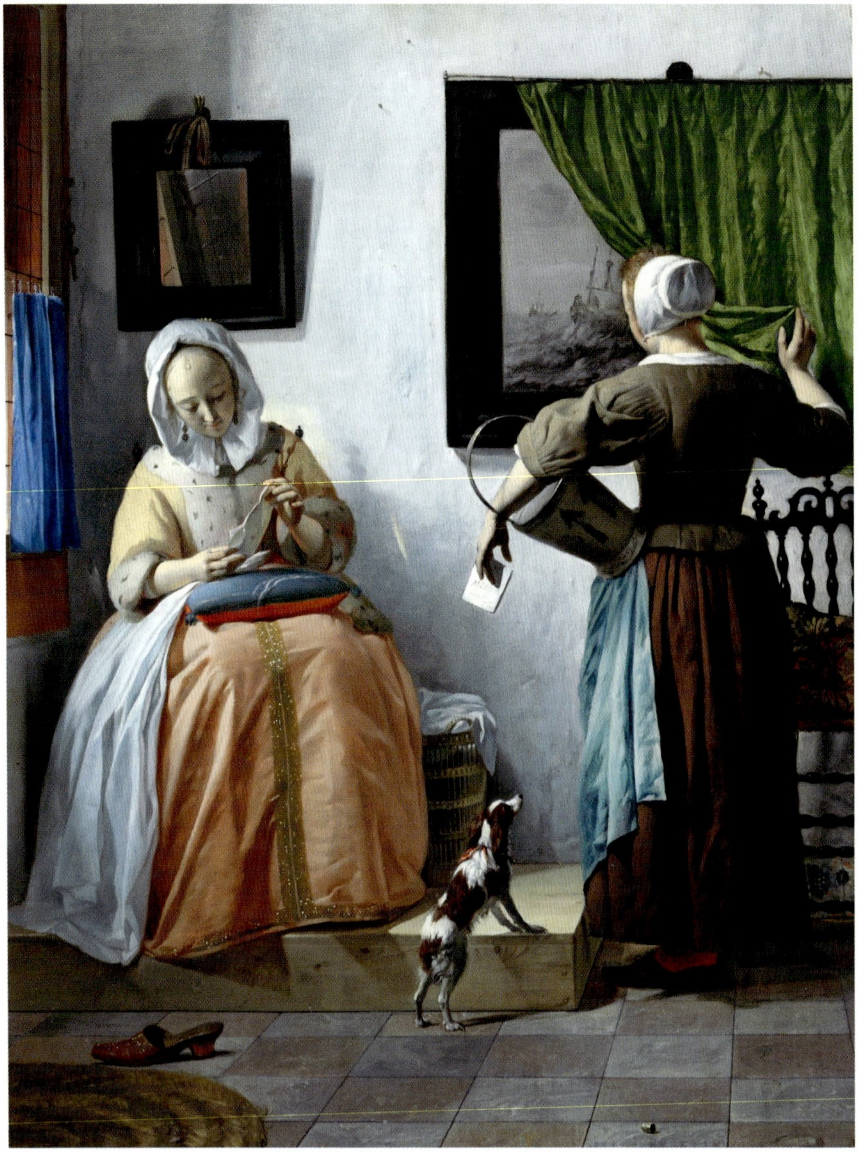

2 Gabriel Metsu, *Lady Reading a Letter*, 1660s. During the nineteenth century this painting belonged to the Hope family, and was shown in Thomas Hope's Flemish Gallery in his London house (different to the room shown in illus. 3). There, many of the pictures were mounted on hinges to allow them to be moved into better light, echoing the way the two women here manipulate a letter and a picture-curtain respectively.

alive, but in the sense of the ancient rhetorical concept of *enargeia* (vivid lifelikeness) which might involve the communal perception of certain traits of a living presence.[17] At a London art exhibition a visitor would be caught up in the crowd's enthusiasm for a novel form of realism, and be guided in their response by what they had read in the critics' reviews. Most importantly, a public picture show would have provided a *cue*, a moment at which to respond – the self-consciousness with which you push through the crowd to finally place yourself in front of Picture X. A visit to see a famous masterpiece at a great museum could without irony be described as a pilgrimage. In this book we will ask how the picture responded to the challenge of living in the home, where such cues were harder to provide. The domestic picture lived in a different flow of time, in which its capacity for lifelikeness often proved as disrupting as it did satisfying.

Anyone used to the modern idea of pictures being rectangles on the wall designed to be gazed upon is unsettled, when looking deeper into the history of art, to realize that prior to the eighteenth century pictures in the home often seem to have been difficult to see. For a start, pictures seem so very often to have been placed high in comparison to later periods. The nineteenth-century advice writers spent much time and effort encouraging their readers to bring their pictures down to eye level. Paintings were often not even pictures by our definition, being integrated into other furniture such as a chest or bed, perhaps in the most private parts of the house. Strangest of all to modern eyes is the phenomenon of the picture curtain, a device designed to prevent a picture being looked at. One can be seen in Gabriel Metsu's *Lady Reading a Letter*, of the 1660s (illus. 2). Here the etiquette of revealing the contents of a picture is elegantly set against that of reading a letter. The picture etiquette, however, remains obscure. Is the maid taking a pleasurable peek while unobserved, or only pretending to look away from the scene of a more interesting intrigue, or maybe just checking on dust levels? Curtains had two key purposes: to protect a valuable picture surface from dirt in the atmosphere and on fingers, but also to provide a temporal dimension to looking.[18] The reveal which the curtain allowed meant that seeing the picture was always a special occasion, an event presumably only to be managed by the responsible adults of the house, bringing even worldly imagery (such as the marine subject in the Metsu) into line with the sacred, devotional pictures in the home which might be looked at intensely at certain times of the day, accompanied perhaps by the lighting of a candle attached to the picture and by certain prayers.[19]

The use of devotional images in Britain, of course, declined drastically after the Reformation, but the curtain remained in use into the eighteenth century, albeit now often popularly associated either with Catholic idolatry or erotic imagery not suited for constant display.[20] Its disappearance was more or less complete as the orthodoxy of our period took hold. Victorian picture curtains became the preserve of artists' studios, gothic fiction and museum collections of light-sensitive watercolours. It was said of John Ruskin's family home in London that the Turner watercolours there were covered over on Sundays as an element of sabbath observance, but it seems rather that the Ruskins simply took their role as custodians of these works very seriously and installed blinds to remove them from the sun.[21] This was exceptional, however, and the great challenge posed to the domestic picture in our period was that – at least in theory – it was supposed always to be ready for inspection.

THE PUBLIC FORUM OF THE PICTURE

In pursuit of the private life of the picture we will often be making comparisons with the public sphere – the debates on hanging, lighting and looking prompted by the new public galleries. As

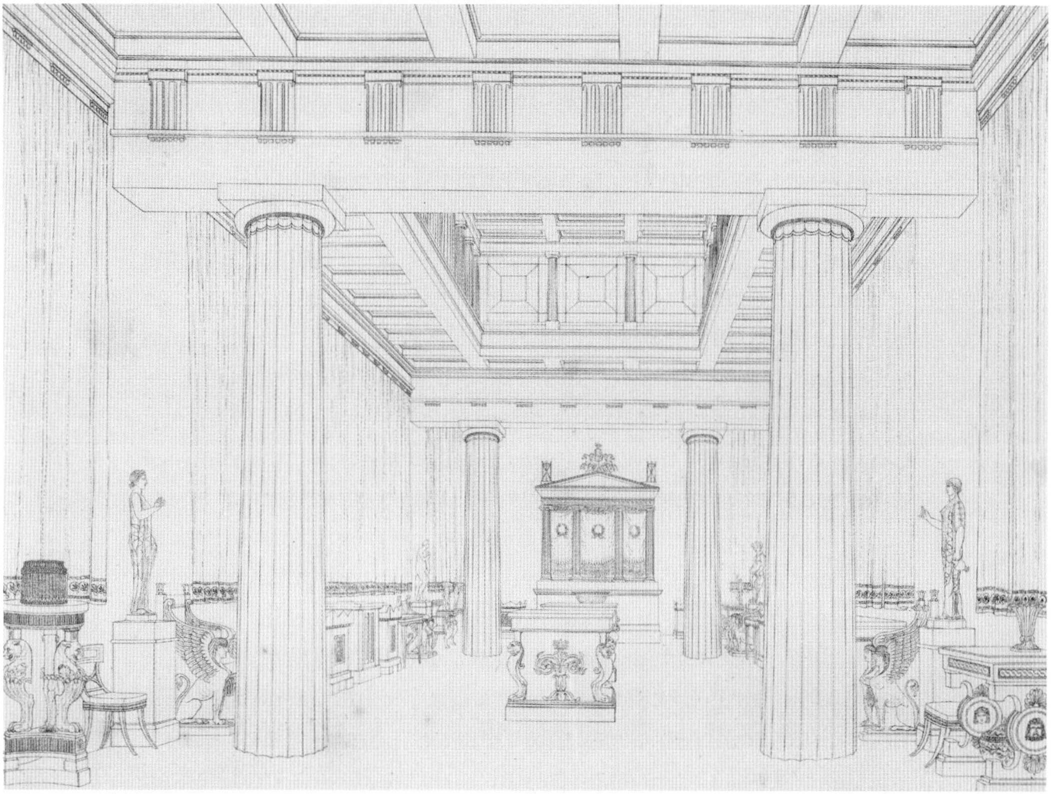

3 Thomas Hope's first picture gallery in his Duchess Street house, as illustrated in *Household Furniture and Interior Decoration* (1807). Hope was proud of the authentic Athenian details of the architecture, designed by himself. Curtains to protect the paintings from direct sunlight are here shown let down, producing the unusual sight of a picture gallery without any visible pictures. Later in the century it became accepted wisdom that sunlight was good for paintings.

our modern idea of a public picture gallery came into being in Britain early in the nineteenth century, it was accepted that such a structure should be a machine for viewing pictures, yet that machine's optimum design was not self-evident. The picture gallery open to visitors grew very much from roots in the private collection, and with rare exceptions, such as John Soane's Dulwich Picture Gallery (opened 1817), was not purpose-built as a public venue. Rather, at first, private houses in London were advertised as being open by appointment to view their owners' pictures. As one such guide of 1802 noted, the massive displacement of paintings during the French Revolution and ensuing Napoleonic Wars had blown a 'hurricane' through European houses, resettling many of the Continent's great masterpieces in British collections.[22] There was a wartime conviction that the resulting embarrassment of pictorial riches needed to be made available to a broader public in some way, and hence the opening in London of the galleries of wealthy men such as banking magnates Thomas Hope and John Julius Angerstein, and aristocrats including the Marquis of Stafford and Lord Grosvenor (illus. 3, 4 and see illus. 60).[23] 'Pictures are scattered like stray gifts through the world,' wrote the critic William Hazlitt in an essay of 1821.[24] He would have preferred the Louvre to have remained a European depot of art gathered by Napoleon's armies, but having the opportunity to visit great pictures in English houses was very much better than nothing. In fact, the opening of these private collections seems to have been somewhat curtailed in the age of Reform, as the privately run British Institution's annual exhibitions of 'deceased masters' (a novelty begun in 1813), featuring paintings borrowed from leading collectors for temporary loan, allowed those owners to be seen to be doing their public duty without opening their houses. By 1835 the *Athenaeum* was describing the Institution's shows as 'the best set-off to the illiberality with which our grand signors shut up their collections from the public – making, in fact, *close boroughs* of their collections'.[25] So the loan exhibition, the staple event of the modern art world, was invented to help overcome the awkwardness inherent in providing public access to important pictures in private houses.

Thomas Hope's house off Portland Place in London comprised some of the most perfect Neoclassical interiors of the age, and his book of 1807 describing them is in turn credited with helping invent the idea of the interior as a work of art. The house's picture gallery was an especially painstaking medley of Athenian motifs, and Hope's account of the room explains that it had wall-height drapes (as opposed to individual picture curtains) to protect the paintings but also, we assume, to allow the architecture to be appreciated unimpeded (see illus. 3). Hope later added to the house another gallery of Dutch and Flemish paintings – including Metsu's *Lady Reading a Letter* – in which many of the works were hinged along one side of their frame to allow them to be moved into the best light, an idea taken further by Hope's friend Soane in his own house (see illus. 23). The National Gallery, meanwhile, was initially established in the house of Angerstein, in one early view of which we can see that a Rubens landscape on display was fitted with a picture curtain that looks like a reminder of another age (see illus. 4).

After the completion of the new, purpose-built National Gallery building on Trafalgar Square at the end of the 1830s, experts sought to address the problem of picture display afresh, from first principles. It was required that a public gallery should no longer look like a private house, and that the pictures should not be arranged on the walls in patterns, 'upholsterer fashion', that is, as they might be in a private house.[26] But this sense that pattern-making belonged in the private sphere extended to some scepticism about the wall itself as a neutral ground. Smaller landscape paintings were thought to require side-lighting to emulate their internal effects, and thus we find Charles Eastlake, Keeper

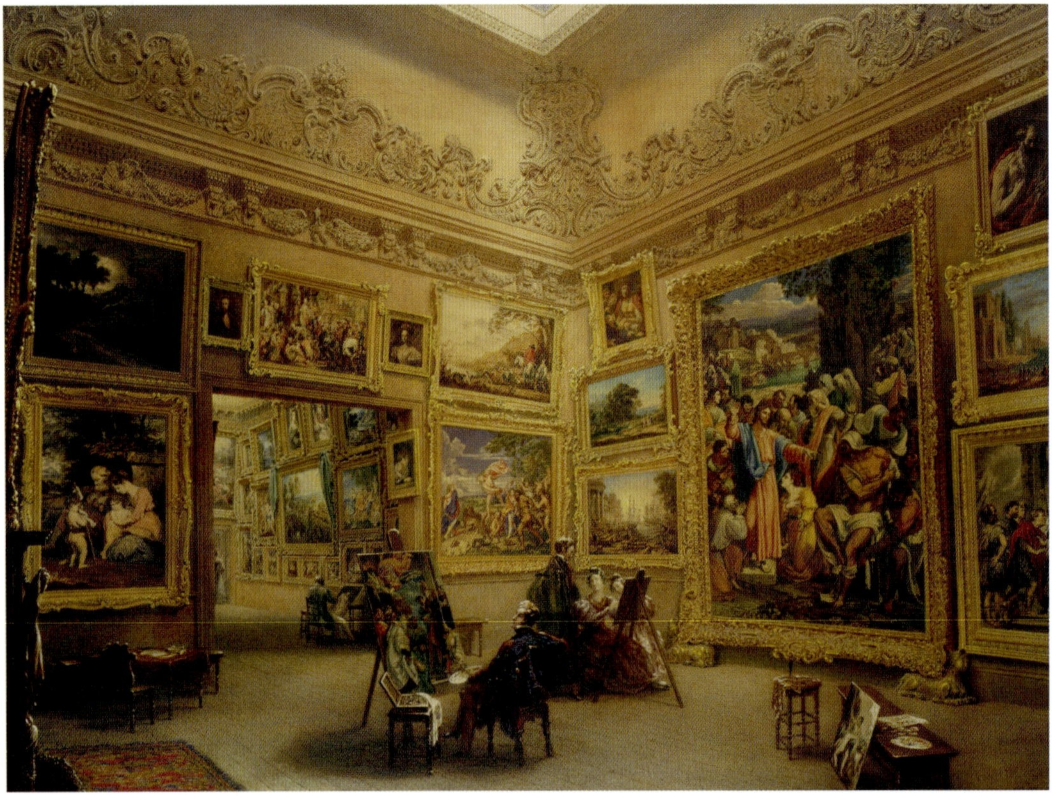

4 Until the National Gallery moved into its purpose-built premises on Trafalgar Square in 1838 the embryonic collection was housed around the corner in the former home of one of the institution's founders, the financier John Julius Angerstein. In this view exhibited by Frederick Mackenzie in 1834, copyists are conspicuous – this being understood to be a principal purpose of the new post-Napoleonic public galleries across Europe. In the further room can be made out a landscape by Rubens protected by a curtain.

of the National Gallery, proposing that such works be hung in circular fenestrated rooms on partitions radiating from a central point.[27] Ruskin, like Eastlake, was associated with the absolutely rational approach to displaying pictures and was, for example, an early advocate of the strict adoption of a single well-spaced row of paintings in public galleries, each offered as a separate experience to the visitor. Ruskin indeed sometimes affected to resent the entire category of the portable easel picture in favour of more civically constant fresco or relief sculpture.

When pondering the ideal future National Gallery in the early 1850s, this very rationality led Ruskin to some extraordinary architectural fantasies. The picture museum should be in the form of a labyrinth – all on one floor, with very long top-lit galleries and each painting in its own recess. The rooms would be so extensive as to absorb any crowd of visitors, dispersed each to his or her own picture. To complete the fantasy, all the museums of Europe would enter a mutual loan arrangement allowing drawings to be united with the paintings to which they related. These, along with any engravings of the pictures, would be made available in display cases near each painting.[28] This was an important thought experiment, as it seemed to suggest that looking with complete seriousness at pictures required architecture to be bent into strange new shapes, and further required the public to be imagined not in the messy aggregate but as a network of scholars each busy researching a single composition. It was an ideal of spectatorship based on a scholar's study extrapolated to gargantuan proportions, and was a hard one to live up to.

Ruskin's successor as art preacher to the nation, Roger Fry, continued the high-minded campaign to get people to really look hard into colours and shapes. He would take his Bloomsbury friends around London galleries, encouraging them to see in a picture's composition as much as he did, but E. M. Forster, for one, concluded that something was wrong with this approach.

This is the opening of his 1939 essay 'Not Looking at Pictures':

> Pictures are not easy to look at. They generate private fantasies, they furnish material for jokes, they recall scraps of historical knowledge, they show landscapes where one would like to wander and human beings whom one would like to resemble or adore, but looking at them is another matter, yet they must have been painted to be looked at. They were intended to appeal to the eye, but, almost as if it were gazing at the sun itself, the eye often reacts by closing as soon as it catches sight of them. The mind takes charge instead and goes off on some alien vision.[29]

Forster encourages our suspicion that looking directly at pictures was far from the straightforward process that common sense seemed to suggest it should be.

THE DOMESTIC INTERIOR

This skirting through some public picture galleries has, I hope, been useful to help focus on our main interest and the alternative to such spaces: the picture in the home. The debate over what an ideal National Gallery might look like coincided with the general perception – actual measurement is difficult – that the British were starting to consume pictures with unprecedented enthusiasm. The *Art Journal* described in 1847 a kind of middle-class version of the hurricane that had previously churned over the aristocratic collections of Europe: 'Within a very few years, we are taken, as it were, by storm; we inundate ourselves with pictures . . . our abodes are becoming museums.'[30] To hang pictures throughout the house was, felt visiting German museum director Gustav Waagen, the most impressive demonstration of 'refined taste' among the British. (Although looking at them was a challenge when 'an impatient housekeeper is perpetually sounding the note of departure by the rattle of her keys', which Waagen found to be sadly typical of grander British houses.)[31] If the British home was starting to resemble a picture museum, then it shared with public galleries a problem with architecture. As soon as a homely room became an *interior* – that is, once it had undertaken to *mean something*, to coherently express an aesthetic preference – then the picture, as a little world of its own, risked becoming an awkward resident. As already noted, Thomas Hope's 1807 book *Household Furniture and Interior Decoration* is often taken as an originating moment in the invention of the interior, and the plate in that book showing Hope's Athenian-styled picture gallery (see illus. 3) seems emblematic of the incompatibility of pictures and interiors. Either the paintings were to be appreciated or the room, but not easily both at the same time. Equally a champion of furniture such as Thomas Sheraton contrasted the dynamic, space-making capacity of chairs and cabinets with the flatly predictable perspectival schemes of conventional pictures (illus. 5).[32]

Tension with the interior, as newly conceived, was an addition to a considerable list of challenges to the private life of the picture. I have already been stressing another, namely, that the domestic picture had to make its impact without the benefits of cues that would set up the experience of looking at it to mean something at a special moment. Furthermore the picture at home risked falling foul of two dominant narratives, of academic art and reformed (rationalized) design respectively, to neither of which it seemed to have much to offer. First, the grand theory of public art, associated with the academies, championed the notion that painting at its best helped define the morality of the nation and literally united people in front of pictorial assertions of the public good. Thus, in eighteenth-century France, the highbrow critic Étienne La Font de Saint-Yenne worried that in private homes pictures had to be squeezed into such tight spaces that their own

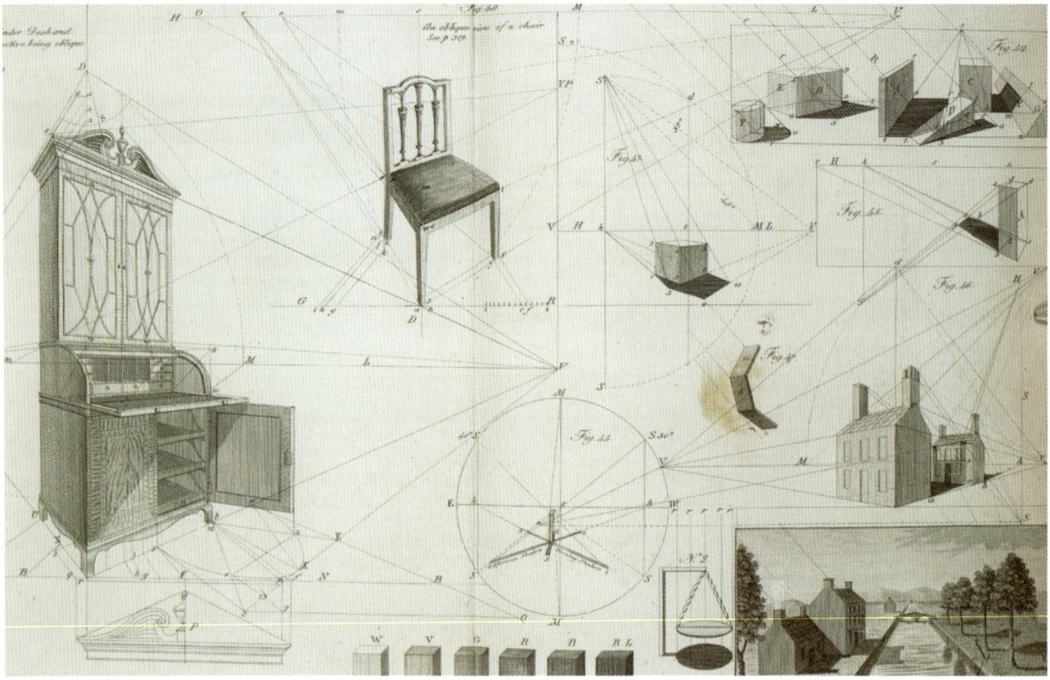

5 Thomas Sheraton's influential *Cabinet-Maker and Upholsterer's Drawing-Book* (1793) is full of exquisite designs for furniture which Sheraton was more interested in drawing than actually making. In this fold-out plate he gives the sense of furniture being dynamic, existing through real space, while a pictorial composition at the bottom right, with its rote perspective, appears lame in comparison.

imagery itself became deformed, leading to what we recognize as the rococo. The twining shapes of such art reflected the fickle narrowness of the selfish interests inevitably dominant in a private house, in contrast to the more stoutly sculptural forms of civic Classical tradition.[33] Saint-Yenne worried further that the newly mass-produced mirrors becoming popular would displace serious pictures from the home as people switched between two types of furniture already, logistically and decoratively, interchangeable

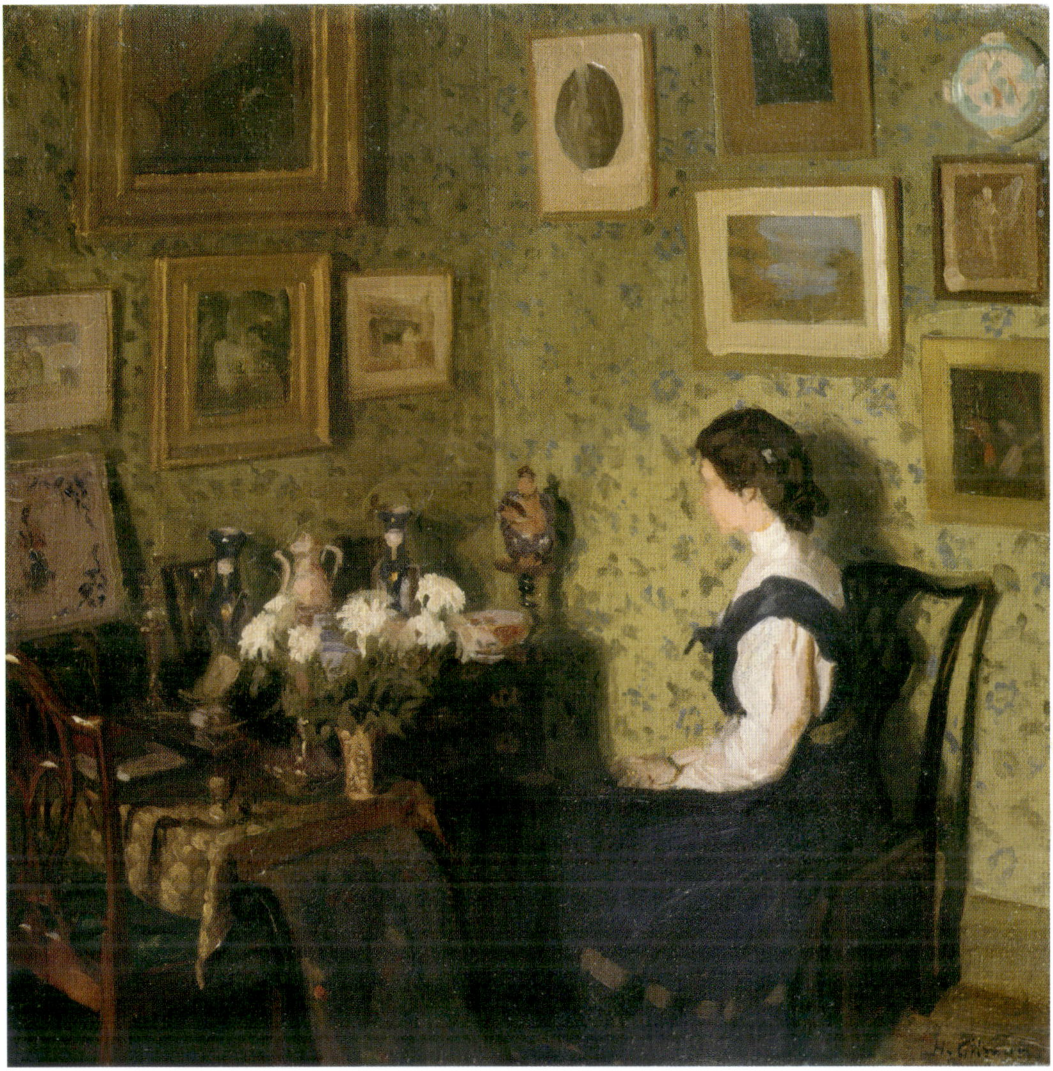

6 Harold Gilman's *Edwardian Interior*, *c*. 1907, shows his sister Irene in their family home, the rectory at Snargate in Kent. She contemplates the Asian-inspired objects on the table, ignoring the densely and rather haphazardly placed pictures on the walls.

(see illus. 1).[34] At least a mirror had associations with speculation and self-reflection, suitable modes of thought for the home to which pictures arguably had less to contribute.

Second, the rhetoric of Victorian design reform insisted that all household objects should openly declare their purpose and under no circumstances affect to look like something at odds with the identity defined by that purpose. Henry Cole, of the South Kensington Museum (later the Victoria & Albert Museum), official dispenser of design advice to the nation, is especially associated with this campaign which abhorred lifelike, perspectival two-dimensional imagery anywhere in the house other than in its proper domain, which was within a picture, the sole purpose of which was, of course, to be looked at and admired as an interesting interpretation of the look of the world.[35] A curtain over a picture became a sign of ancient superstition, and indeed it became standard Victorian domestic advice that sunlight was good for paintings – wishful thinking that, however, seemed to naturalize pictures' desire to be seen. Few if any writers on art or design in our period dared to disagree with this unexceptionably rational position: a picture was put up to be looked at. But this apparently self-evident statement in practice risked dooming the domestic picture to opprobrium because who, truthfully, really looked at the pictures in their home on a regular basis? The scene shown in Harold Gilman's *Edwardian Interior* was surely more common – the pictures reassuringly present but the occupants' attention fixed rather on the tangible, operable objects of the home (illus. 6).

The life of the domestic picture was thus not easily a happy one, its *raison d'être* threatened on all sides. Nevertheless that life was carried on regardless in countless homes across Britain throughout the nineteenth century, and the form and function of this species of furniture warrant investigation that art historians have been reluctant to undertake in the past, assuming, perhaps, that pictures either belonged in museums or were not worthy of scholarly notice. They have been deterred too, of course, by the fact that uncovering the history of any aspect of private life is necessarily challenging.

WRITING THE HISTORY OF THE PICTURE AT HOME

Earlier efforts to write accounts of the art collections of 'ordinary' people have had their roots in the radical intellectual tradition of the 1960s and '70s. There seemed then to be the possibility of a heroic history of working-class picture-owning in which images bypassed the art world of formalist qualities to take on tasks more urgent and meaningful, perhaps expressing a yearning for a more

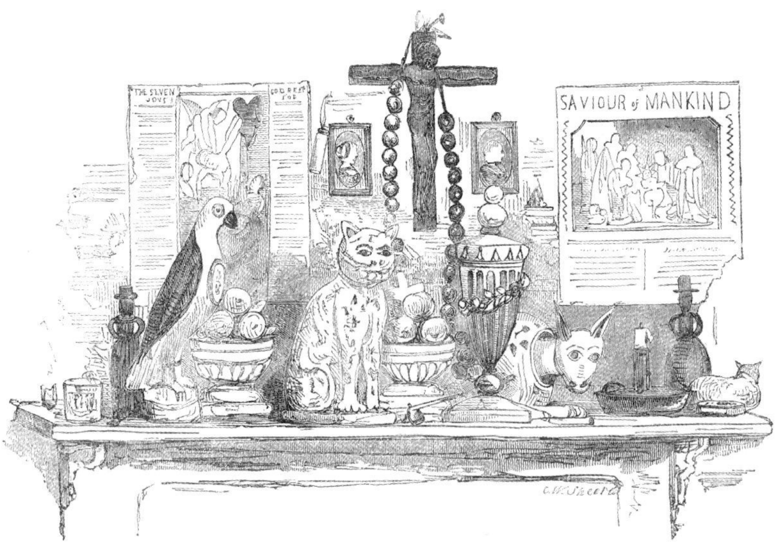

7 Religious imagery – prints combining scenes from the life of Christ with text, a crucifix and rosary – along with zoomorphic knick-knacks decorate the mantelpiece of a London slum: from George Godwin, *Town Swamps and Social Bridges* (1859).

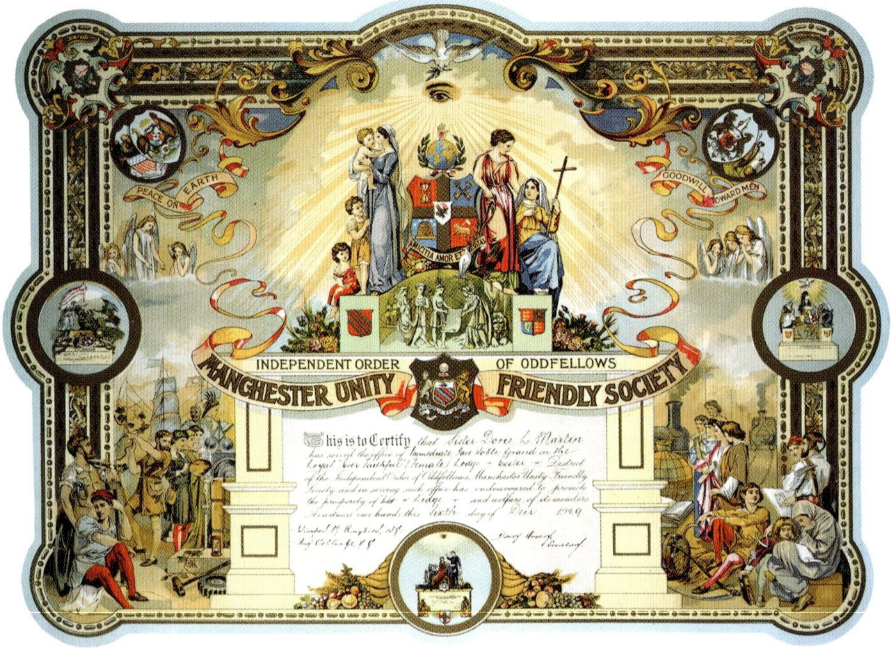

8 The rich iconographic tradition associated with trade unionism and friendly societies was an important source of pictures in working-class homes. This example, a certificate awarded to a member of a female lodge of Manchester Oddfellows in 1929, is the kind of thing a writer in the *Manchester Guardian* had in mind when in 1932 they referred to 'those amazing coloured "emblems" packed with as much hieroglyphic symbolism as a totem pole'.

self-determined culture. To be sure, there was sociological interest in the pictures of the poor going back well into the nineteenth century, when Victorian slum visitors reported in emotive terms on the use of pictures to help salvage some kind of respectable living conditions (illus. 7).[36] But the idea that such pictures might be an index of an overlooked, rich and politically potent visual culture is a twentieth-century enthusiasm. In even broader terms we should see this interest in the light of Surrealism's conviction that true art lay buried somewhere beyond the gallery – in asylums, children's paintings and, of course, the unconscious. Was the art beloved by the proletariat a form of *Art brut* – raw, unprofessionalized but more sincere? A rare success in bringing such an approach to fruition is David Halle's *Inside Culture: Art and Class in the American Home* (1993), based on interviews with art owners in New York City and Long Island, a thorough work of sociological reportage.[37] In Britain it is perhaps instructive that the research project that might have resulted in a work parallel to Halle's remained unpublished. Colin Painter's 'The Uses of Art: A Comparative Study, in Newcastle-upon-Tyne, of the Objects and Images that the Fine Art Community and the General Public Hang on the Walls of Their Homes, and Their Attitudes towards Them' (1986), based on an approach more or less comparable to Halle's, was not developed beyond a PhD thesis.[38] Its title immediately announced its aspiration to be a rejoinder to Richard Hoggart's *The Uses of Literacy* (1957), the landmark study of working-class literary culture. No study of pictures to match Hoggart's on books has appeared, although we can point to John Gorman's beautiful *Banner Bright* (1973), which was the first to fully address the kind of allegorical iconography adopted by trade unions, friendly societies and the like, which so fascinated and mystified observers of the homes of the respectable working classes in our period (illus. 8).

In researching this book I have not taken a sociological approach, mining archives to compile lists of pictures actually owned by samples of householders. That would be a labour of years that would surely produce interesting findings. In order to create a readable text evoking something of the rich history of emotion and ideas attaching to the domestic picture, I have relied more on writers who sought to generalize, pontificate, advise and chastise in regard to the home – typically, domestic advice writers, critics and novelists. More rooted in concrete cases are the illustrations, the majority of them representations of actual interiors showing

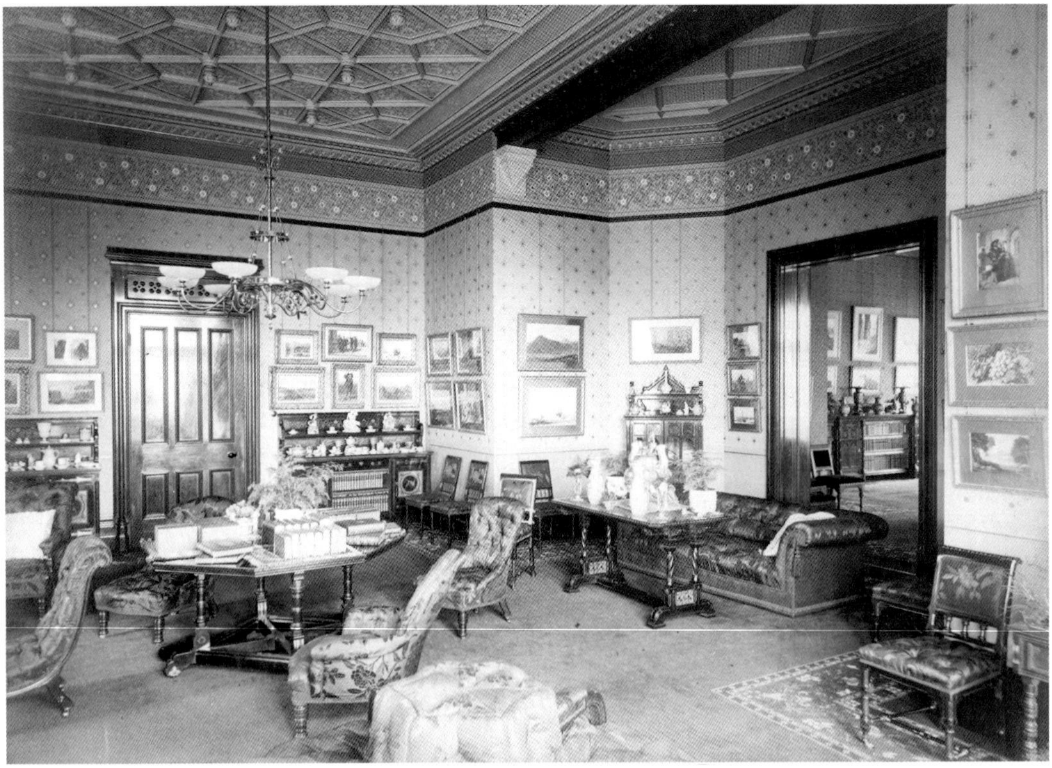

9 The drawing room at Allerton Priory, built in the 1860s by Alfred Waterhouse for Liverpool industrialist John Grant Morris. Watercolours dominate the walls, their blocked hang helping give shape to an otherwise rambling interior. Comparing this 1875 photograph with a painting of an interior of the same year (illus. 10), we can see how the latter was able to include windows, daylight and reflections in its composition, whereas the photographer of the interior typically pointed their camera away from the window, resulting in images which risked giving Victorian rooms that sense of claustrophobia of which the twentieth century never tired of complaining.

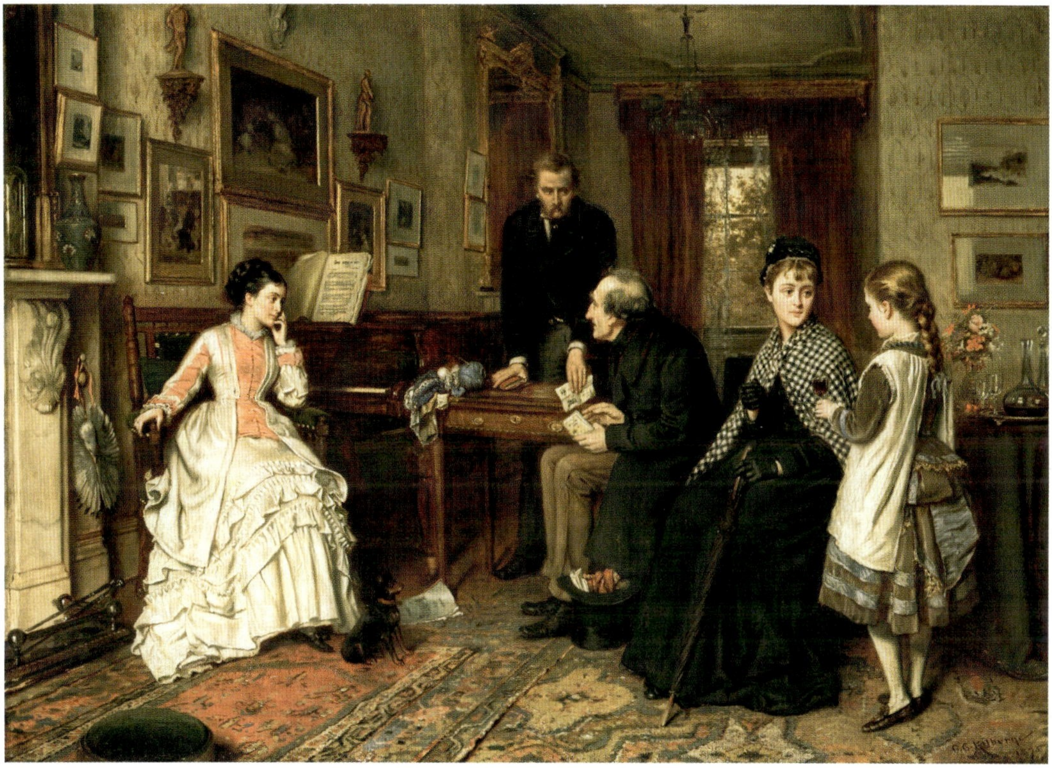

10 George Kilburne was primarily a painter of watercolours, and in this conventional oil subject of 1875 (*Poor Relations*) he seems to be demonstrating how to display such products. The adoption of both gilt and plain white mounts is used as a further means of creating pattern and symmetry in the hang.

the pictures displayed there. The rich photographic archives of Historic England and the Royal Institute of British Architects proved invaluable as representing, cumulatively, a visual record of the domestic picture since around the 1870s. For earlier decades we are more dependent on painted representations of interiors, those beguiling images in which minor artists often seem to have given the best of themselves. In George Kilburne's *Poor Relations* (illus. 10) we have the same fascination with recording an interior as we see in the work of Bedford Lemere & Co., Britain's go-to specialists in architectural photography in the decades around 1900.[39] But beyond that we are given here – in addition, of course, to the narrative scene – an idea of how a Victorian artist would have liked to see their works used in a home, and a depiction of the flow over the pictures of the natural light which photographers typically had to close out when shooting interiors (illus. 9).

The Private Lives of Pictures is structured as a walk-through of a house, with plenty of digressions prompted by issues raised by the pictures encountered in each room. I have in my mind something like this (unbuilt) design of the 1860s for a London terraced house by the architect Robert Kerr (illus. 11) – a house with an extensive but still readily recognizable list of different room types.[40] The house is narrow and tall – five storeys plus a basement accommodating the 'offices': that is, the kitchen, associated functional spaces and servants' day-rooms. On the ground floor are the entrance hall, library (often seen to be a masculine realm) and dining room for formal mealtime gatherings. On the first floor are two drawing rooms, for sitting (withdrawing) with family or guests, especially in the evenings, one of them also designated a boudoir – literally a place to sulk – a room for the lady of the house to have some real privacy. Above are the bedrooms – for the family, guests and servants, with the servants at the very top of the house, where there are also the day and night nurseries for the children. Note the presence of functional passages in the basement and upper floors, but not on those levels dominated by the reception rooms (ground and first floors). Note also that some room types are missing: for example, there is no parlour. This was the room kept for best in more modest houses, or alternatively (and paradoxically) a parlour might be found in grand houses with so many rooms that every type of designation was required to distinguish them from one another. I have not kept strictly to this plan, and

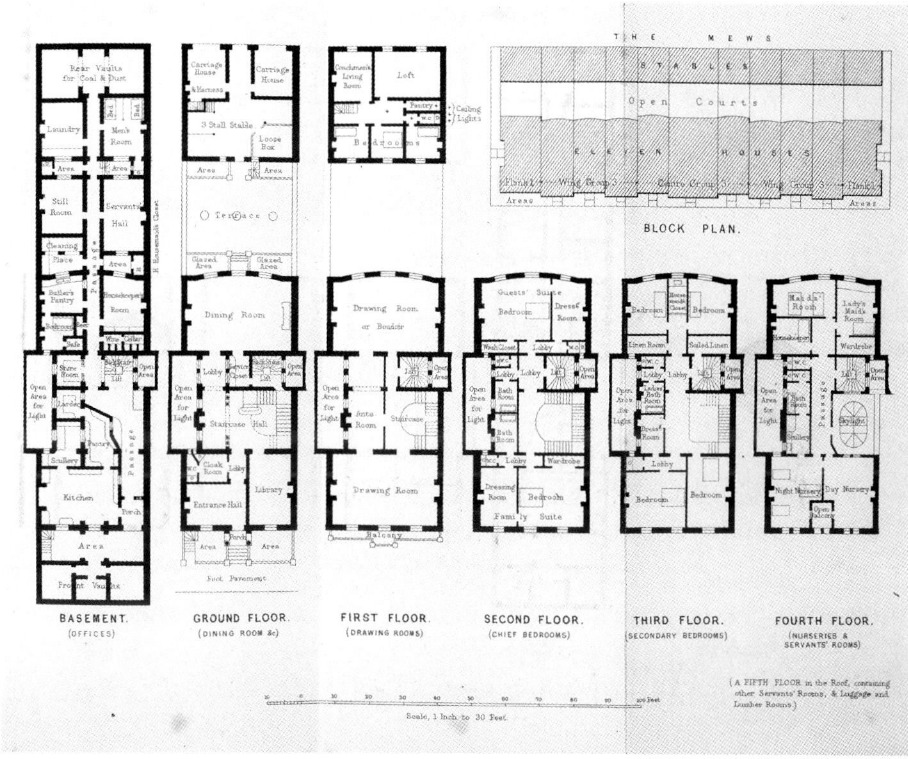

11 The architect Robert Kerr published these floor plans for a London terraced house in 1865 (in his book *The Gentleman's House*). The basement (at left) with kitchen and other functional spaces extends through the entire depth of the property, while there is a two-storey stable at the back. The dining room at ground level opens to a modest terrace. There are a pair of drawing rooms on the floor above, with the bedrooms and nursery on the upper floors.

will regularly be issuing warnings that the traditional function of a drawing room, boudoir and so on was a vague thing varying from house to house. These categories represented *ideas* of how to divide up shared space, and each category, as we will see, had its own particular requirements in regard to pictures. These ideas of space with which we are dealing are essentially Georgian, dating from the mass urbanization of the eighteenth century, and indeed Kerr's house might have been designed a couple of generations earlier: it is in a particular town-house tradition. The huge growth of the suburbs in the nineteenth century generated properties in different shapes, typically of course smaller than ours, and one central theme of the Victorian domestic advice writers was how to maintain the gendered and functional articulation of rooms configured in less generous structures.

This house of Kerr's is clearly for those some way up the social scale. Generally, the examples of homes referenced in this book are from the upper middling sorts of society, in which there would be hired help from servants who might or might not live in, and where we might find the aspirational books and magazines about the domestic arts that I cite throughout – the monthly *Art Journal*, for example, or the series of books on 'Art at Home' published by Macmillan from the later 1870s. Such improving literature, then as today, flattered its readers by imagining them to live in rather grander places than many of them must in fact have occupied. Our writers are thinking about how a home should ideally be organized, however humble. (Again, our illustrations offer more in the way of specific examples of how rooms and their pictures were in fact arranged.) Those writers are overwhelmingly British, with several American authors cited where the issues addressed were common across the Atlantic, and in a few cases European writers are introduced because they make significant points important to the discussion.

In order to think in a more focused way about the picture's relationships with its immediate physical environment, we will then proceed for most of this book room by room through our house, essentially imagined as arranged in illus. 11 but which will morph considerably in terms of location, period, shape and social class as we pursue commentary on the domestic picture. It is fundamental to our definition of it that the picture itself moves about. This is what allowed the canvases of Caravaggio gradually to become better known than the frescoes of Raphael and caused Ruskin (and many later writers) to condemn the 'contemptible piece of work' that was 'Your little Dutch landscape, which you put over your sideboard to-day, and between the windows to-morrow'.[41] Such indeed had always been the easel picture's nature. Painstaking scholarship has confirmed that pictures in seventeenth-century Dutch houses did not match their rooms in any predictable iconographic way, as Ruskin's criticism of pictures' inveterately peripatetic character suggested they never could.[42] Thus when Early Modern writers proposed menus of pictures for certain rooms, there is a definite dash of ironic humour involved in the very idea of such tidiness. In one of the earliest English-language teach-yourself art manuals, William Sanderson's *Graphice* of 1658, the hall of the house is said to be the place for pictures of peasants and milkmaids, and of fowl and fishes 'fitted for the cooking'; on the staircase, to be paused over by guests making their way up the house, should be architectural scenes and picturesque ruins. Obscene pictures, representing '*Centaures, Satyrs Ravishings, Jupiter-scapes*' should be avoided entirely, while the portraits of one's female relatives should be hung exclusively in the most private parts of the house lest 'an *Italian*-minded Guest gaze too long on them'.[43] The compiling of catalogues of which pictures suited which rooms was something of a minor genre of *belles-lettres*, at least until the more serious, largely female, writers of domestic advice became prominent from the 1860s. Invited to advise on the dispersal of pictures around an ideal villa in the 1840s, Charles Eastlake got as far as the proposed breakfast room before giving up, as such a narrowly purposed chamber 'supposes a degree of order in the family migrations to which the muses [i.e., the pictures] could hardly be expected to accommodate themselves'.[44] Nevertheless there were certain expectations around which pictures suited which types of room, conventions evolved during the seventeenth and eighteenth centuries and which the advice writers were fond of recalling, if only on occasion to squash them with their ruthless logic of household management.[45]

In the absence of any obvious body of theory describing the private lives of pictures, Chapter One is based around the nearest thing to such a theory, to be found in the earlier part of our period, to which we can point: Leigh Hunt's 1834 short essay, 'Put Up a Picture in Your Room'. Here Hunt, a journalist of Romantic and radical sympathies, opens up the fundamental questions of why and how someone might hang a picture. He considers the emotive power of the domestic picture, and emphasizes the print – a picture existing in multiple copies – as particularly suiting the home. Chapter One develops Hunt's themes to describe the fundamental issues at stake for the private lives of pictures. The tour of the house gets properly under way in Chapter Two, 'The Picture and the Interior', with an account of the pictures to be found in the dining room and drawing room – the reception rooms on the ground and first floors of our plan. These spaces had strongly characterized, and thoroughly gendered, traditional formats to which pictures were key. Yet as the design reform movement evolved into the Arts and Crafts late in the nineteenth century, the picture's position within the interior became acutely problematic: how could this over-priced commodity carrying its own space within itself ever be part of an integrated decorative scheme? Chapter Three, 'Picture Galleries of the Memory', continues the tour up the stairs, along passages and into the nursery and bedrooms. Here it is argued that, rendered an alien by the emergence of the modern interior, the picture is displaced into a gothic mode, haunting the home. This last chapter goes on to explore the picture's role in remembrance of home, both as a sign of affection for a lost paradise but also as a worryingly fickle basis of memory.

I
Put Up a Picture in Your Room

Often, when I have had a picture well framed or have hung it in the right surroundings, I have caught myself feeling as proud as if I had painted it myself.

Ludwig Wittgenstein[1]

INSIDE

'May we exhort such of our readers as have no pictures hanging in their room to put one up immediately?' So opens a short essay of 1834 by Leigh Hunt (illus. 12), a rare and much-cited attempt to investigate the special properties of the domestic picture. In this first chapter we will be taking Hunt's themes as starting-points for our own attempt to open up the private lives of pictures.

Hunt was the distinguished veteran of British radical and Romantic history, one who had served time in prison for libelling the Prince Regent and had attended the cremation of Shelley on a Tuscan beach. Hunt was the original keyboard warrior, a fiery orator and editor of the outspoken *Examiner* but, on his own account, one whose 'habits have always been of the most domestic kind' and who was 'not accustomed to be from home a day long'.[2] His notorious attack on the Regent may have been prompted by

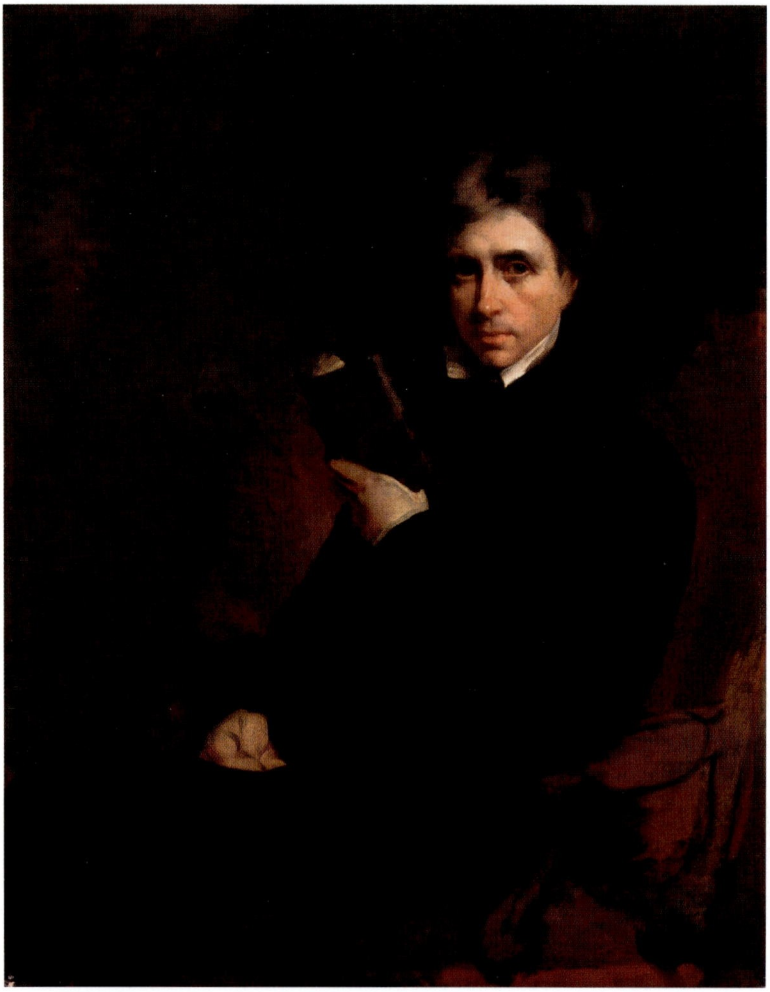

12 The author and editor Leigh Hunt in a portrait of about 1837 by Samuel Laurence. Shown a few years after the publication of his essay 'Put Up a Picture in Your Room', Hunt appears an almost clerical figure rather than the dangerous radical he had been twenty years earlier.

sympathy for colonized Ireland, but the vocabulary of the indictment was homely. The Prince was 'a libertine over head and ears in debt and disgrace, a despiser of domestic ties, the companion of gamblers and demireps'.[3] Hunt and his elder brother John, the stoic publisher of the *Examiner*, were sentenced to two years, cruelly separated to different prisons, Leigh at the Surrey County Gaol on Horsemonger Lane in Southwark and John at Coldbath Fields in Clerkenwell. Leigh Hunt was soon in sentimental correspondence with his jailer. It was to Mr Ives of the Surrey Gaol that Hunt described himself in the terms quoted above, and it was to him that he addressed requests that his wife and infant sons be permitted to join him in jail and that 'his friends be allowed to come up to his room during the daytime'. These requests were granted, and Hunt's pair of rooms in the infirmary were transformed into one of the most celebrated salons in London, welcoming, among others, Lords Byron and Brougham, and the historical painter Benjamin Robert Haydon, who somehow managed to bring with him his picture of *The Judgement of Solomon*, all 120 square feet of it, 'to relieve the tedium of confinement'.[4] The decoration of these spaces has often been recalled. Hunt's son remembered the wallpaper 'representing a trellis of roses' which elided with the 'small enclosed garden' to which a door gave direct access. Among the items of furniture were bookcases carefully adjusted to Hunt's requirements with a bust of Homer on one of them, a piano and a lute and, presiding over this makeshift home, above the mantelpiece, the portrait of his brother John.[5]

These legendary rooms, made from little or nothing, seem to offer an origin myth for the entire history of the modern interior, evocative spaces generated through only the loyalty of friends and the emotive power of a small number of things, crucial among which were pictures. For later writers on the modest 'house beautiful', the Romantics offered the prototype for tightly focused spaces of affection, and of political and poetic enthusiasm, where a little was enough.[6] Hunt's prison rooms suggested an ideal for the writer himself ever afterwards. The diminutive cosiness of his little house on Hampstead Heath, taken in 1816, was recalled with pride in the 1830s. 'I defy you', wrote Hunt to a friend,

> to live in less of a cottage than I have done; yet it has held Shelley and Keats, and half a dozen other friends in it, all at once; and they have made worlds of their own within the rooms. Keats's *Sleep and Poetry* is a description of a parlour that was mine, no bigger than an old mansion's closet.[7]

Keats had spent the night at Hampstead as a guest not long after Hunt's arrival there. A bed was made up for him in that parlour, which functioned also not only as a study-library but as a spare bedroom as well. Keats's first collection was published the following year, with a dedicatory sonnet to Hunt. The last and longest poem in the book, 'Sleep and Poetry', concludes with what has been termed an 'inventory of the art garniture of the room'.[8] Hunt's modest collection of black-and-white engravings combined an innocently erotic Arcadian imagery ('fauns and satyrs taking aim/ At swelling apples with a frisky leap/ And reaching fingers, mid a luscious heap/ Of vine-leaves') with a more austere line in portraits of poets ('Round about were hung/ The glorious features of the bards who sung/ In other ages – cold and sacred busts/ Smiled at each other') and of historical heroes, including King Alfred and the Polish patriot and anti-slavery campaigner Tadeusz Kościuszko. The inspired Keats remained awake throughout the night, during which 'there came/ Thought after thought to nourish up the flame/ Within my breast' so that in the morning he felt, despite his sleeplessness, 'refresh'd, and glad, and gay,/ Resolving to begin that very day/ These lines'.[9] These special pieces of furniture were evidently able to clarify an otherwise ambiguous space – to fix a welcoming character to a room with uncertain purpose. Well might Hunt, writing not so very much later but now with Byron, Shelley and Keats all dead, urge that we each of us should put up a picture in our room without delay.

It is a clear indication of Hunt's later status as grand old man of the Left that his 1834 article appeared in a newspaper titled simply *Leigh Hunt's London Journal*. The paper's motto – *To Assist the Inquiring, Animate the Struggling, and Sympathize with All* – perhaps suggests a mellowed temperament no longer so inclined to fire off invective as the Hunt brothers had been in the polarized and violent post-Waterloo years. But the act of putting up a picture, he suggests, is still something of urgent importance, a means of effecting that marvellous splicing together of the fireside with the great wheel of history turning beyond. As his own heroic penal history would have led his readers to expect, Hunt addresses this domestic question from the very basics up. First, where to hang your picture? In your 'principal sitting-room', answers Hunt, which on his own Romantic terms meant a space of multiple roles, all, however, centred on the life intellectual. A picture he defines 'in the child's sense, meaning any kind of graphic representation' in any medium, and he declares that a frame is not strictly necessary: 'Better put up a rough, varnished engraving, than none at all – or pin, or stick up, any engraving whatsoever, at the hazard of its growing never so dirty.' His guidance is to use the print and then replace it when necessary – anything rather than keeping fine images hidden away in portfolios: 'We are no friends to portfolios,' for 'How should you like to keep your own heart in a portfolio?' By being placed in the room, the picture takes on, suggests Hunt, the character of a special kind of looking-glass, but one that reflects back something better than our own image. Pictures will 'correct our infirmities at their mirror by modesty and reflection; in short, even the admiration of a picture is a kind of religion, or additional tie on our consciences, and *rebinding* us (for such is the meaning of the word religion) to the greatness and goodness of nature'. Living alongside pictures provides us with 'the going out of ourselves' that we might all benefit from ('Anything is better than the poor, small unit of a man's selfish self'), conduits which, we infer, were essential to the homebound person for whom 'a picture is a companion'. Hunt had a human companion in his wife, Marianne: her alcoholism and his poor nerves were among the reasons for their living such a stay-at-home life.

Hunt offered the outline of a theory of the domestic picture, aware that he was writing against the grain of academic traditions. There were few, if any, prior authorities for him to reference in pursuit of his theme. He does, however, cite his late friend William Hazlitt (illus. 13). Hazlitt was the first regular British essayist on the fine arts to write for an extensive periodical readership and a close ally of the Hunts' circle. The art world he wrote about was dominated by certain opulent private collections which, openly accessible to a greater or lesser extent, effectively constituted too Britain's public art world.

The son of a dissenting clergyman, Hazlitt's passion for painting had been fired in 1798 by seeing the magnificent Orléans collection in London, where it had been brought from Paris for sale; in the same year he met Coleridge and Wordsworth. For a few frustrated years Hazlitt sought himself to become a painter at a moment when the isolation of Britain during the Napoleonic Wars gave impetus to a pictorial naturalism resonating with the earthy language of the Lake Poets. He took advantage of the temporary truce of 1802 to visit the Louvre, and although his commitment to an alternative career in letters was soon confirmed, Hazlitt's writing was always to be informed by the bitter-sweet memory of having tried and failed to paint like the Old Masters over whose canvases he had swooned as a young man. In 'Put Up a Picture in Your Room' Hunt recalls Hazlitt outlining the effect that the picture of a morally or physically beautiful person might have. He

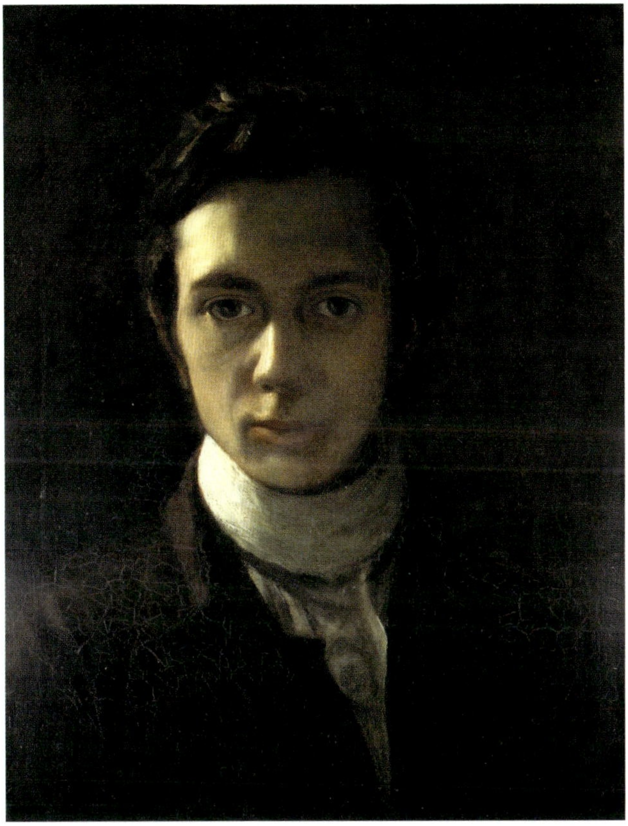

13 The critic, and onetime painter, William Hazlitt in a self-portrait from around the time of his 1802 visit to Paris to study the masterpieces of the Louvre. Hazlitt watched his own eyes and mind as they studied art – hence the continuing fascination of his writings for us.

quotes Hazlitt's art tour of Windsor Castle, during which he had been moved by Van Dyck's allegorical portrait of Venetia Digby. 'You are introduced into the presence of a beautiful woman of quality of a former age,' wrote Hazlitt, 'and it would be next to impossible to perform an unbecoming action with that portrait hanging in the room.'[10] The portrait of John Hunt which Leigh had in his prison room must have fulfilled a similar function, providing a link between the brothers across the Thames but also helping the younger, more emotional sibling keep his spirit firm.

When John Hunt was returned to Coldbath Fields in 1821–2 for having suggested that Parliament was full of 'criminals', his picture of choice for the mantelpiece of his room was lent to him by Hazlitt. This was the portrait of an elderly woman, in the manner of Rembrandt, that Hazlitt had himself painted near Manchester in 1799 – in fact, the very picture whose creation Hazlitt describes so carefully in his 1820 essay 'On the Pleasure of Painting'.[11] It cost him 'numberless sittings' and, while no marked success, it 'taught me to see good in every thing, and to know that there is nothing vulgar in nature seen with the eye of science or of true art'. The experiment is remembered in Hazlitt's essay as the moment at which his entire philosophy of art is established, as through his immersion in decayed skin he 'understands the texture and meaning of the visible universe, and "sees into the life of things"' (a quotation from Wordsworth's 'Tintern Abbey'). The picture, never finished, became for the young Hazlitt a kind of icon of realism: 'I used to set it on the ground when my day's work was done, and saw revealed to me with swimming eyes the birth of new hopes, and of a new world of objects.' The outcome was an exalted notion of the artist as one able, through their attention to nature, to escape their 'own vanity or interest, or the opinion of the world'. This pre-echoes Leigh Hunt's account of the purpose of domestic pictures and underlines the meaning of this particular picture for John Hunt during his second imprisonment, which he saw as a duty to be undergone in the cause of speaking truth to power whatever the personal costs.

But if there was something of the martyr in John Hunt, then there was something morbid too in Hazlitt's aesthetic, which exalted the idea of the artist to such unattainable heights. The painter was 'the best of scholars', a philosopher of nature and of human character, 'a critic as well as a connoisseur'; painters were worldly, gregarious and yet able always to fall back on their 'individual sagacity', and, as practitioners of a mechanical craft, also healthy, hearty and happy. It is a youthful aspirant's vision of future bliss, and once Hazlitt had renounced painting as a profession, no other living artist could ever satisfy his criteria for a true painter, and only a few from the ranks of the Old Masters. The critic Peter George Patmore visited John Hunt in prison in 1822 with Hazlitt and later wrote about the study of the old woman. Before giving it to John Hunt, Hazlitt had kept it, says Patmore, 'as a precious relic, not of his success, but of his *failure*, as a painter', just as he also treasured, in his way, two copies after Titian that he had made in the Louvre in 1802 which 'used to hang in or stand about his rooms, without frames, covered with dirt'. These Hazlitt

> cherished with a personal fondness that seemed to give them in his eyes all the character of living objects; they seemed necessary to his very existence, and to preserve, as it were, that personal identity with his early life, in the absence of which he would scarcely have felt that he continued to live at all.[12]

Set against such a melancholy philosophy of painting, Leigh Hunt's article, 'Put Up a Picture in Your Room', sounds determinedly cheerful, almost an injunction to anyone who, like Hazlitt, might be minded to leave their pictures sitting on the floor or in portfolios, to buck up and try harder to get out of themselves. While Hazlitt's studies of Titian lay about his spartan rooms, unappreciated by any but himself, and his critical aesthetic of rare genius developed in such apparent contradiction of his otherwise democratic principles, Hunt recruited the great masters of the past to his own brisk pictorial egalitarianism:

> The greatest knave or simpleton in England, provided he is rich, can procure one of the finest paintings in the world tomorrow, and know nothing about it when he has got it; but to feel the beauties of a work of art, or to be capable of feeling them, is a gift which often falls to the lot of the poorest; and this is what Raphael or Titian desired in those who looked at their pictures.

'Put Up a Picture in Your Room' was much reprinted during the Victorian age: for example, among selections from Hunt's writings, in several women's magazines and in a book accompanying the vast Manchester Art Treasures exhibition of 1857. It was cited approvingly by domestic advice authors and by campaigners seeking to bring art into ordinary homes. But surely the finest accolade awarded the essay was its being plagiarized by Samuel Smiles, of *Self-Help* fame, who silently helped himself to chunks of the text in his later book *Thrift*.[13] As a rare example of a famous writer addressing the question of art in the home, 'Put Up a Picture in Your Room' became a conspicuous reference point for later commentators on the same theme, an unexceptionable call for all to join in the picture culture that no Victorian seems to have doubted was anything but a good thing, as public art galleries multiplied across the country. As will typically happen with any piece of journalism allowed a lingering afterlife, however, much of Hunt's original sense of psychological urgency dissipated in these rehearsals. Hunt's appeal was for each of his readers to select the images to which they wished to aspire. That appeal's power lay in its assuming both the humility of each picture owner and their right to choose their own ideals. Pictures were portable, exchangeable, yet once selected and hung they functioned, for Hunt, as constants, persisting while their fickle owners too easily changed. The allegorical Venetia Digby, with her complex symbolic attributes, was scarcely going to change her character, any more than was a certain picture of a saint which, according to Hunt, was covered with a veil whenever its owner, a Catholic money-lender, 'was going to cheat a customer'.[14] This unchanging character seems allied to Hunt's lack of interest in designating specific rooms for pictures, their proper place simply being wherever the owner spends their time. If that was in an office away from home, then that room too needed a picture; in fact, it might need a minimum of two – a professional ideal, say the portrait of a senior judge in a lawyer's office, but also something to indicate broader sympathies, 'to show his client that he is a man as well as a lawyer'.

MOVING PICTURES

With Hunt's sense of the domestic picture as something to live up to, as a fixed route out of oneself, came a particular approach to the affective properties of this species of furniture. By emphasizing its persistence, its steadying function, the owner – in Hunt's theory – is not invited to displays of emotion in relation to their pictures. Who indeed would such a display be for, and what would be its cue? The aesthetic of the domestic picture was centred on its stabilizing role. This nature is brought out in a witty late eighteenth-century satire on the alternative: looking at your pictures too hard and allowing bursts of emotion to follow the encounter with each in turn. Xavier de Maistre, a young Savoyard army officer, balloonist and amateur chemist and landscape painter, spent a period under house arrest (for duelling) in Turin in 1790. He whiled away some of the time in writing a travelogue covering the entirety of the room to which he found himself confined. *Voyage autour de ma chambre* was published in French in 1794 and first translated into English in 1818 by Mrs Outhwaite. When this translation was reprinted the following year in the *New Monthly Magazine* it was claimed that

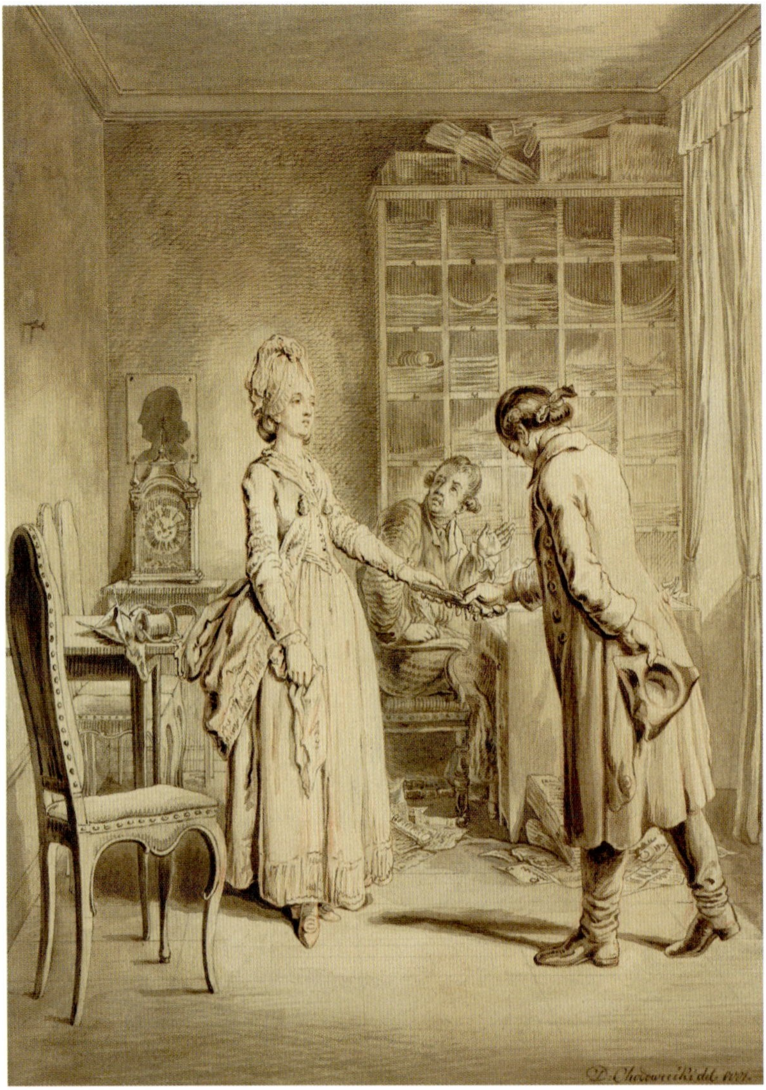

14 The illustration to Goethe's *Sorrows of Young Werther* which so infuriated Xavier de Maistre during his confinement. Werther receives from his beloved Charlotte the pistol with which he will shoot himself. Her husband Albert waves blandly from his bureau. This is the original 1770s design by Daniel Chodowiecki from which the print was derived.

'No work in the style of philosophic badinage ever merited or obtained such vast success in France and other countries.'[15] The brief narrative, in dainty chapters, takes place in a room which, being used for reading, working and sleeping, is comparable to the parlour-library-study-bedroom prepared for Keats at Hunt's Hampstead cottage. Trapped in this narrow space but unable, like Hunt, to transform it socially, the adventurous de Maistre undertakes a tour using the pictures on his walls as staging posts. Confronting the images singly, directly and in choreographed sequence has the unnerving result of cueing excessive responses. After an elaborate prelude, during which the author takes down the portrait of his mistress, dusts it and calls his servant to help him rehang it, he finally sets off.

First de Maistre encounters what can be identified, from his description, as one of Daniel Chodowiecki's illustrations to Goethe's *Sorrows of Young Werther* (illus. 14), in which the luckless hero collects from his beloved Charlotte the pistol with which he will shoot himself, while her older husband, Albert, waves him off nonchalantly. 'Many a time have I been tempted to break the glass that covers this engraving, that I might tear Albert away from the table, rend him to pieces and trample him under foot.' The tone of horror and violence within this otherwise comfortable apartment is already set. Next up are Ugolino in prison, about to eat his sons; Captain d'Assas being skewered by 'a hundred bayonets' as he bravely raises the alarm at the Battle of Kloster Kampen in 1760; an abolitionist print of an enslaved woman holding her baby under a palm tree; and finally an ostensibly idyllic scene of 'a young shepherdess tending her flock alone in the Alps' which, however, also sends our captive into a panic as he imagines soldiers advancing unseen behind her and the roar of cannons heard even here, up in the mountains, 'for no longer is repose to be found in this sad earth!' Prints after Raphael's noble portraits of himself and his mistress, Margarita Luti, calm the narrator briefly, yet he is soon dwelling on the story, emphasized in the spurious *Vita inedita di Raffaello da Urbino* recently published by Angelo Comolli, that Margarita had in effect murdered the great painter and deserved to be held responsible for the loss of all those sublime works of which the world was thereby deprived.

De Maistre offers a spoof on looking at domestic pictures too hard, and on the absurdity of having in one's home images of cannibalism, suicide and slavery, things suited possibly to book illustration or public exhibitions but hardly apt to cheer the hearth – a complaint often to be heard in the nineteenth century, although abolitionist imagery was frequently to be found in homes, especially those of Quakers, where religious scruples otherwise restricted pictorial imagery.[16] The narrator has certainly selected an especially gruelling tour through the iconography of eighteenth-century sensibility, a collection of engravings that contrasts sharply with the Arcadian classicism and portraits of poets that Keats found in Hunt's cottage. De Maistre's memorably acute responses are, of course, generated by a fictive narrative, a story, however self-consciously digressive and ironic, and so the encounters with the pictures have their due moment, their cue to receive a reaction, allowing them access to the temporal dimension so much more readily achieved in other art forms.

Poets and biographers have often made use of the idea of family portraits to help generate affective moments, but these typically required a *mise en scène* that bring picture and viewer together on a prepared cue. William Cowper's plaintive late poem 'On the Receipt of My Mother's Picture' was prompted by the sudden reappearance of a face unseen for decades, while a (far cruder) poem that appeared in the *Edinburgh Literary Journal* in 1832 (signed only 'Gertrude') imagines a bereaved son making up his mind to enter his late mother's room to gaze passionately upon her portrait.[17] The portrait of a lost loved one, when hung on the wall, can scarcely have been allowed constantly to evoke such feelings – indeed, family portraits were often seen as suited to the dining room, where those who had departed might still, through their pictures, vicariously rejoin the company. An 1869 watercolour, *Her Mother's Portrait*, by Charles Green (often an illustrator of Dickens), shows a young woman clutching her hands before the picture, a response surely impossible to replicate every time the portrait was encountered. We are told that the eighteenth-century prison reformer John Howard constantly spoke to his late wife's portrait to beg forgiveness for his harshness to her, but this was recalled by a Victorian psychiatrist posing the question of whether Howard had been technically mad or simply very eccentric.[18] To produce an acute moment of feeling, the portrait of a loved one might be taken down from the wall and held, as in the case of the picture of de Maistre's mistress. A fabulously self-conscious example appeared in the American *Sixpenny Magazine* in 1863, where the narrator ('Charles Florida') describes taking down a portrait of an early friend – an angel in man's clothing, he says – and places it on his desk, so that whenever he looks up to see it, 'a thrilling sensation runs through every fibre of my body, and it seems as though we were together again'. The writer confesses his love for young men, and his regret that his jealous wife will not have them in the house, yet it is precisely the affection he continues to feel for the man in the portrait that keeps him from falling into self-pity and bickering.[19]

The history of crying before pictures suggests that private moments during visits away from home offered the most likely occasions for tears. The classical archetype for such a moment appears in the *Aeneid* when Aeneas and his fellow refugees from Troy land at Carthage and find there a temple newly erected by Queen Dido, decorated with scenes from the war they had themselves not long left behind. Following 'ex ordine' – in proper sequence – these pictures' narration of his own story, which in actuality was yet to find its resolution, brings tears to the eyes of the hero.[20] The immediate prelude to resolution, in pictures as in music, provided the sweet spot for emotion, as in the imagery of sensibility in which we are shown suffering yet to be concluded by either redemption or tragic demise, a drama that seems to invite our own urgent response. The painter David Wilkie, a contemporary of Leigh Hunt although no political sympathizer of his, found ways to continue that eighteenth-century tradition of unfinished drama, creating domestic genre scenes with unmatched technical mastery that were among the great Royal Academy crowd-pleasers of the early nineteenth century. His biggest hit was a complicated composition showing Chelsea Pensioners and their neighbours receiving news of the outcome of the Battle of Waterloo, a commission from the victor, the Duke of Wellington, himself. Shown at the Academy in 1822, the painting required a railing to protect it from the ranks of visitors pressing close around it, an intervention prompted by the duty of care owed to the picture's famous owner. Yet the most emotive response to the picture, among the very many recorded, was that of the artist Théodore Géricault, whose *Raft of the Medusa* had recently completed a tour of Britain and Ireland and who saw *The Chelsea Pensioners* alone in Wilkie's Kensington studio. Géricault immediately grasped the subtle dramatic twist, a young woman desperately searching the text of the despatch for news of her husband's fate. A spike of anguish through the patriotic jollity, her pose and expression, wrote Géricault, 'wring tears from the eyes, however one might hold them back'.[21]

Few of us today will find it difficult to imagine such responses to portraits of our lost friends and family, or even to fictional dramas of everyday life, especially those relating to the separation of families. But the emotive potential of landscape imagery has surely waned to the point that few now would follow John Constable in saying of Gainsborough's landscapes, 'on looking at them we find tears in our eyes and know not what brings them'.[22] As a professional painter himself, Constable was, of course, scarcely a typical viewer of landscape imagery any more than was Turner, who surprised the collector John Julius Angerstein by bursting into tears before *Seaport with the Embarkation of the Queen of Sheba* by the seventeenth-century master of poetic landscape Claude Lorrain, 'Because I shall never be able to paint any thing like that picture'.[23] Not long afterwards, in 1824, Angerstein's house and his pictures became the National Gallery (see illus. 4), amplified by further gifts including the collection of Sir George Beaumont, who, however, could not bear to part, during his lifetime, with his own Claude, *Landscape with Hagar and the Angel*, which he kept with him when moving between his different homes.

Claude's pictures, with their elegiac, receding distances, were able to evoke especially emotional reactions in our period. So appealing was their vision of space and time that they were often taken as an optic for the appreciation of actual landscapes by travellers, for the laying out of parks at home and for the continued practice of landscape painting itself. Claude's pictures encapsulated the very definition of the picturesque understood as seeing the world through a picture – the world tidied into composition through being imagined as an image.[24] Yet the gently swaying recessional movements of Claude's perspectives leading to soft, setting suns were also interpreted, not as meandering back again to a viewer reassuringly confirmed in their place, but rather as not stopping, as flushing us out into the beyond. They were, in a word, sublime, as the Romantic professor of painting at the Academy, Henry Fuseli, insisted, an authority often appealed to by the landscape painter Samuel Palmer.[25] Palmer was fond of repeating the story of the maid cleaning at Cleveland House, where the aristocratic Stafford Collection was on semi-public exhibition. Found leaning on her broom before a 'wondrous Claude', she had forgotten her duties not merely to enjoy the picture but because 'she thought she was in Heaven'.[26] So the power of landscape pictures was not, as art historians have perhaps too often assumed, all about flattering the viewer's circumstances but also about the emotion inherent in the viewer's sense of separation from their horizon.

For Hazlitt, that connoisseur of disappointment, not only did the modern city of Rome – when he saw it in 1825 – fail to live up to the imagery he had arrived carrying in his memory, not least Claude's, but even the master's paintings themselves missed the mark. Coming to live at Winterslow, near Salisbury, at his new wife's cottage in 1808, Hazlitt struggled to paint his own landscapes, tacking his canvas to a tree as the ultimate rustic easel, and created a studio-study decorated with engravings after Claude. One print in particular, after *Landscape with the Arch of Constantine* (illus. 15), Hazlitt recalled some years later when describing the Grosvenor Collection, another of the capital's public-private galleries (see illus. 60), where he found the original painting: 'but this is to us a bitter disappointment. A print of it hung in a little room in the country, where we used to contemplate it by the hour together, and day after day, and "*sigh our souls*" into the picture.' No, he insists obtusely, 'This is not the picture, the print of which we used to gaze at enamoured – there is another somewhere that we still shall see!'[27] The engraving was a better version of Claude's image because its own distance from the absent original better echoed the landscape's sense of an ever deferred promised land.

Elsewhere Hazlitt has more conventional things to say about the relationship between reproductive engravings and the paintings from which they were derived – that the former were memoranda of the true 'flesh and blood' of the 'bright originals'. Yet the prints do not disappoint – they tantalize with the aura of absent paintings – while the originals, when encountered in the great private collections of London, depended for their impact on the sense of a privileged visit: 'Throw open the folding-doors of a fine Collection, and you see all you have desired realized at

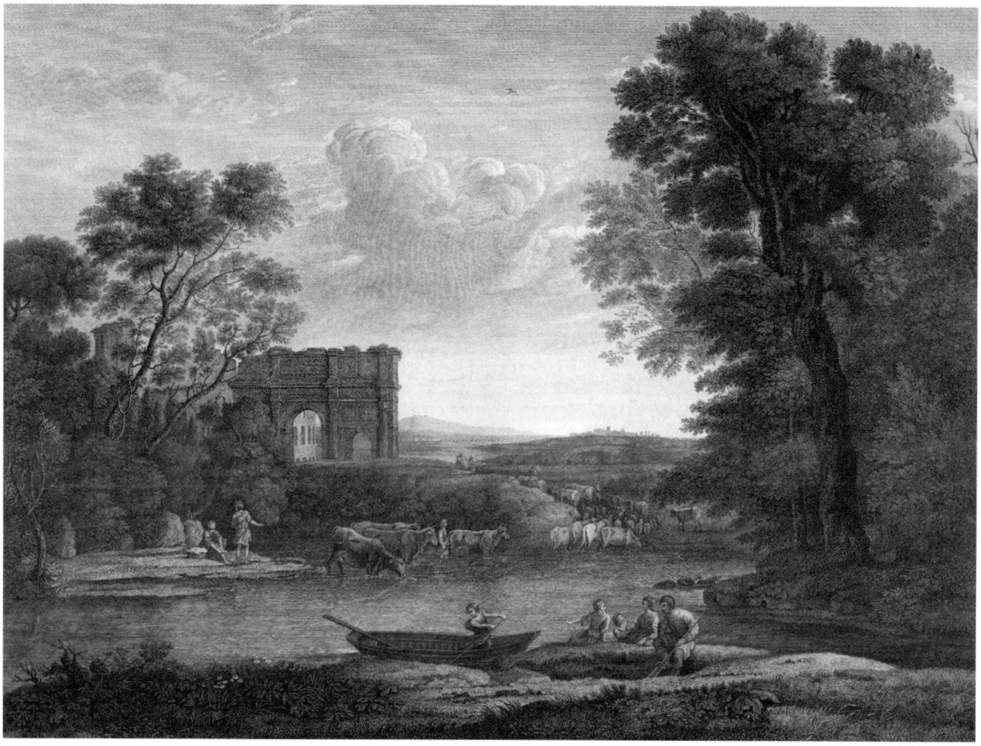

15 James Fittler's 1782 engraving after Claude's *Landscape with the Arch of Constantine*, one of Hazlitt's most treasured possessions. The original seventeenth-century painting was a capriccio in which a famous monument of ancient Rome was imagined as reappearing mysteriously out in the Campagna.

a blow.' Realized, but not possessed, for Hazlitt claims to pity the lordly owners of these great paintings for whom the pictures' glories must inevitably become quotidian. Those lords should in fact themselves envy the visitor of taste, able for a precious brief measure of time to enjoy 'the true and exclusive enjoyment' of the pictures' beauty.[28] This enjoyment entailed the suppression of all proprietary desire, including noting down facts such as title, location, measurements and the like, for even this was 'pilfering something from the pictures'.[29] For Hunt, pictures in the home were signposts out of it, links to other places and people, forming a network that mapped a self broader than the one sat indoors. But not, it seems, for Hazlitt, whose sighs were directed back 'into the picture' and who was able to form only complicated relationships with those things – Rome, the original oil painting, the pictures of Claude's modern follower Turner – to which his favourite engraving ostensibly pointed.

A biographically minded historian of Romanticism might simply say that Hunt was gregarious and Hazlitt notoriously awkward. This is certainly true, and Hazlitt's philosophy of pictures had little to do with any public discourse or larger communion.[30] His more private aesthetic has some resonances with pre-Enlightenment practices of picture-looking. For example, his apparently perverse preference, in Claude – the past master valued above all for his ethereal, glowing perspectives – for a relatively flat engraved image over the hues of the oil itself, recalls the phenomenon, identified in Italian Renaissance households, of sacred images that eschewed pronounced perspectival depth. Scholars have suggested this relates to an instinct to want to trace meaning across the plane of the picture surface, a habit ingrained through the devotional use of prints, sometimes keyed to texts that guide a metaphorical or physical finger over the paper in pursuit of a spiritual narrative, especially the sufferings of the saints and the Passion of Christ.[31] We have noted Hazlitt's habit of placing his own painted studies on the floor rather than hanging them, and indeed his nailing his landscapes to trees when first executing them. Such habits suggest Hazlitt's need to dematerialize pictures, to void their possessable substance as furniture in order to arrive at 'a set of chosen images, a stream of pleasant thoughts passing through the mind' – his ultimate definition of pictures (in 'On a Landscape of Nicolas Poussin'). 'It is a luxury to have the walls of our rooms hung round with them', he goes on to say in the same essay, but 'no less so to have such a gallery in the mind'.[32] Hazlitt knew how to enjoy a visit to a collection of pictures, in one of the grand private houses of London or at the loan exhibitions of the British Institution. We imagine him entering such rooms feeling as if he wanted, as was said of Coleridge, to 'shake hands with his pictures'.[33] Yet he was content to remain a visitor, and to find fuller satisfaction at home with his prints and distilled mental gallery.

The heirs to Hazlitt's mental gallery were to be found among the aesthetes of the later nineteenth century. Hunt's more social explanation of the reasons to put up a picture, on the other hand, was echoed by many Victorian writers whose readers were imagined to devote their lives to their homes: for example, Robert Kemp Philp, Chartist and compiler of domestic advice literature. In his *Lady's Every-Day Book; A Practical Guide in the Elegant Arts and Daily Difficulties of Domestic Life* of the 1870s, between entries on controlling beetles and making gruel, can be found guidance on pictures, which should be 'such as we can truly sympathise with' and thereby 'have a moral effect, and at times prevent our going astray by their silent monitions'.[34] But before moving on to meet those Victorians, first we will look more closely at the question of physical intimacy with the domestic picture – and at its fundamental relationship to a room – by asking: how exactly was it that one was supposed to put up a picture?

PUTTING UP THE PICTURE

If a picture is of its nature peripatetic, designed for easy manoeuvrability, then to fix it in place immediately creates a point of tension – literally, in the strain of physical suspension, and aesthetically through the awareness that the picture may not stay put. For Leigh Hunt the essence of the domestic picture was that it was a constant, projecting its identity resolutely, whatever the emotions of its owner. That constancy was entirely compatible with, indeed dependent on, the picture's urge to keep moving: it demonstrated its constancy by being the same wherever it went. As the mechanics of picture-hanging became a lively field of innovation and experiment from around 1800, many solutions were proposed to establish a balance between fixity and flux.

We should start by recognizing that the supposed standard means of knocking a nail into a wall and suspending a picture from it with string or wire was not so straightforward. Finding a timber stud behind the plaster was assumed to be necessary by some guides, and a series of aborted attempts to find one through brittle plaster might easily end in a pockmarked wall. Then, beyond the individual picture's place within any kind of 'hang' or arrangement, there was the problem: to tilt or not to tilt? Long tradition suggested anything large fixed to a wall, a mirror or picture, should tilt forwards, and this practice was adopted for the upper tier or tiers of pictures at the new, closely hung London exhibitions of pictures beginning in the 1750s and '60s. In the case of public shows, tilting pictures placed high up on the walls for greater visibility was an obvious solution, maintained at Somerset House, the Royal Academy's base until their exhibitions moved to the new National Gallery building in Trafalgar Square at the end of the 1830s.[35] With the longer walls available there, and at the Academy's subsequent premises at Burlington House on Piccadilly, tilting became rare, while the newly lateral sense of the hang encouraged instead a wrap-around installation in which pictures were often fitted in at 45 degrees across the corners of the rooms. This latter practice seems to have been more or less unheard of in private houses, other than in cases where a religious picture might be placed high in a corner following Orthodox Christian tradition.

In the home, the issue of tilting immediately invited the awkward question, easy enough to answer at an exhibition: is this

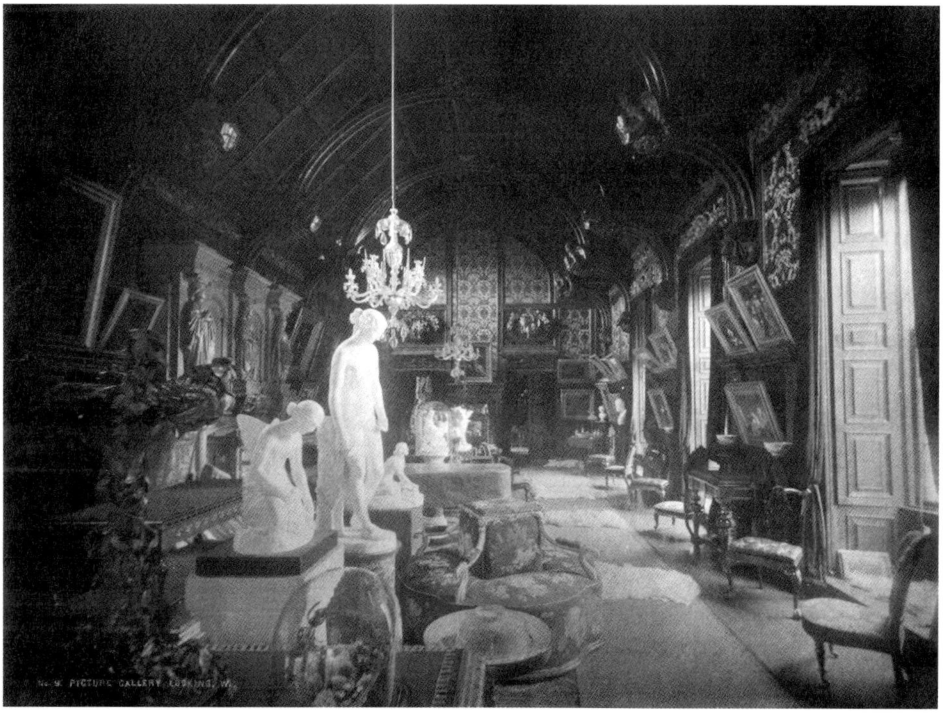

16 The artist Patrick Allan and his wife Elizabeth Fraser rebuilt Hospitalfield outside Arbroath following their marriage in 1843. In the baronial Picture Gallery the paintings – mostly by the owners' friends – had an adjustable degree of tilt which was used to the full, to judge from this photograph published in *The Book of Hospitalfield* (1894).

picture really intended to be looked at? Did hanging a picture entail giving the occupants of the room the best opportunity to see it without glare, shadow or distortion, or was this to privilege the picture too indulgently in relation to the rest of the room? The question was answered confidently by writers on the home in general, and especially anyone concerned with the integrity of the interior *per se*: to tilt was old-fashioned, unhygienic (dust got down the back of the picture) and risked extra damage to

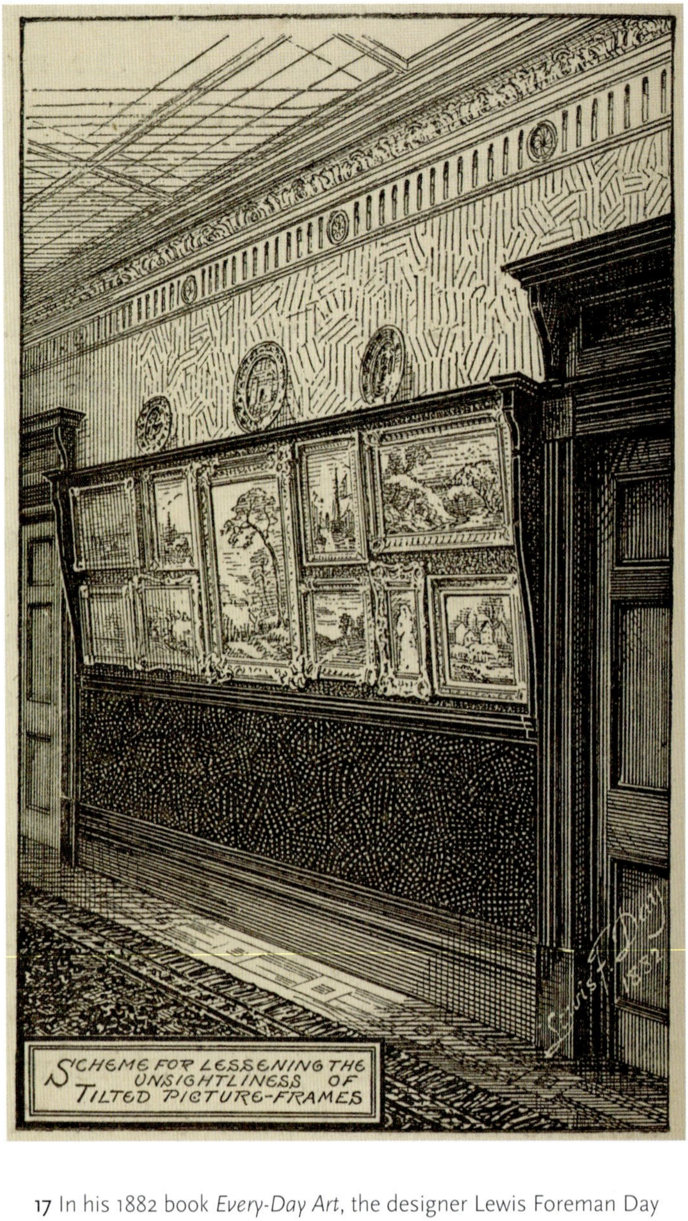

17 In his 1882 book *Every-Day Art*, the designer Lewis Foreman Day proposed this 'Scheme for lessening the unsightliness of tilted picture-frames'. The rake of the modestly tilted paintings is mitigated by being enclosed within a kind of meta-frame topped out with a plate rail.

the wall if the canted picture's lower edge needed more nails to rest on.[36] Edgar Allan Poe, for instance, an early champion of the ideal bourgeois interior, described his preference in his 1840 essay 'The Philosophy of Furniture' (the only domestic advice text, to my knowledge, to open with a quote from Hegel). Pictures, thought Poe, should 'lie flat upon the walls, and . . . not hang off with cords. The designs themselves may, sometimes, be best seen in this latter position, but the general appearance of the chamber is injured.'[37] Henry Mogford, in his *Handbook for the Preservation of Pictures*, the most readable early Victorian text of its kind, claimed that the 'most desirable way of placing pictures would be to fasten them to the walls, without any visible appearance of the machinery of their suspension' and that tilting was especially objectionable, 'like living under tottering crags, or overhanging cliffs – an uncomfortable insecurity oppresses every one'.[38] Yet it is clear that the kind of tidiness preferred by writers, who after all had to offer up some kind of logical argument, was not in fact practised. Many Victorian photographs show pictures tilting, some at the kinds of alarming angles feared by Mogford. At Hospitalfield, outside Arbroath, remodelled from around 1850 by the well-married painter Patrick Allan-Fraser, pictures did not so much tilt as collapse towards the presumably seated guests (illus. 16). Generally, tilting was later seen as emphasizing the separateness of pictures from the interior, and therefore associated with old-school connoisseurs of painting, which lent the practice a certain kudos even after its explicit condemnation by the design reformers, to whom also picture cords creating unruly diagonals across walls were anathema. Illus. 17 shows a proposal by the designer Lewis Foreman Day for a kind of wall cabinet to tidy up, and protect from dust, a group of pictures for those who could not resist the temptation to tilt.

Prior to the early nineteenth century the nail-and-cord system involved simple but often decorative fittings. Brass nails, sometimes with fancy heads (still available late in the century: illus. 18), were combined with 'hempen cords, covered with coloured worsted'.[39] As for the frame, this part of 'the machinery of . . . suspension' was also supposed to be decorative but restrained, although it very regularly defaulted.[40] The single most cited authority on interior design of the later nineteenth century was *Hints on Household Taste* (1868) by Charles Locke Eastlake, the nephew and namesake of the Eastlake of the early National Gallery (confusingly the younger Eastlake was also later Keeper there). His book embodied the principles of applied common sense and truth to purpose and to materials that were to help guide much of the later design reform movement. 'These conditions seem simple enough', wrote the younger Eastlake of what was required of the frame, 'but how frequently are they violated in modern work!'[41] Eastlake openly called out what others complained of more discreetly – the collapse of craftsmanship in frame-making during the nineteenth century. Patterns from the two previous centuries continued to be reproduced but now with the raised decoration not carved but applied as a moulded plaster 'compo', resulting in frames that were 'so brittle that, instead of protecting the picture . . . [they] have to be handled more carefully than the glass [covering the picture] itself'. It was a cliché of both design literature and fiction that the vulgar preferred these showy frames to the pictures themselves. Heavy frames, wrote Henry Mogford, were 'more indicative of purse-proud parvenuship than of a refined intelligence; it is exhibiting the weight of money instead of mental expansion'.[42]

The frame, then, was over-ripe for reform. For some ambitious painters, such as Dante Gabriel Rossetti or James Abbott McNeill

18 In their 1885 catalogue of apparently infinite varieties of fancy goods, the London firm Silber & Fleming offered a wide range of picture-tackle including cords gauged to prescribed maximum load weights.

CORNICE POLES, PICTURE RODS, AND FITTINGS.

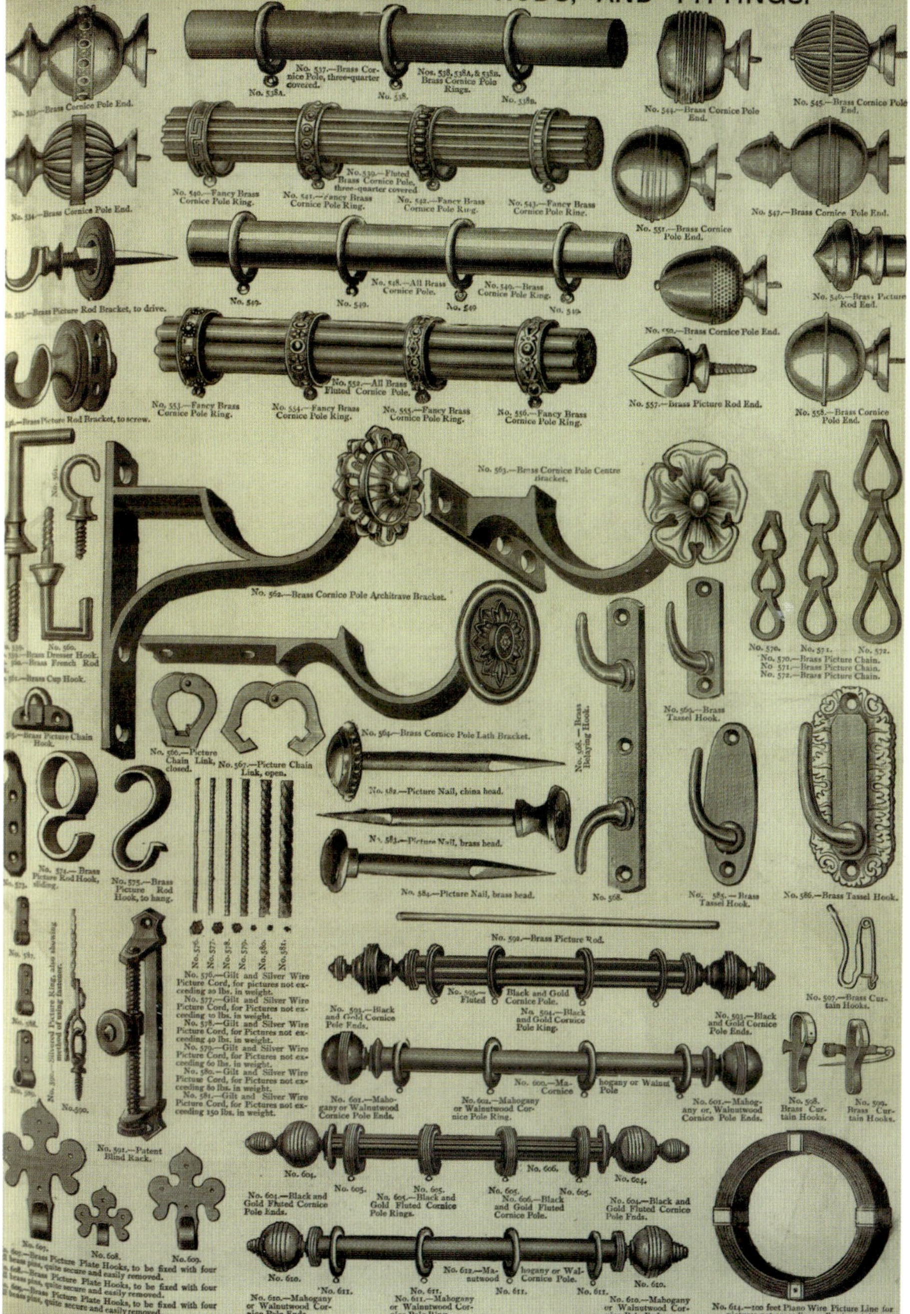

Whistler, this was something they were ready to take into their own hands, with frames that made clear they were on the side of the picture-field in its battle with the interior. Such bespoke fixtures were permanently married to their pictures, and no one was likely to mess about with an artist-designed frame which would always go where the picture went. The idea that picture frames formed links between pictures and interiors was only true of newly furnished rooms in very wealthy homes where all the carpentry might be ordered as a suite, or in a grand collection where the frames were all of a high quality and of a similar period (for instance, at the National Gallery: see illus. 4). Such beautiful creations as the frames designed by Rossetti and his friends and followers are now the stuff of thorough art-historical research, but less familiar are the more openly extravagant kinds of 'rustic' frame designs that completely ignored the traditions of the craft in favour of decoration resembling, or actually using, twigs or roots. An example can be seen on a Dutch painting in a family portrait of the 1830s (illus. 19). The professional decorators could not abide this sort of thing, Lewis Foreman Day expressing the hope that '[s]ober Englishmen need scarcely be warned against' them.[43] Yet many other authors championing DIY over the services of professionals such as Day felt that here was a job anyone could take on at home, often recommending the addition of floral decoration, especially ivy. Various images survive from the nineteenth century showing sprigs tucked behind pictures to give a festive air, but it was commonly proposed that picture owners go much further in this line, setting creepers to grow from bottles placed behind pictures, sending their tendrils along the frame and out into the room to create a 'fairyland effect' that allowed an interior to be unified from the root point of the picture.[44] The ultimate fusion of pictures with the new enthusiasm for amateur gardening was described by Shirley Hibberd in his book *Rustic Adornments for Homes of Taste*, first published in the 1850s. This was a large room for displaying flowers on collapsible stands that in moments could be transformed into a picture gallery. Copies of famous paintings made on canvas were rolled up like drop scenes at a theatre, with 'the rollers and cords . . . hidden with a cornice, and when the pictures are shown, they fall down into gilt mouldings, so as to appear like great oil paintings in handsome frames'.[45] Rather like pictures festooned with ivy or morning glory, the idea of pictures that were hung but still moved in some way may seem like something made up by a refined art critic to scandalize their peers. But that the picture should be kept moving was in fact a common aspiration in the earlier part of our period.

As private picture galleries became places of public interest from around 1800, more systematic display apparatus was adopted involving fixtures attached to multiple works. The picture pole, adapted from the principle of the curtain pole, only becomes common from this period, evident, for example, in the designs by Charles Heathcote Tatham for the picture galleries of aristocratic clients, where the poles, tucked just beneath the cornice, allowed a tidy sequence of parallel chains or cords to descend vertically to the paintings in pairs.[46] The picture pole or rod has ever since retained associations with grander homes, despite later being produced in volume for the catalogue shopper (illus. 18) and despite efforts on the parts of several inventors to adapt the basic principle for more intricate use in modest homes. The builder Charles Vokins evolved the picture rod into a grooved track along which ran pulleys from which in turn descended adjustable cords to be attached to the backs of pictures that might thereby be shifted laterally and vertically without touching the walls against which they were suspended. A design for this appeared in the various editions of John Claudius Loudon's *Encyclopaedia of Cottage, Farm, and Villa Architecture and Furniture* from 1835 onwards (illus. 20). Essentially the same idea formed the basis for a patent granted in 1840 to the Birmingham brass-founder William Potts, which

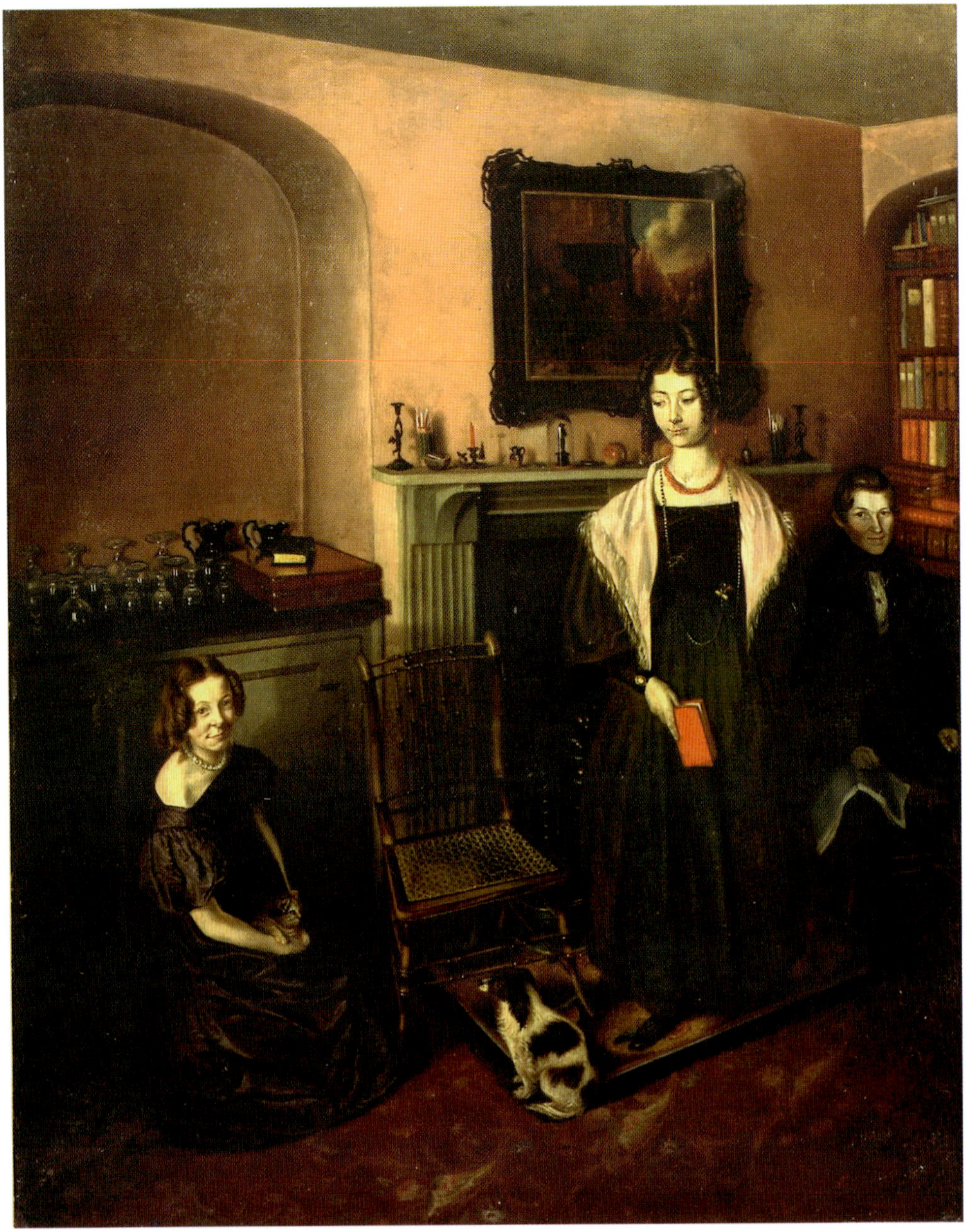

19 John Petherick, Welsh ironworks manager and amateur artist, painted this family portrait in the 1830s. Over the fireplace is a seventeenth-century Dutch genre scene with an extraordinarily fragile-looking bird's-nest-style frame.

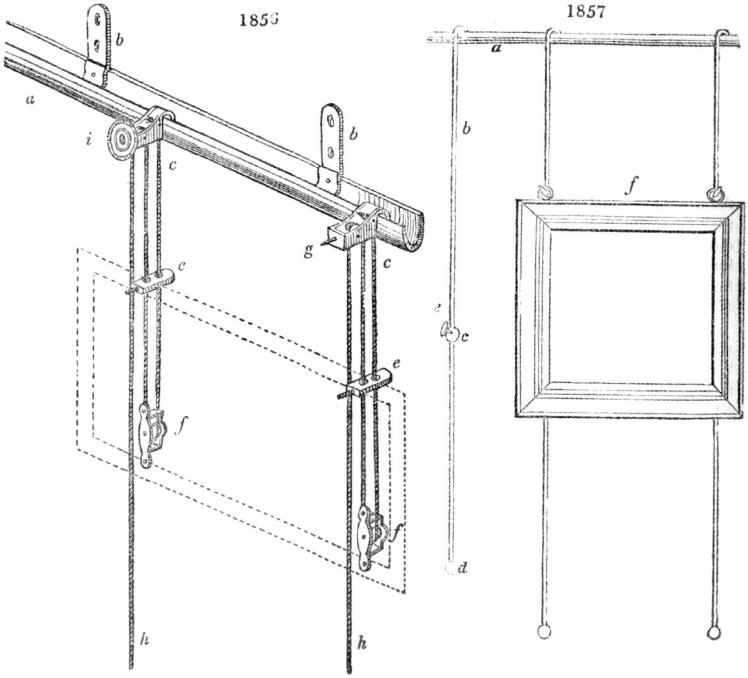

20 John Claudius Loudon's *Encyclopaedia of Cottage, Farm, and Villa Architecture and Furniture* of the 1830s featured several suggestions from the builder Charles Vokins. One of them was for this adjustable picture-hanging system.

added the further refinement of a miniature windlass that could be turned to adjust the tilt of the picture (illus. 21).[47] Despite energetic promotion in the press and at trade exhibitions, there appears to be little evidence that the Potts Patent Picture Rail proved any more popular than Vokins's contraption. For the middling sort of homeowner it was only when the grooved timber picture rail – attached as a moulding to the wall rather lower than the conventional height of a pole, and used with *S*-profiled hooks – became a standard architectural fixture from the 1870s that any popular viable alternative to the nail and cord was found

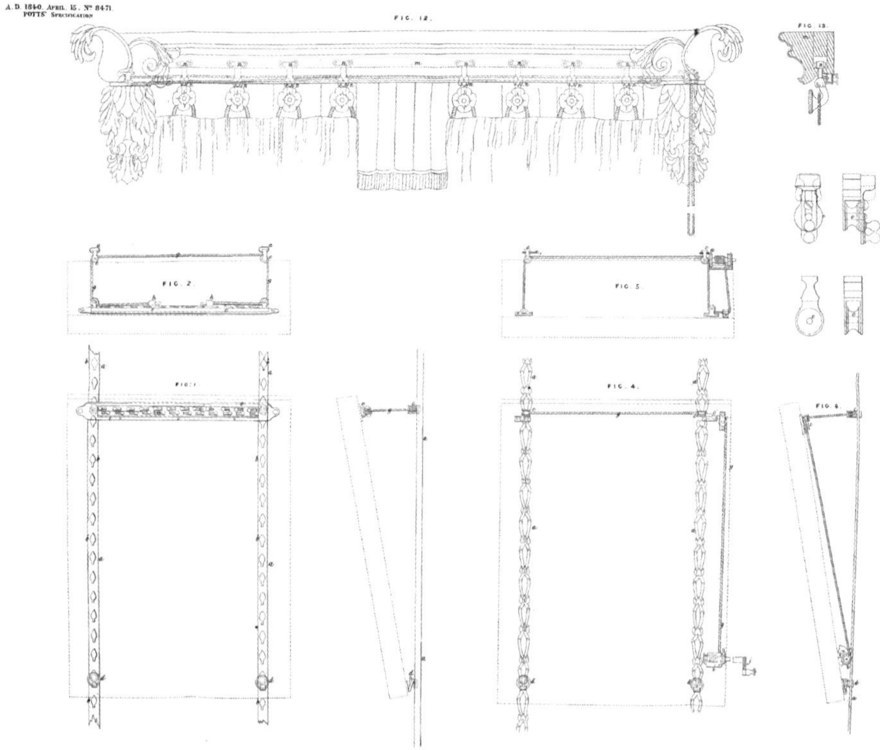

21 Soon after the appearance of Vokins's proposal, the Birmingham brass-founder William Potts patented this comparable rail for curtains or pictures: for the latter it featured the added attraction of an adjustable degree of tilt (patent no. 8471, 1840).

(illus. 22). Design historians wondered how such an apparently obvious solution could have been so far delayed, starting with Hermann Muthesius in his survey of *Das englische Haus*, of 1904: 'it almost amazes one that such a simple substitute has not been thought of long ago.'[48] The explanation, as we will see in Chapter Two, relates to the picture rail's embodying the ghost of a frieze, its existence dependent on developments in interior design that postponed its conception.

So much for the history of the picture's placing against the wall; but that was not the whole story. We saw in the Introduction that when, in the 1840s, Ruskin and the elder Eastlake were thinking through the display of pictures around the time of the opening of the new National Gallery building, they found that the wall, a permanent uniform field against which to hang, was not enough. Eastlake liked the idea of screens radiating axially from a single point, while Ruskin fantasized about pictures fixed into coffered partitions suggestive of the architecturally dramatized sequence of images that so moved Aeneas. Their apparent readiness to believe that pictures might demand more from a wall than an inert ground upon which to await approval was surely influenced by the practice, carried on previously in private houses for at least several decades, of mounting pictures so that they remained minimally movable in order to swing them into the best available light.

Two early examples of this idea were recorded by late eighteenth-century female tourists. In 1786 Caroline Lybbe Powys

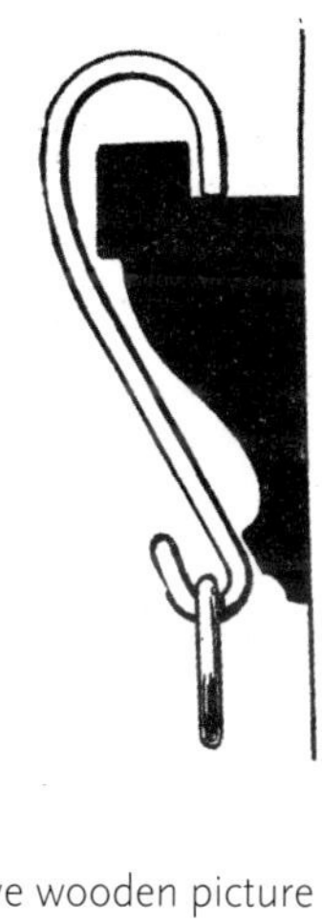

22 The simple and effective wooden picture rail, fixed directly into the wall and used with S-hooks, was introduced widely from the 1870s. This diagram appeared in a comprehensive account of picture hanging in *Every Woman's Encyclopaedia*, published between 1910 and 1912.

visited Stourhead in Wiltshire, where in a small room or closet she found 'a number of fine paintings . . . hung in a most clever manner, the frames having hinges fasten'd to the walls on one side as a door is, and [the pictures] may be pulled forwards as the light is required'.[49] A few years later the German novelist Sophie von La Roche visited the print-seller John Boydell in his old-fashioned house on Cheapside, where, among a great many other options, the print after Claude's *Arch of Constantine* (see illus. 15) could be had for ten shillings. The irregular rooms had led to an 'invention' whereby a sequence of doors took up the length of a wall, each opening to reveal, on its inside, pictures that could be exposed to full light before being shut up again away from the dust that was a perennial worry to the possessor of any precious object.[50] Possibly such attention to lighting related to the novel popularity of *plein-air* painting in the later eighteenth century, but the design and carpentry involved cannot have been especially demanding in comparison to the kinds of elaborate furniture being produced by elite cabinet-makers for their clients' libraries, the folding leaves of which were clearly a model for some of the apparatus adopted in private London picture galleries in the immediate post-Napoleonic years. This was a heroic age of public museum-building in Europe as national collections were redefined and rehoused in the wake of the massive churn of displacements following the French Revolution. In London, however, the private sphere outpaced the public. As the compiler of an upmarket guidebook to London had written in 1802, introducing a list of the private galleries open to visitors by appointment,

> The commotions on the continent have operated as an earthquake on the productions of genius, and the finest works of ancient and modern times have been shook out of their old situations. Many, very many of them have been consigned to this country, and are now in the private

> collections of our nobility and gentry, in and about the metropolis.[51]

In several such collections the pictures were indeed still moving, recognizing their inherent portability, which had been so traumatically emphasized by recent history.

Thomas Hope, of the vastly wealthy international banking family, had fled the revolutionary wars to London in the 1790s, and his famous house on Duchess Street was one of those advertised as viewable 'by application' in 1802. The house was celebrated as the *ne plus ultra* of scholarly Regency Neoclassicism, but by the early 1820s visitors could also see there the Flemish picture gallery, built to Hope's own designs and housing masterpieces including Metsu's *Lady Reading a Letter* with its picture curtain being drawn aside (see illus. 2). Along the middle of this fifty-foot room ran a kind of double-sided dwarf bookcase with compartments for books and prints but also supporting a substantial screen on which were fixed twenty of the 'choicest' cabinet pictures hinged on one side to be swung out for better viewing, as in our eighteenth-century examples.[52] It has been suggested that this was the inspiration for John Soane's picture gallery of 1824, surviving in his house-museum in Lincoln's Inn Fields, where screens of paintings fold out in a modestly scaled room to create the sensation of being trapped within a giant piece of furniture, a fairy-tale experience only enhanced by the view, revealed by the released screens, down into the Monk's Parlour, one of the architect's most fantastic creations (illus. 23).[53]

Meanwhile, overlooking St James's Park was the exquisite house and collection of the banker, poet and patron Samuel Rogers, whose drawing-room collection of paintings appeared conventional, other than in their exceptional quality, until the frames were gently tugged so that 'by very simple machinery' they would 'advance from the wall and turn in almost every possible

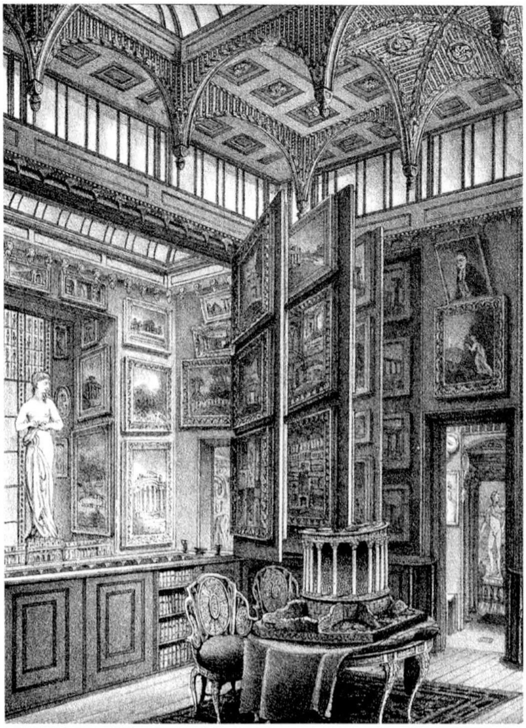

23 The house of the architect John Soane survives in Lincoln's Inn Fields as a museum. Still to be seen there is the modestly proportioned Picture Room fitted with folding screens allowing, as Soane boasted, as many pictures to be shown there as in a much larger gallery, with the added advantage of it being possible to move them into the best light for viewing.

direction'.[54] This was evidently one of many attractions for the guests at Rogers's famous weekly breakfasts, in one imagined view of which Turner is shown gingerly levering out one of the pictures (illus. 24). Such arrangements were in part a more ambitious extension of the practice of adding hinged glazed panels to the frames of smaller, especially precious, paintings that, when unlocked – of course, only by the proprietor-keyholder – released

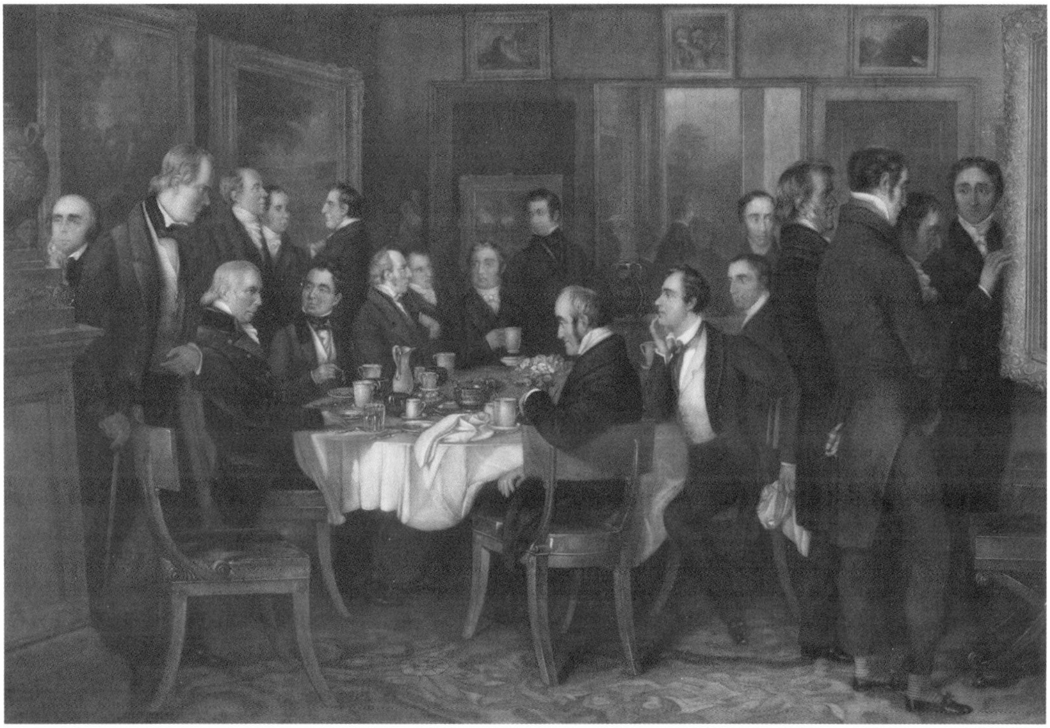

24 The banker, poet and wit Samuel Rogers held famous breakfasts for distinguished artists, writers and politicians in his London house throughout which was displayed one of the choice art collections of the age. In this engraving, among the guests imagined to have been present simultaneously in 1815 are Wordsworth, Byron, Walter Scott and (second from the right) the painter Turner. Turner's hand is shown playing with one of Rogers's paintings, some of which were hinged to the wall to allow them to be moved into better light, like those at Soane's house (print by Charles Mottram after John Doyle).

the pane of glass like one protecting a clock-face to allow a period of intimate inspection.[55] By the 1860s this added interest of 'movableness' offered by hinged glazing was being recommended to the middle-class readers of *Cassell's Household Guide*.[56]

Hinged pictures like those of Hope or Rogers were sometimes to be found in public museums of this period – for example, in the Galleria Palatina at the Palazzo Pitti in Florence, opened in 1828 – a feature felt necessary for the benefit of copyists. But it was in private collections that the more interesting experimentation evidently took place. Here the desire to fix a picture in a room while also allowing it to retain some of its instinct to roam could be more safely managed. One of the last commissions received by the unfortunate Benjamin Robert Haydon – the house artist to the Leigh Hunt circle in their youth – was from the sixth Duke of Devonshire for a pair of window shutters for Chatsworth House. It was not obviously the most epic project for the self-proclaimed saviour of historical painting, yet these panels showed, from behind, Wellington surveying the field of Waterloo and Napoleon musing upon a sunset on St Helena. They were installed in the South-East Sitting Room just in time to form part of the tour of the house narrated by the Duke for his sister and privately printed in 1845.[57] Here he instructs his reader to sit facing away from the window, enjoying via a mirror the magnificent view beyond, in the company of the distinguished men flanking it, thereby generating the ultimate fusion of the picturesque and the sublime. Framing the experience of single or paired pictures in this way was a further refinement of the principle of keeping them in movement. It was said of Goya's pair of clothed and naked *Majas* that an early owner had them rigged up so as to be viewable in sequence, the more modest lifting from its place to reveal its erotic version behind – although modern historians find the story to be suspiciously poorly documented.[58] Other contraptions gave up altogether on walls and screens in favour of something more

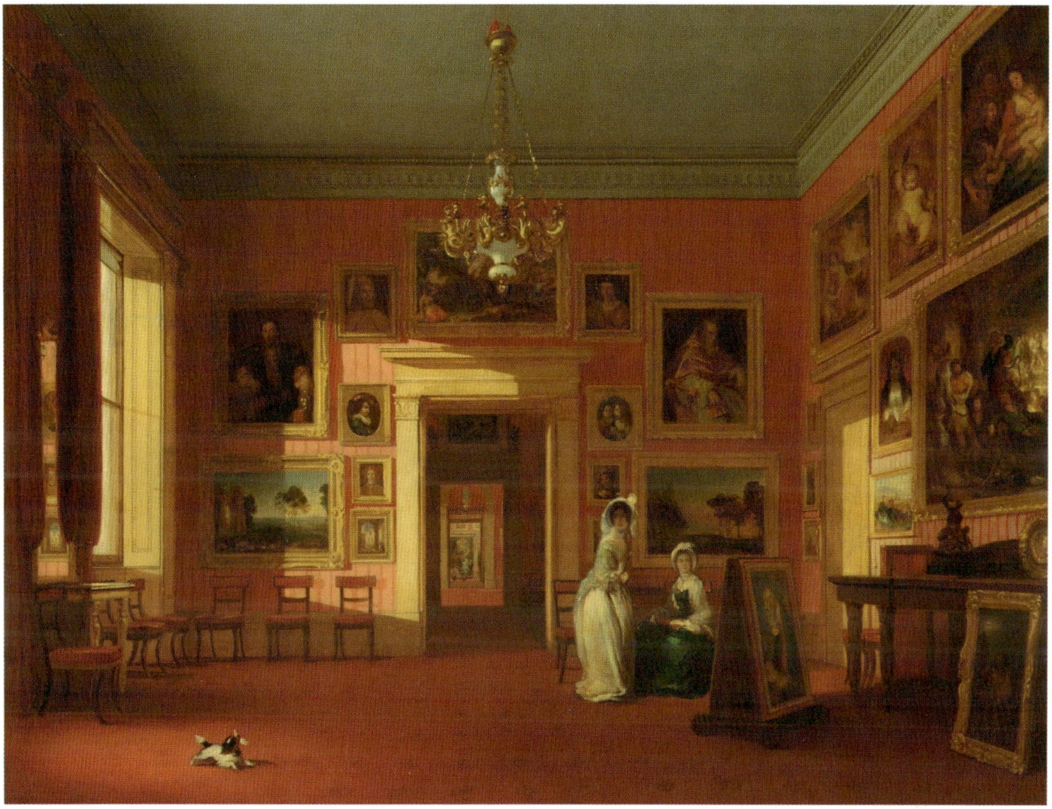

25 John Rushout, 2nd Baron Northwick, was, like Samuel Rogers, a wealthy bachelor collector. His later home, Thirlestaine House in Cheltenham, became something of a museum devoted to the display of his pictures. The Botticelli on the trundling easel was acquired by the National Gallery of Scotland in 1999 (painting by Robert Huskisson, 1847).

frankly portable, such as the *pinacotheca* described by Loudon in his *Encyclopaedia*, a shallow glazed display cabinet on wheels for pictures that kept the works dust-free while being trundled about larger rooms for inspection.[59] A much simpler version, simply a low-lying double easel on castors, can be seen in an 1840s interior view of the gallery of Lord Northwick at Thirlestaine House in Cheltenham (illus. 25).

Watercolours necessarily had an especially troubled relationship to walls, given that long exposure was known to cause fading. When Ruskin considered the problem of providing access to the vast quantity of works on paper that came to the nation with the Turner bequest in the 1850s, he proposed the fragile works be minimally framed and stored in boxes at perhaps a dozen at a time. A box, something between a Wardian case carrying a botanical specimen and a DJ's jobbing selection of twelve-inch vinyl, could then be issued to the visitor, who would be directed to tables where empty gilt frames were permanently fixed. The student would insert the drawings one at a time into the fixed frame in order to study them to best advantage before returning the sheets in their box to the invigilator.[60] This method of focused, sequenced looking at pictures, reminiscent of a lantern show, long remained an attractive ideal, not least for Modernist architects hoping to wean clients from cluttered interiors, a theme we return to in the following chapter. For now I will close this section with a word from Charles Dickens, reflecting on the mammoth Manchester Art Treasures exhibition of 1857, intended to bring pictures to the working people of the industrial north, the starting-point in many ways for the campaigns that would follow in the decades ahead to install beauty in the lives of all citizens. But Dickens was pessimistic: 'they want more amusement, and particularly something in motion' – the cavernous display of pictures on walls was simply 'too still after their lives of machinery'.[61] That insight might be applied too to the many wealthier collectors for whom the dynamic act of putting up a picture did not signal the curtailment of their pictures' mobility or of their own opportunities to handle them.

FINGERING PICTURES

There was a humorous tradition of men being bad at hanging pictures. That humour expressed the tension between two gendered assumptions – that the owner of the pictures and the house was probably male, but that the person better suited to arranging the pictures was female. For example, a memoir of the court of George II tells of the king's sophisticated consort Caroline taking advantage of his absence in Hanover to switch some of his execrable pictures in Kensington Palace for very good ones of her own selection. Through sheer vanity, upon his return, the king demanded the bad pictures be put back.[62] In Jerome K. Jerome's 1889 comedy of suburban romantics *Three Men in a Boat*, Uncle Podger's efforts to hang a picture allow him to exercise a preposterously uneconomic tyranny over his household – having everyone run errands to help in what he presents as a massive logistical challenge – that has sometimes been recalled during exchanges of insults among politicians.[63] Early in the twentieth century Muthesius reported that it was in fact now the norm for women to take the lead in the English house, and, significantly, the most completely illustrated account of hanging pictures in our period is to be found in the Edwardian *Every Woman's Encyclopaedia* (see illus. 22).[64]

Once it was in place, looking after the picture was certainly considered women's work, although advice differed over where lay the division of labour between the maid and the ladies of the house. Mrs Beeton says the maid's early-morning whisk-through should include the picture frames, although she should use only a feather duster, advised Florence Caddy, for, as several of their fellow authors warned, it was all too easy to knock out lumps of

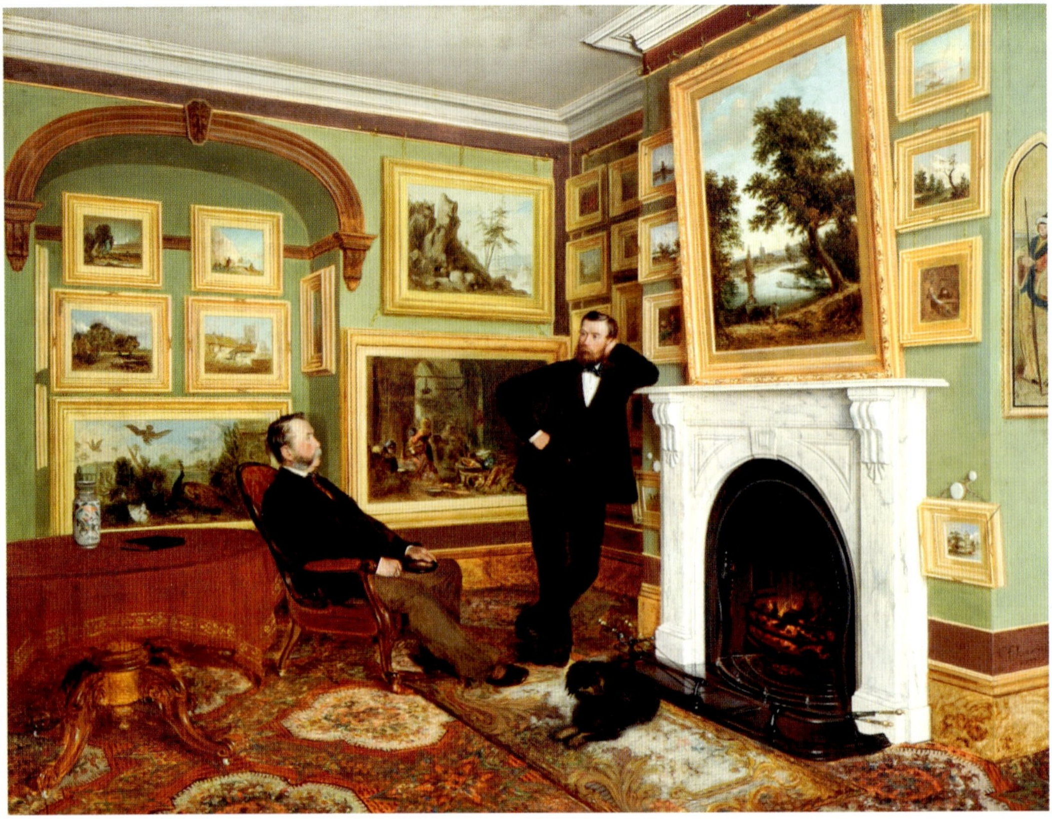

26 Charles Eastwood (standing) and his brother David (seated) were brush-makers in Victorian Leeds. The location is supposed to be Scotton Grange, Charles's house near Knaresborough where he displayed his extensive collection of paintings. A 1900 catalogue of the collection lists some 231 pictures, the last entry being for this portrait by Charles Lowcock, dated 1877.

compo from the frames.[65] However, advice more directed towards the art collector (that of Mogford, for instance) assumed the staff will be kept away from precious things, the pleasures of tending to which the mistress and her daughters will wish to appropriate to themselves if only to please the man of the house.[66] Florence Nightingale, who broadly condemned dusting as merely 'flapping' particles from one surface to another, recommended the practice only in the case of pictures, to prevent dust settling on their surfaces.[67] It was assumed pictures would be taken down for an all-over dusting only once a year during the spring clean.[68] Pictures were essentially low-maintenance. This portrait (illus. 26) of two gentlemen in a room filled with pictures, and little else, suggests a pleasure in being entirely independent, even of servants, whose exclusion is suggested by the bell-pull to the right of the fireplace – intended to summon domestic help – reassigned as a fixture from which to hang a small picture. All these examples, however, pre-date the general adoption of the picture rail, which, for all its being an elegantly simple solution to an old problem, was acknowledged to be a lethal dust trap.[69] The picture rail was indeed, claimed Miss E. P. Hughes in the *Journal of the Royal Sanitary Institute* in 1913, one of those offensively labour-generating devices inflicted on home-makers that would not be overcome 'until we have good women architects, in sufficient numbers, to plan good houses for us'.[70]

Beyond talk of dust, Victorian advice on picture preservation emphasized the mortal dangers of damp and the life-giving properties of light. Damp would destroy frames, canvases and especially panels, and as a consequence pictures were not truly safe in their proximity to many domestic walls. One recommended solution was to set corks at the rear corners of the frame to keep the picture off the wall and allow air to circulate around the entire object. Devices such as those invented by Vokins and Potts also had this advantage. The management of damp was something that

British householders could be expected to pride themselves on, but advice writers felt it necessary to stress, as news, the guidance relating to sunlight. Pictures needed sunlight, it was standardly advised: without it they would fade and perish, while a strong dose of solar rays could even revive deadened pigment. Scientists came to understand the damage that ultraviolet sunlight ('chemical rays', in the nineteenth century) did to skin only in the 1890s, and to oil paintings later still. For centuries prior to this, painters had used full sunlight to dry out pictures once first completed, and the belief that direct sun literally allowed pictures to live, common in the nineteenth century, may have been strengthened by the arrival of photography, through which sun pictures were miraculously fixed by light.[71]

Conservators today accept that light, aside from its deleterious impacts, prevents the darkening of linseed oil. But the nineteenth-century enthusiasm for the benefits of sunlight demonstrates above all a self-consciously rational, literalist approach to the rhetoric of the picture, according to which it was intended to be looked at directly – a far from unproblematic assumption. Thus *Cassell's Household Guide* of 1869, standard middle-class fare, while not recommending constant exposure to strong sunlight, stressed that without daylight colours would fade and the oil and pigment start to separate, in which case the only remedy was to take the work to a professional conservator 'who will expose the picture carefully to the sunshine, until the fading colours become revived'.[72] Another domestic encyclopaedia claimed that this need for light set oil paintings in a class by themselves, distinct from other types of furniture and works on paper, all of which suffered by the rays of the sun: paintings were so far more akin to living beings than inanimate household objects.[73] Charles Savory's more specialist book on pictures and frames repeated the notion of restorative sunbathing for paintings: 'We have recently found this to be very beneficial to a pair of portraits, looking very much as if the artist had painted a post mortem representation, which came out in the course of nine or ten weeks in blooming health.'[74] According to several authors, the practice of sheeting pictures, or merely shuttering rooms, when a house was empty should be abandoned for fear of damaging the pictures through deprivation of light, 'which is their very life'.[75] Covering pictures was now akin to both superstition and economic obfuscation. To take just one literary example from late in the century: in Henry Nevinson's class-based collection of short stories *Neighbours of Ours*, an older East Ender visits the pretentious home of his socially aspiring daughter, where he notes, in the parlour, 'two pictures covered over with yeller gauze to keep the flies off', rendering them thereby entirely useless as pictures.[76]

As well as keeping dust and flies off, picture curtains had been intended to prevent touching. The exposed surface of the modern picture signalled that any potential viewer would be trusted to keep their fingers to themselves. The opening and shutting of picture curtains aligned them with a model of vision based on the mechanics of the camera obscura, the image conjured only at the opening of the cloth or aperture. As historians suggest, from the early nineteenth century the understanding of vision shifts to the viewer him- or herself, as 'the visible escapes from the timeless order of the camera obscura and becomes lodged in another apparatus, within the unstable physiology and temporality of the human body'.[77] Indeed, in the case of the picture, the question now was how to manage the entire body's involvement – how to train viewers *only* to look as it became recognized that their bodily instinct was to engage across the senses.[78] To consider this tension in the home, it will be useful first to make another brief excursion to the museums of London to listen to what was being discussed in the public sphere.

The protection of pictures from flies, soot, industrial effluvia and human debris became a question of government policy once

Britain became the owner of a national gallery from 1824 and especially once this had its own new building from the following decade. The Gallery's painfully public learning curve regarding the cleaning of its pictures, as these accumulated at Trafalgar Square after spending the previous centuries in private homes, has often been described.[79] The Romantic notion of the deep-toned picture, its surface a sedimented landscape of delicate layers of paint, each successive stratum more transparent as it neared the eye, allowing views into murkier layers beneath, collided with the urgent call to sanitation. That affection for hidden sublimities was routinely mocked by those campaigning for more thorough cleaning of the nation's pictures, calls echoed by writers of domestic advice literature who felt that the experience of private picture owners, especially in London, was clear evidence that pictures needed regular cleaning. Once put in decent shape, the National Gallery paintings needed to be protected from their own audience by attendants, barriers and glass. Official reports published during the 1840s and '50s effectively constituted explicit guidance that artworks were absolutely not to be touched, human proximity to pictures being described in deliberately disgusting terms. Surveying this great enclosure of public pictures, Henry Cole of the South Kensington Museum (later the V&A) testified that

> The public sneeze upon the pictures, and the saliva runs down on the pictures, and positively eats away the surface of them . . . we had great difficulty in preventing them expressing the emotions that they felt at looking at a picture, and they will touch it; they say 'Look at that expression.'[80]

Cole gave the particular example of a highly finished work by the genre painter William Mulready covered in a film of snot, and it was the similar art of Wilkie which, as already noted, caused the Academy to erect a barrier before one of his pictures at their 1822 exhibition. The privately managed British Institution installed barriers throughout its rooms a few years after its loan exhibitions began in 1813, but the grand private collections by and large made do with the ottomans that were promoted by Regency furniture designers for use in picture galleries, 'their projections from the wall preventing the pictures being fingered, which is too often practised'.[81]

The urge, when confronted with a picture, to engage the senses other than sight was now thoroughly consigned to the category of the primitive or superstitious. At the Reformation a royal decree of Henry VIII had proscribed the 'kissing or licking' of images and relics, a sensory restriction now, in the age of state picture galleries, rolled out to cover these secular spaces too.[82] The solution of Henry Cole at the V&A and the elder Eastlake at the National Gallery, in response to their picture-devouring visitors, was a massive campaign of comprehensive glazing.[83] Museum-goers were encouraged to police one another by notices such as those in the picture galleries of the V&A which pronounced the visitor 'a shareholder in the property' and called on them to protect that property 'in the event of any attempt at injury on the part of evil-disposed persons'.[84] The way was clear for the eventual triumph of an official art history that would absorb the tactile into the visual, that recognized the necessity of the former to first teach the latter but which saw the authority of the eye as the culmination of civilized experience, as expressed archetypally, around 1900, in the apotheosis of Cézanne's art and in Bernard Berenson's account of Italian painting.[85] The rare recorded examples of people contravening the new rules now imagine their subjects as heretics, eccentrics or criminals, with the home often a refuge for them all.

How many people kissed their pictures in private? Surely more than let on, is probably all we can answer. Thomas De Quincey, in his *Confessions of an English Opium-Eater*, was one to own up.

An unhappy teenager at Manchester Grammar School in 1802, he became devoted to the print or copy after Van Dyck's *Duchess of Somerset* that hung over the mantelpiece of his study-bedroom: 'I had a thousand times laid down my pen, or my book, to gather consolation from it.' Resolved to run away, on the night of his escape he fixed his 'parting gaze' on her until he heard the clock strike four. 'I went up to the picture, kissed it, and then gently walked out, and closed the door for ever!'[86] Haydon, ever proud of his empathy with the great masters of the past, made a special study of a depiction of Christ dining at the house of Simon the Pharisee, attributed to Jacopo Bassano, exhibited at the British Institution in 1838. He recorded in his diary having looked into it 'till I smelt its color . . . What an eye, what a verve for Color! How I sucked it in! How I tasted it on the tip of my tongue!'[87] But even the overwrought Haydon had to kiss the picture synaesthetically, vicariously. After all, it was not his. The wealthy Victorian collector William Graham was fond of both early Italian art and his contemporary Pre-Raphaelites, the latter finding it a charming eccentricity that his affection for his pictures was such that he would actually pucker up to them, perhaps in self-conscious emulation of an imagined pre-Reformation practice in keeping with his taste in imagery.[88]

Touch of the fingers, too, might feel less inappropriate in such cases. The author Richard Jefferies, in a short story of the 1870s, imagined a country squire whose passion, like Graham's, was the fashionable aesthetic of the early Italians, pictures that his neighbours found hopelessly unrealistic: 'Some sensitive persons rather shrank from seeing him handle these painted panels with those peculiar scratchy finger-nails; it set their teeth on edge.'[89] A special case of fingering pictures was that of blind art lovers whose vision may have deteriorated after their collections were formed, meaning they were still able to enjoy the presence and touch of their pictures. One such was Samuel Joseph, who went on to commission a painting from the artist William Quiller Orchardson in the early 1890s *after* losing his sight. Orchardson obliged with a picture of a young woman in a conservatory looking as though she risks overdosing on the floral scents surrounding her. Orchardson's daughter narrated the story:

> When I saw it in the studio I remarked on the sadness of painting for a blind man, and then added some shy words in praise of the exquisite beauty of the little picture, and my Father answered: 'Yes, most sad, and, of course, one painted one's best just because he would never see it. I painted that with my heart's blood. But I think that he knows my work well, perhaps he will see it quite clearly in his mind's eye, with his wife's detailed description, and her hand guiding his over the picture as she always does.'[90]

We rarely hear of pictures themselves smelling, however olfactorily exquisite the scene represented may have been, for this would have been to allow the basest of senses to interfere with their optical purpose.[91] And a picture was, above all, silent: for it to generate any sound would be to risk speaking over the narrative it carried. Art talk generally has always had a bad name, and the mark of a true connoisseur was often that they were able to remain silent before pictures for long stretches.[92] How grateful a picture must have felt to meet such a quiet visitor, imagined the Goncourt brothers, one of whose aphorisms was 'The thing that hears more nonsense than anything else is perhaps a picture in a museum', which at least allowed the hope that there might be fewer idiots to be endured at home.[93] When the picture itself did speak, or rather was ventriloquized, its voice was annoyingly whiney, like that of a neglected pet. In *A Voice from a Picture, by a Female Artist of the Present Day*, the prominent landscape painter Harriet Gouldsmith (who had been a pupil of Mulready) has a painting lament its being kept moving from place to place and urge greater patronage of British art. 'The Pictures' Petition', doggerel that appeared in *Punch* in 1853, demanded reprieve from the 'sand-papering and scraping and scouring' that had allegedly been inflicted on the National Gallery paintings since the restorers had been given free rein there.[94]

The silence of the picture, its discretion, helped fit it for a role as partner in crime (not the same thing as its being the victim of crime, as in the much glamourized tradition of high-value art heists). The records of the Old Bailey attest to a long tradition of hiding shameful things behind pictures, the one place above all others where one did not look. Tickets or tokens for pawned stolen goods were commonly to be found tucked into the back of frames, but other cases mention pistols, bullets, stolen linen and jewellery, counterfeit coins and notes, a thief's 'pocket Book, wherein was an Account of the Robberies committed by him in the Year 1716' and, in 1907, most of the miniatures taken from the Belgrave Square house of the banker and clubman Alfred Farquhar.[95] More distressing are the examples of pictures' roles in acts of domestic violence – a man writing out on the backs of their pictures a confession and plea relating to an attack on his wife; a woman using a picture as weapon on her partner; and, saddest of all, a disturbed young man whose mother testified that

> I had some pictures in my parlour – he broke every one of them, and put them into the fire – one of them was a portrait of his brother – I valued them, because the parties were dead, and they were my mother's – he knew I valued them on that account – he himself valued his brother's picture very much – I told him of it afterwards – he was extremely sorry then.[96]

PRINTS, PORTRAITS AND PROGRESS

Having considered some of the means and ends of putting up pictures, I would like to return to Leigh Hunt's 1834 essay 'Put Up a Picture in Your Room', and to another of its key themes: the print as the archetypal domestic picture. Relatively few people could afford original oil paintings, but Hunt urges his readers not to let that get in their way and to make a piece of paper into a picture by putting it up on their wall. 'Better put up a rough, varnished engraving, than none at all,' he writes, 'or pin, or stick up, any engraving whatsoever, at the hazard of its growing never so dirty.' Under the heading of 'picture', Hunt stresses, he includes reproductive engravings – it is the *idea*, after all, the 'memorandum', that matters. Put one up, enjoy it and then 'get a fresh one when you are able'. Here Hunt and Hazlitt essentially agree: we have already seen how Hazlitt preferred his print of Claude's *Arch of Constantine* (see illus. 15) to its original. A similar aesthetic is at work in Hazlitt's appreciation of what were the most famous pictures in Britain – Raphael's huge cartoons on paper at Hampton Court Palace showing scenes from the lives of SS Peter and Paul. These grandiose preparatory coloured drawings were initially made up of grids of small sheets, then cut into strips when first used as models for tapestries, and much knocked about ever afterwards. They were nevertheless, Hazlitt declared,

> the more majestic for being in ruin: we are struck chiefly with the truth of proportion, and the range of conception: all the petty, meretricious part of the art is dead in them; the carnal is made spiritual, the corruptible has put on incorruption, and, amidst the wreck of colour, and the mouldering of material beauty, nothing is left but a universe of thought, or the broad, imminent shadows of 'calm contemplation and majestic pains!'[97]

Such a vision of sublime putrefaction was diametrically opposed to the new languages of sanitary public responsibility promulgated through the new museums of the early Victorian age. But in the private house the much more humble reproductive engraving, while of course smaller, cleaner and simpler than 'the Cartoons' (as they were reverentially known), might still bring into the home something of their mysterious separation from a finished product and their purified expression of an *idea* – in a word, the domestic sublime.

Hunt's insistence that a print could be put up with nothing more than a few tacks deliberately rejected the tradition that to make an image on paper into a picture assumed its being glazed: that is, its frame having a thin sheet of glass added to it. While apparently present for protection, just as importantly the glass made good the lack of solidity entailed by the absence of a stretcher on which a canvas would be mounted prior to framing, an absence that also often led to the print or drawing being pasted down onto a stiff board before being assembled with its glass and frame. The practice only became common during the eighteenth century: we quoted above Xavier de Maistre's desire to break the glass to get at a villain in one of his framed prints. While glazing might suggest the greater appreciation of the art of the printmaker, connoisseurs were apt to read the development as the degradation of the print as art. As the publisher and antiquary John Nichols complained in the 1780s,

> The scarceness of the good impressions of Hogarth's larger works, is in great measure owing to their having been pasted on canvas or boards, to be framed and glazed for furniture. . . . The majority of these sets being hung up in London houses, have been utterly spoiled by smoke.[98]

Nichols objects to fine engravings being treated in the same way as, for example, political prints, which could have little purpose if not displayed. Thus when in 1761 there was published, as a print, Pitt the Elder's letter on his resignation, below a portrait head of the statesman – scarcely a work of art – it was advertised as being 'Proper to be Framed and Glazed'.[99] Hunt would have all prints put up on the wall, even without frame or glass and only a layer of varnish to stiffen the sheet: they had a job to do in making sense of the home into which they had been brought, and should get on with it regardless of safety measures.[100]

Prints had to be framed and glazed to be shown in an exhibition. At Somerset House a ground-floor room was reserved each year for the display of sculpture and glazed drawings as part of the Academy exhibition. But this necessarily side-lit space resulted in the pictures suffering 'a vicious glare dazzling upon them', causing them to resemble as a result 'so many pier glasses'.[101] In the home, however, this doubled nature, as picture and mirror, came into its own, as is brought out clearly in the painted representations of interiors, in which artists make explicit the glazed print's capacity to reflect and thereby expand and reform the space around it. George Kilburne's *Poor Relations* (see illus. 10), for example, allows a clearer sense of the room depicted through the reflections in the glazed paper works on the right, revealing the garden doors behind the viewer. An especially striking example of such objects being used to add life to interior scenes that otherwise risked being compositionally static is Edward Matthew Ward's 1853 portrait of the historian and politician Thomas Macaulay in his study (illus. 27). Here a framed engraving reflects a dramatic slash of red from the curtain on the other side of the sitter, thereby providing a subtle chromatic symmetry. This emphasis on the power of a domestic picture suited Macaulay, who had written to Leigh Hunt a few years earlier that he felt unable to love the huge *Raising of Lazarus* by Sebastiano del Piombo in the National Gallery

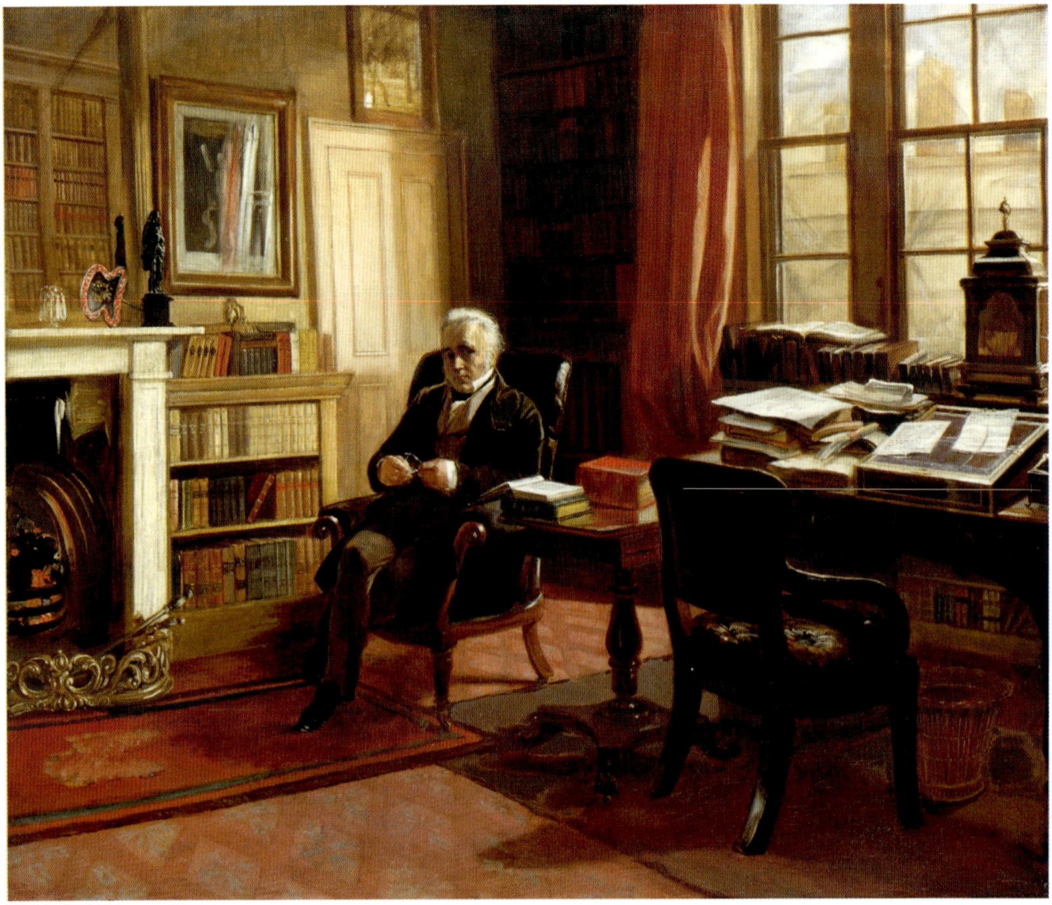

27 The historian and statesman Thomas Macaulay in his London flat in 1853, one of a series of portraits of writers in their studies painted by E. M. Ward. Macaulay's room is functional, and was said, in terms of pictures, to contain only 'half a dozen fine Italian engravings from his favourite great masters', one of which, over the bookcase, reflects the scarlet curtain.

(conspicuous in illus. 4) and 'should be very little concerned if I heard that it was burned'. He preferred the idea of pictures of much lesser value which 'I would hang over my fire-place, and look at half-an-hour every day'.[102]

If a framed-up black-line engraving intriguingly existed simultaneously as ghost of an absent original, feat of craftsmanship and looking-glass, then a colour print was something else altogether. 'Chromos' – mass-produced colour lithographic copies after crude original paintings – were things of such horrendous bad taste that it is still often assumed by British writers that they were a peculiarly American problem. Certainly chromos were energetically promoted in the States, not least by Louis Prang, whose products were endorsed by writers as distinguished as Harriet Beecher Stowe as appropriately economic items for the modern American home (see illus. 47). C. L. Eastlake (the nephew), whose *Hints on Household Taste* was massively influential in America, disapproved of them, yet catalogue retailers such as Silber & Fleming offered extravagant varieties of garish chromos to the British public in addition to other services such as the copying, in oils on canvas, of any photograph at any size.[103] Only when seen against this contrast can the copperplate etching or engraving be fully appreciated as the rarefied production it was perceived to be. Again it is in the interiors described by artists that this appreciation is fully expressed, as in Millais's portrait of the wife and daughter of the Oxford framemaker and print publisher James Wyatt (illus. 28), where engravings after Raphael and Leonardo, hung as a triptych, establish a space and a tone both sober and tender.[104] Several of Whistler's best-known paintings include representations of framed prints, among them *At the Piano* (1858–9), in which hulking examples with very broad mounts form the backdrop, reflecting a lively jumble of hues, and the portrait of Thomas Carlyle (1872–3), in which more modestly presented etchings accompany the sitter, hung so low as to be improbably convenient to the seated sage (illus. 29). In both cases Whistler is careful to give us slightly too little visual information to be able to identify the prints confidently, so that they do their compositional work as it were anonymously, and indeed they are typically overlooked in scholarly discussions of the paintings.

This fading of pictures into pictures appealed to Marcel Proust, who, we are told, only tolerated one picture in his bedroom in his family's apartment in the rue de Courcelles, a reproduction of Whistler's *Carlyle*. This print embodied three levels of imagery, in keeping with Proust's fascination with the different 'layers' of representation ('"épaisseurs" d'art') made available through varying combinations of painting, printmaking and photography.[105] In his declared faith in masterpieces but everyday preference for reproductions, and disdain for the art of the interior, Proust appears the heir of Hazlitt. But the print as an exquisitely domestic work of art, perfectly at home in the most carefully refined interiors, is a theme across Europe at the turn of the twentieth century, from the painted interiors of Vilhelm Hammershøi to the reproduction after Burne-Jones placed over the fireplace in the frosty perfection of the White Room in arch-Symbolist Fernand Khnopff's Brussels studio-house.[106] This was an acutely aesthetic approach to the print, taking pride in knowledge of its analogues in different media and comfort from its suggestion of controlled, sequenced distance from brute actuality. In its focus on the *single* print as a complex work of art, this self-conscious way of hanging a reproduction was informed by exhibition culture in which exhibitors almost always sent in their works singly. The picture in the home, on the other hand, was, historically speaking, far more often required to be a member of a pair or larger team, irrespective of the original intention of its maker. A writer familiar with the grander, long-established British private collections of paintings has even claimed that most of these collections contained at least some pictures that over the years had been enlarged or reduced

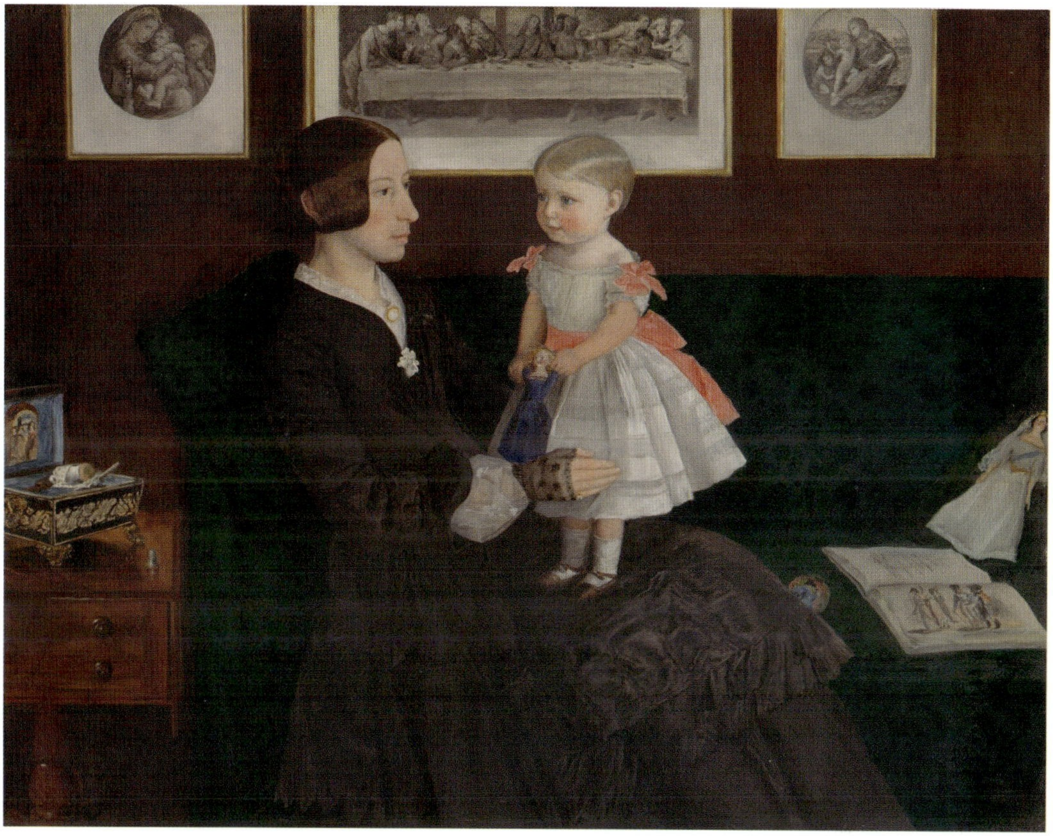

28 The young Millais provides a lesson in Pre-Raphaelitism by contrasting the impossibly elegant contours of Raphael's Madonna and Child prints with the reality of a young mother coping with a toddler just learning to walk. Over their heads, the centrifugal composition of Leonardo's *Last Supper* offers a further contrast to the sitters' rigid engagement (*Mrs James Wyatt Jr and her Daughter Sarah*, 1850).

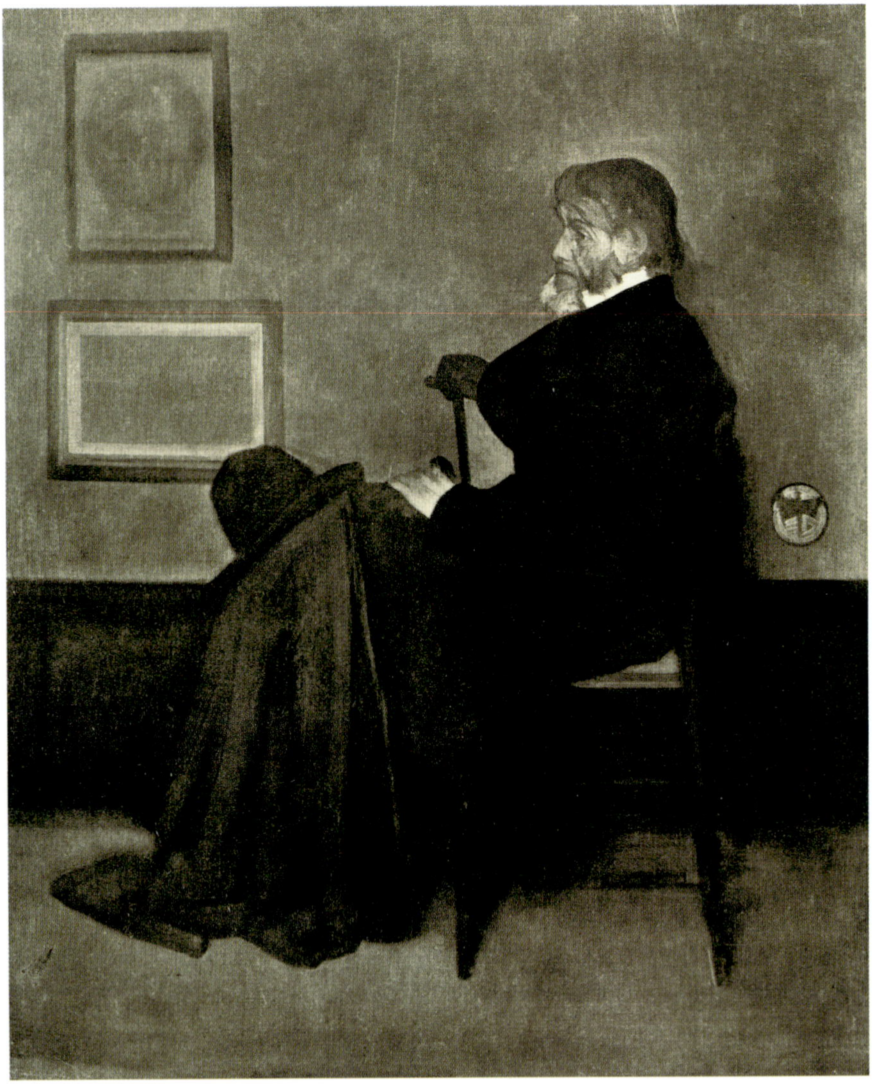

29 Whistler's 1873 portrait of Thomas Carlyle has often been seen in terms of fading – of colour, light and the fire of the writer's youthful wrath. Two framed prints accompany him, just vague enough to be invisible as subjects in their own right. A reproduction of the portrait was the only image allowed into Proust's bedroom (early twentieth-century photogravure after *Arrangement in Grey and Black, No. 2*).

to fit them to sets.[107] While the exhibition changed this approach to paintings, insisting on their singularity, the furniture print continued its habit of married life. One popular memoirist of country life around 1900 recalled that:

> Every house had a few pictures, mostly coloured ones given by grocers as almanacks and framed at home. These had to be in pairs, and lovers' meetings, lovers' partings, brides in their wedding gowns, widows standing by newly made graves, children begging in the snow or playing with puppies or kittens in nurseries were the favourite subjects.[108]

These were the '"kitschy" pictures in the house' lamented by Nikolaus Pevsner in 1937, a time of mass culture and mass politics, when the ambitions of the design reform movement initiated by the mid-Victorians seemed more urgent than ever.[109]

One of Pevsner's responses to kitsch, very much in a tradition of Victorian social improvement, was to encourage real (modern, unsentimental) pictures to be displayed in state schools. The late Victorian faith in such processes of bringing culture, specifically pictures, to the people was so enthusiastic as to seem an almost theological swing-back against the iconosceptic traditions of the Protestant churches. The Settlement Movement of slum-dwelling intellectuals often brought culture with them, as at St Jude's Church in Whitechapel where the Revd Samuel and Mrs Barnett held art exhibitions in their schoolhouse from 1881.[110] In Manchester, Thomas Horsfall established the Ancoats Museum of art and design for the aesthetic education of locals, wrote pamphlets to help them appreciate pictures and sought to get reproductions of great paintings into schools. His theory of art was based squarely on the affective equivalence of beauty in pictures and in actuality that we have seen was the Victorian norm:

> Show people the best pictures you can get of beautiful common things; make them notice the beauty of form, all the curves and combinations of lines, and the beauty of colour, and when they next see the thing which the picture represented, they will see in it the beauty which, but for the picture, they would not see.[111]

Many of the great and the good – Ruskin, and the artists George Frederic Watts and Frederic Leighton – lent their names and their pictures to these and similar ventures. Watts cheerfully made multiple versions of each of his grandiose allegories so he always had one handy for loan, while Leighton, also generous, made to Horsfall the intriguing but impracticable proposal that great paintings should be represented, to those who had not the means to travel to see them, by both an accurate photograph and a copyist's oil sketch to give the colour of the absent original. This meant in effect offering the cartoon and *ébauche* (colour sketch) that academic theory posited as stages in the development of an ambitious picture, with that final *tableau* to be produced in the imagination of the working-class connoisseur.[112] As for art in the homes of the poor themselves, at Ancoats, Horsfall had on display a Model Sitting Room, with some help from the initially sceptical William Morris, which included small pairs of (unidentified) pictures.[113]

The dynamic expansion of the illustrated press from the 1840s offered plenty of opportunities for the kind of DIY picture-making advocated by Hunt. Carrying imagery of modern life in wood-engravings based on original drawings or photographs, periodicals such as the *Illustrated London News* brought a new visual culture of contemporary reportage into modest homes. *The British Workman*, established in 1855 to promote temperance and progress among the working classes, carried full-page engravings of sturdy folk suited for pasting or pinning up as pictures, and in

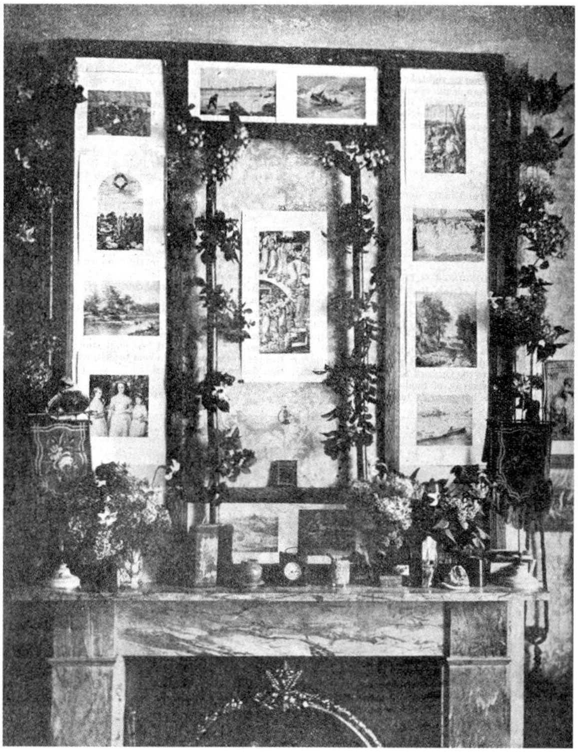

30 In 1900 the campaigning journalist W. T. Stead launched a plan to offer cheap reproductions of famous paintings to all his readers. In his magazine the *Review of Reviews*, he gave a suggestion of how to display them, but risked undermining his own claims for the power of the pictures by admitting that they looked 'rather bare' before the addition of bamboo sticks and flowers.

the 1860s a conservative writer fondly imagined that such humble but decent images 'now adorn the cot of honest poverty'.[114] From this period date the earliest mass-produced photographic reproductions of artworks, although it was some time before aesthetic philanthropists recruited such photomechanical printmaking processes to their campaigns, discouraged by the strong preference for handmade prints among collectors and curators. W. T. Stead was the heroic campaigning editor of late Victorian London. In 1885 he had spent time in prison following his demonstration of how shamefully easy it was to hire a child prostitute. In 1900 he turned his attention to art. Borrowing Leigh Hunt's 'Put Up a Picture in Your Room' as his slogan, Stead declared that now 'the treasures of art' had been 'brought within the reach of the poorest in the land' through modern reproductive techniques, Hunt's ideal was truly achievable.[115] Stead launched a series of portfolios of reproductions of favourite Old Masters at affordable prices, and suggested how these might be displayed using a photograph of his own seaside cottage decorated with the prints (illus. 30). His *Review of Reviews* was soon carrying endorsements such as that from Charles Dyall, founding curator of the Walker Art Gallery in Liverpool, to whom the portfolios were useful in his own campaigns, which evidently involved a kind of roadshow version of Horsfall's model room. 'I have for many years been trying to teach the working class how they can acquire beautiful things at a minimum of cost,' Dyall told Stead, 'and have lectured on "Art in the Houses of the People", with illustrations, fitting up a room on the platform and decorating the walls with art objects costing from 6d. to 5s.'[116]

Stead aligned his efforts with politically progressive movements, and indeed gave them such a flavour by citing Hunt as his inspiration. There were soon more openly commercial initiatives on very similar lines, offering domesticated versions of the famous masterpieces of the great galleries of the world, such as those issued in instalments by the department store Whiteleys. For at least one Edwardian working-class memoirist, tacking up a selection of these in his new lodgings was a symbol of having escaped the slums.[117] But for fiction writers – especially those with purported inside knowledge of working-class life – such quick-fix domestic art was often represented as a sign of a culturally passive household. To take just one example, D. H. Lawrence's drama *A Collier's Friday Night* opens with a lengthy stage direction describing a working family's 'kitchen or living-room' where over the mantelpiece hangs a picture of Venice 'from one of Stead's Christmas Numbers'.[118] The room, says Lawrence, is 'nevertheless, satisfactory enough' despite this intrusion of false art.

George Gissing, another working-class novelist and intellectual but of an earlier generation than Lawrence, was especially fascinated by missionary aesthetics, in which, however, he ended up having little faith. The books and pictures of a given home are frequently referenced in his stories as a barometer of its culture, yet always with the worry that they represented too an emasculating excess of domesticity.[119] Gissing's own pictures comprised the kinds of modest but highbrow prints after the great Italian masters (plus Dante Gabriel Rossetti from among the moderns) that were more or less standard among intellectuals up to and including one as sophisticated as Walter Pater.[120] Because the print by definition existed in many impressions it lent itself to self-expression, perhaps paradoxically, through that very quality. By displaying an image with some degree of common currency, one became the sort of person who liked this or that kind of picture, one's choices speaking a shared language of signs. For better or worse, prints allowed a person to be judged. There were, for example, plenty of no-nonsense types ready to smirk at all the newly admitted female undergraduates at Oxford having the same Burne-Jones autotypes as recommended by the better class of advice writers. In contrast to this, more urbane critics enjoyed mocking the suburban attachment to prints of absurdly cruel imagery, ostensibly so inappropriate for family life, such as the hunting scenes of Landseer or the various reproductions of paintings showing noble souls on their way to execution.[121] Children, with their sense of their own home as comprising the world, might be astonished to find the same pictures in other houses. In her autobiography the artist Gwen Raverat recalled gradually realizing that the tasteful print after George Mason's *Harvest Moon* that hung in her family home was also to be found pretty much everywhere else, having been the picture of choice around the mid-1880s.[122] For the adult owners, however, this sharing of an image was presumably one of its charms – it aligned them with the right sort of people. Earlier we mentioned the engraved letter and portrait of William Pitt of the 1760s, which was 'Proper to be Framed and Glazed' precisely because it signalled an allegiance to other sympathizers, an outgoing feeling of the kind that Hunt suggested would flow from putting up the picture of those one admired. Art historians have often worried over the political allegiances of painters and sculptors, rarely acknowledging that the public exhibition was widely recognized as a politics-free environment. That is not to say that artists had no opinions: rather, that the critical discourse surrounding picture shows meant that their opinions were rarely considered by those commentating. Private homes were much more likely venues for pictures to express politics, whether in the most immediately dynastic sense of placing and editing a line of family portraits or in the more abstract sense of putting up pictures of political figureheads.

Many, in the decades around 1900, who wished to declare allegiance to secular principles beyond those attended to by mainstream politicians were drawn to prints after the portraits and subject pictures of G. F. Watts. The huge reputation enjoyed by the sage of Kensington, the most noble-minded of all the great and the good Victorians, has often puzzled historians who look in vain for answers in Watts's ungainly allegorical canvases. The explanation lies in the ways his images, as reproductive prints, were semantically flexible enough to be adopted privately by vast numbers of individuals and adapted to their own homes and circumstances (see illus. 72). *Love and Life*, *Hope* and suchlike concepts were expansively inclusive and yet could suggest criteria of conduct and policy that demanded precedence over the

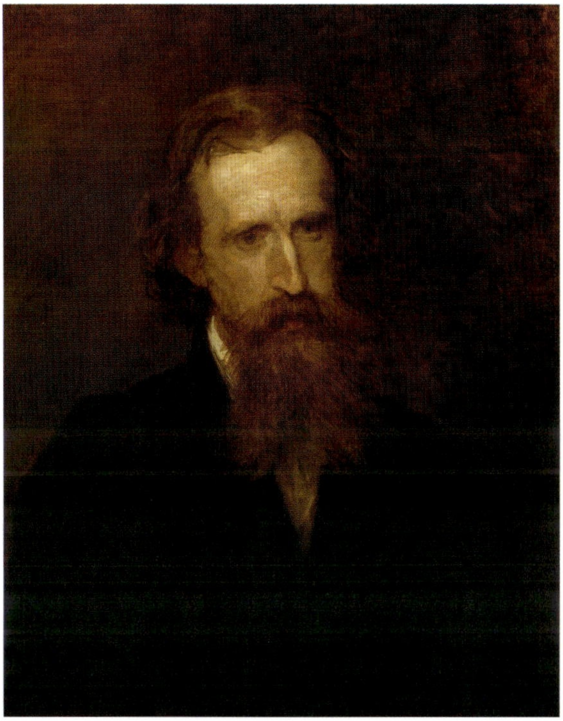

31 The writer and mountaineer Leslie Stephen shared with the artist G. F. Watts a quasi-religious belief in progress in human ethics. Their perspective attributed huge importance to the biographies and portraits of great men as representing the truest record of national history. Stephen's daughter Virginia Woolf recalled how vain he was of this portrait by Watts, of which the novelist Henry James owned a reproduction.

established order. In their appeal to absolute yet human constants they were inherently liberal and progressive.[123] Watts's portraits of public figures, painted over many years for the National Portrait Gallery, equally eschewed representatives of formal authority in favour of heroes of culture – intellectuals whose images naturally held great appeal for other intellectuals. Watts's *William Morris,* for example, was to be found in the studies of W. B. Yeats and

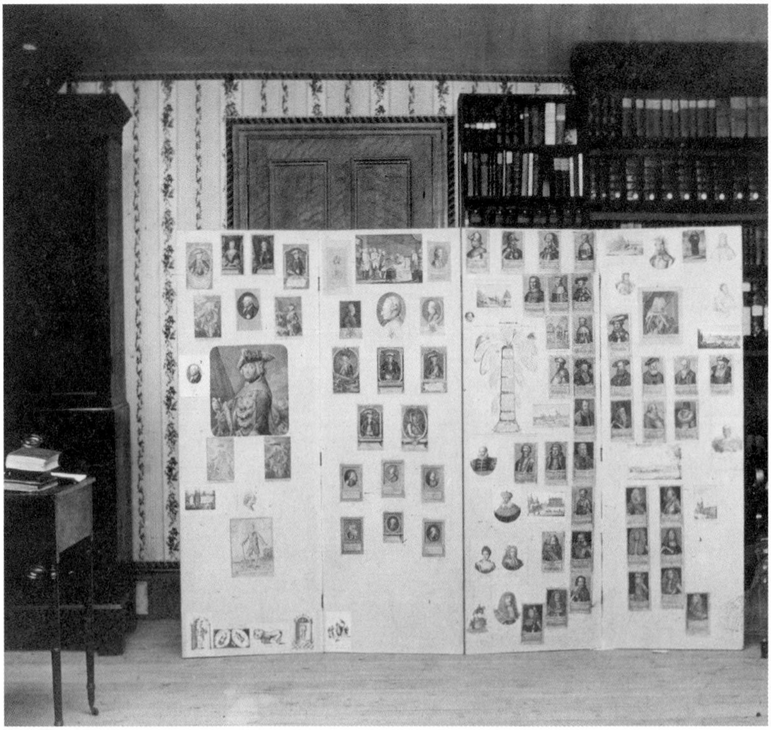

32 An early biographer of Thomas Carlyle opened his book with a description of Carlyle's Chelsea study in the 1850s when he was at work on his *History of Frederick the Great*: 'One side of the room was covered from floor to ceiling with books; two others were adorned with pictures of persons or battles' (M. D. Conway, *Thomas Carlyle*, 1881; photograph of picture screen dated 1857).

Clement Attlee, while Henry James owned a reproduction of his portrait of the historian and biographer Leslie Stephen (illus. 31).[124]

Cheap reproductions of portraits of writers, campaigners and scholars allowed anyone to plot their own intellectual family tree, however socially modest. This was a portraiture of progress stretching into the future, not limited to reinforcing the authority of the present. It was a mode of imagery especially suited to science. Thus Lord Kelvin, in his Glasgow study, had portraits of Darwin, Joule and Faraday, while in Darwin's own study at Down House were his friends and fellow scientists Joseph Hooker and Charles Lyell (plus his grandfather Josiah Wedgwood).[125] So portraiture, for intellectuals at least, provided a chain of personal inheritance analogous to the series of dynastic portraits of earlier generations. Emily Dickinson hung the portraits of George Eliot and Charlotte Brontë.[126] Another, earlier, poet, Felicia Hemans, in her Liverpool home, prioritized regional literary pride in putting up the portrait of local man William Roscoe, banker and biographer of Lorenzo de' Medici.[127] The Classical scholar and Scottish nationalist John Stuart Blackie, meanwhile, compiled in his Edinburgh house what was in effect a proto-Scottish national portrait gallery. As a wide-eyed visitor recalled, 'There were portraits everywhere, on the walls, in the chairs, on the tables; some of them rested on the floor', the greats of Scottish literature and history organized in shifting arrangements with a larger cast of European worthies. Blackie even demonstrated how this veritable laboratory of portraiture might operate, taking portraits of himself and Gladstone – the latter initially placed below the former – and, in a show of deference, switching them.[128]

One of the foremost motivators of the creation of the London Portrait Gallery, Thomas Carlyle (see illus. 29), also had a study overflowing with portraits, most of them of the same person – Frederick the Great, whose image multiplied by the dozen over walls and across screens during the years Carlyle was at work on his biography (illus. 32). For a British intellectual, being committed to a heroic version of historical progress often meant selecting individuals who had no significant formal role in the British state but who had helped make culture and history, rather than merely passing it on. Hence the great popularity in Britain of portraits of Napoleon Bonaparte, an apparently paradoxical phenomenon that regularly struck commentators such as this writer on print-sellers' shop windows in 1854: 'the shade of Napoleon would doubtless be gratified to find how often the light of his Imperial countenance is cast on our pavements.'[129] A radical could curate their own portrait gallery of individuals who had dissented. Mary Augusta (Mrs Humphry) Ward, a socially conservative novelist, described with careful horror the home of an English couple living together out of wedlock in Belgium:

> The walls, hung with the faded damask of a past generation, were decorated with a strange crop of pictures pinned carelessly into the silk – photographs or newspaper portraits of modern men and women representing all possible revolt against authority, political, religious, even scientific, the Everlasting No of an untiring and ubiquitous dissent.[130]

Such personalized political galleries were not the preserve of *rentier* radicals or those with private libraries where conventionally 'such prints as are hung in the walls ought to be memorials of learning, and portraits of men of science and erudition'.[131] Dan Cullen, a London docker thrown out of work for his union activism, was found dying in his filthy Whitechapel room around 1900, looking up at his collection of cheap portraits of Engels, John Burns and other heroes of labour.[132]

Leigh Hunt had imagined the domestic picture remaining static as a marker for its wayward owner. But of course the problem with progress is that it keeps changing. Virginia Woolf lived her early life immersed in the social circles whom Watts specialized in painting. She recalled especially the portrait – the original oil, naturally – of her father, Leslie Stephen (see illus. 31): 'a flattered, an idealized picture, up to which father would lead admiring ladies; and pause and contemplate it, with some complacency'.[133] For all their mournful austerity, Watts's portraits of suffering male

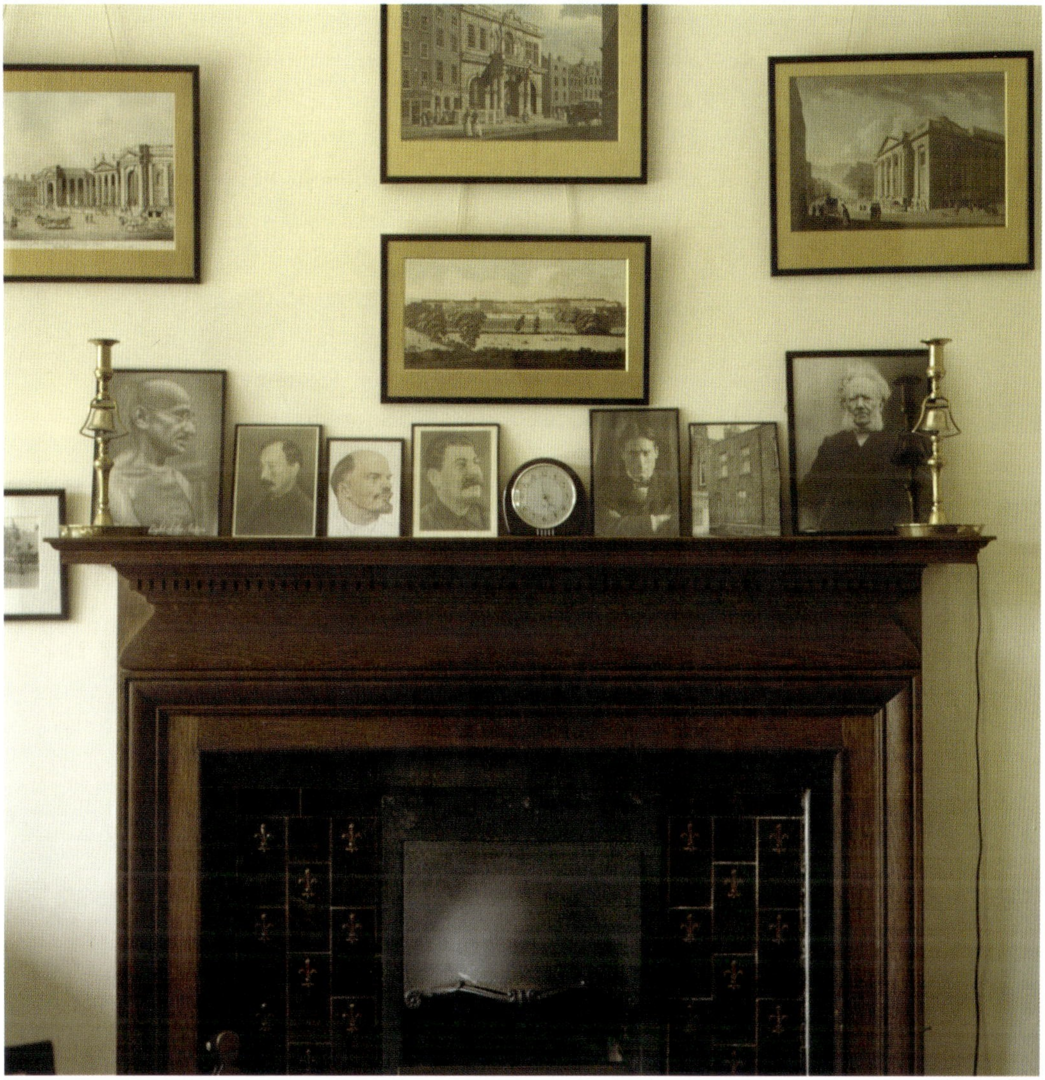

33 The mantelpiece in the dining room of the home of playwright George Bernard Shaw offers a salutary warning against identifying progress with great individuals. Among the heroes informally celebrated here are several men now considered among the greatest criminals of modern times. Even Gandhi (on the left, facing the founder of the NKVD), is – at the time of writing – becoming a controversial figure again.

intellectuals, perceived Woolf, were part of the comfortable upholstery of the late Victorian liberal home: 'Mounds of plush, Watts' portraits, busts shrined in crimson velvet, enriched the gloom of a room naturally dark and thickly shaded in summer by showers of Virginia Creeper.' This was at Hyde Park Gate. The Stephen family's relocation to the literally and metaphorically more enlightened Gordon Square in Bloomsbury allowed her to see the Watts portraits and other furniture properly for the first time. That very visibility seems to have hastened their demotion. When Woolf recounts the famous moment in which Lytton Strachey opens a frank conversation about bodily fluids, marking an epoch in the visibility of sex, she sets the scene by recalling, with self-conscious mythologizing, that 'The Watts portraits of my father and mother were hung downstairs if they were hung at all.'[134] But heroes other than those portrayed by Watts took their place for later intellectuals, most of them now, for us, at least as distasteful as Tennyson or Cardinal Manning became for Bloomsbury. George Bernard Shaw, like Hunt and Watts, a grand old man of the Left in his later years, shared with Watts a fascination with strong men that it is no longer possible politely to overlook as naivety.[135] At Shaw's home in Hertfordshire can still be seen the selection of portraits he placed over his fireplace. The actor Harley Granville-Barker is there, and Ibsen, along with the anti-Imperialist Gandhi (illus. 33). Their neighbours, however, include Lenin, Stalin and even the early Soviet chief secret policeman, the murderous 'Iron Felix' Dzerzhinsky. Shaw died in this room in 1950, with what comfort derived from such mixed company we can only guess.

2
The Picture and the Interior

. . . that detachment from their surroundings which makes the picture too often appear an alien in the decorative community.

M. H. Baillie Scott[1]

PARLOUR

If you have come to talk, then of course you should come into the parlour: that, nominally, is what it is for. A parlour was set apart for sitting with others. In American parlance it was in effect what was known in Britain as the drawing room – somewhere to withdraw to. In grand British houses where room names were necessarily multiplied and therefore used less precisely, it might be any kind of sitting room. But in its classic usage the parlour is the front ground-floor room kept for special occasions, somewhere that immediately signalled social aspirations among those of limited means – an irrational, because rarely used, space from which children were barred and where significant visitors, were there any, would be received. It was also (although already we risk giving it more of a fixed character than it can have had) legendarily where the best, and again rarely used, china and furniture were kept. Its pictures, likewise, were not to be used – that is, carefully examined – but were there to support more abstractly an aura of unexceptionable respectability.[2] The idea of an unused room containing all the house's best things was anathema to anyone approaching the home from a rationally economic point of view, as did domestic advice writers from the 1860s. In America, in particular, the evolution of the parlour into the all-purpose 'living room' was celebrated as a national event of characteristically practical enlightenment.[3] Once challenged by the logicians of household management, the parlour survived in fiction as an admission of the failure of a home's self-sufficiency, a place waiting for something to happen to it. Back in the real world of home-making, however, Mass-Observation's wartime *Enquiry into People's Homes* noted the general abolition of the parlour in recent housing developments, but also residents' continued expression of 'a very deep-seated feeling in favour of having a special room for these "best" occasions, where visitors can be entertained and the best furniture kept'.[4] A helpful warning of the limits of rationality in matters of the home.

The classic picture for the parlour was an engraving of an earnest subject. The novelist Somerset Maugham, imagining the ultimate in tasteless rooms, the 'outrage to decency' that was a British missionary's parlour in China in the 1920s, suggested you might find there prints of James Sant's *The Soul's Awakening* or Luke Fildes's *The Doctor*, both massively popular images centred on a noble, pensive figure.[5] Such imagery implied that the hosts were taking seriously whatever it was their visitors had to say, and if the parlour was where one found those historical trial scenes evidently so very popular as engravings, then again the location made sense as a place where words were carefully weighed (illus. 34). Among the transcripts of trials held at the Old Bailey is one of 1863 in which a complicated police operation to bring to book a network of banknote forgers was finally successful when officers opened up a hole into a suspect's parlour 'and hung a little

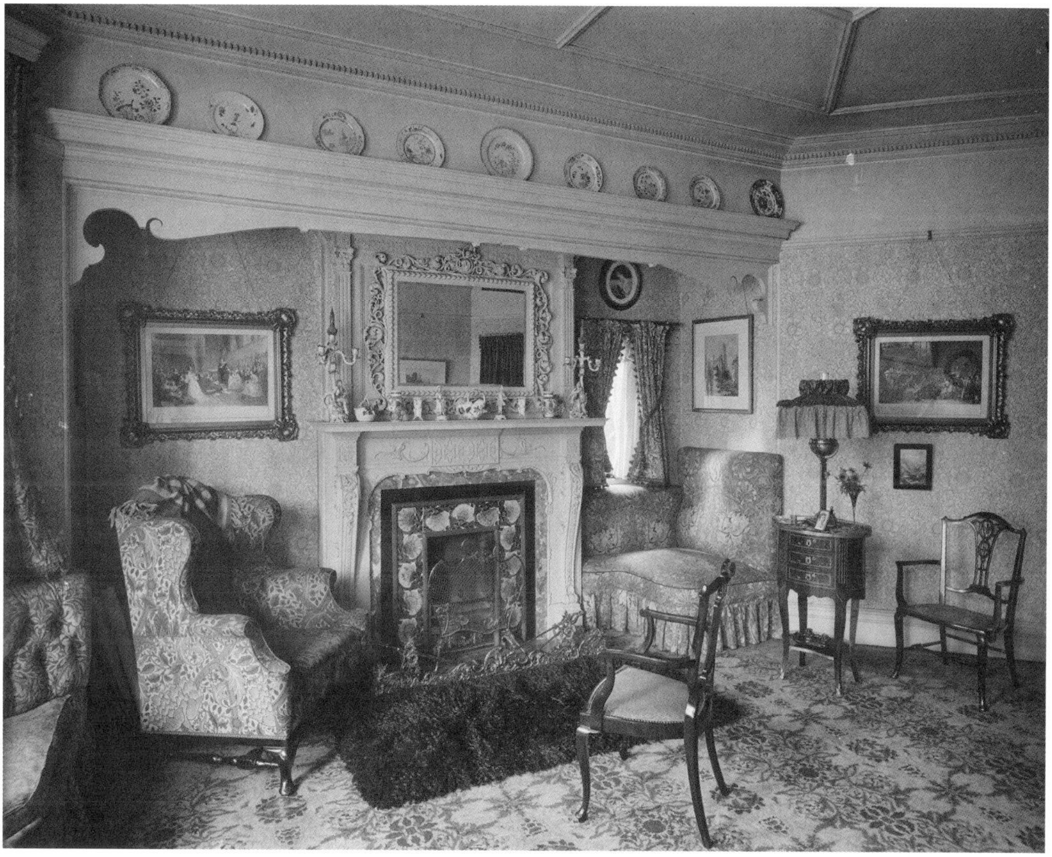

34 A newly furnished drawing room in a leafy Birmingham suburb, 1897. The two large pictures are engravings of Victorian paintings of seventeenth-century trials. On the left the royalist Earl of Strafford confronts Parliament, and on the right William, Lord Russell, vice versa, is condemned by a royalist court. The lesson is perhaps to listen carefully to both sides.

picture, a print, over the hole, so as to avoid any person seeing it'. Incriminating conversation duly ensued and the forgers were taken into custody: the carefully attentive parlour picture was in this case fully true to its character.[6]

The very pointlessness of the parlour from an economic view gave it an almost sacred meaning when its association with 'best' meant bettering oneself. Whither would the working-class autodidact retreat to study other than the parlour? For George Gissing the parlour was a site of dramatic tension where the intellectual's dreams would be fulfilled or broken. The absence or presence here of 'books and pictures' – such a common phrase in Gissing – was a question of the life or death of the mind. In the parlour used by Richard Mutimer, the protagonist of Gissing's *Demos: A Story of English Socialism*, the pictures are convincingly random: 'A striking landscape of the Swiss type, an engraved portrait of Garibaldi, an unframed view of a certain insurance office, a British baby on a large scale from the Christmas number of an illustrated paper.'[7] We have the sense that it is the task of Richard and his kind to grasp this flotsam and jetsam of passively acquired, commercial visual culture – the 'meaningless pictures' that Gissing describes elsewhere – and to mould it into something meaningful and lasting (he has already made a start on the books in the same room, which are better chosen and coherent as a collection).[8] In another novel of the same period Gissing describes a funeral party in a parlour in which there are the conventional images of judgement – the seventeenth-century trials of the Earl of Strafford and Lord Russell along with John Martin's *Fall of Nineveh*. There was even, exceptionally, an oil painting, pathetically retained despite its dilapidation to the point of illegibility: 'the canvas bulged forth from the frame; the subject appeared to be a ship, but was just as likely a view of the Alps.'[9] Here was another important purpose of the parlour, too easily overlooked by planners and reformers – somewhere to lay out a body for a wake, as Emily Dickinson's was, among the 'chastely cold' engravings in her parlour, in 1886.[10]

DINING ROOM

Historians of domesticity tell us that it was a nineteenth-century principle to define the uses of the rooms of a home more clearly, or at least to emphasize how in theory each might aspire to a different character. The parlour, in its splendid isolation, was defined against the more immediately functional rooms of the house, while the dining and drawing rooms enjoyed a special relationship of complementarity. The dining room (illus. 35) was – to broadly summarize the received wisdom of our period – masculine and the drawing room feminine; the dining room was dark, symmetrical and its occupants static, while the drawing room was light, picturesquely varied in decoration and fluid in personnel.[11] The dining room contained oil portraits of family members and probably pictures of animals and foodstuffs, both dead and alive; the drawing room would have works on paper and any picture that repaid close attention. The theory of the dining room, so to speak, envisaged it as a richly painted oil based on transitions from light to dark, the drawing room resembling rather a watercolour with its details lucidly and evenly lit. Jacob von Falke, a dynamic figure in the development of German and Austrian museums, put it elegantly in his comprehensive *Art in the House*, first published in 1871. In the dining room all interest, light and society are focused: 'The chandelier in the centre, the faces of the guests with light falling full upon them, the dark background against which they are relieved – all this makes the whole room and the persons in it look like a picture with a concentrated light in the manner of Rembrandt.'[12] That 'dark background' was where the pictures of the dining room had to live: it was indeed their duty to contribute to the sense

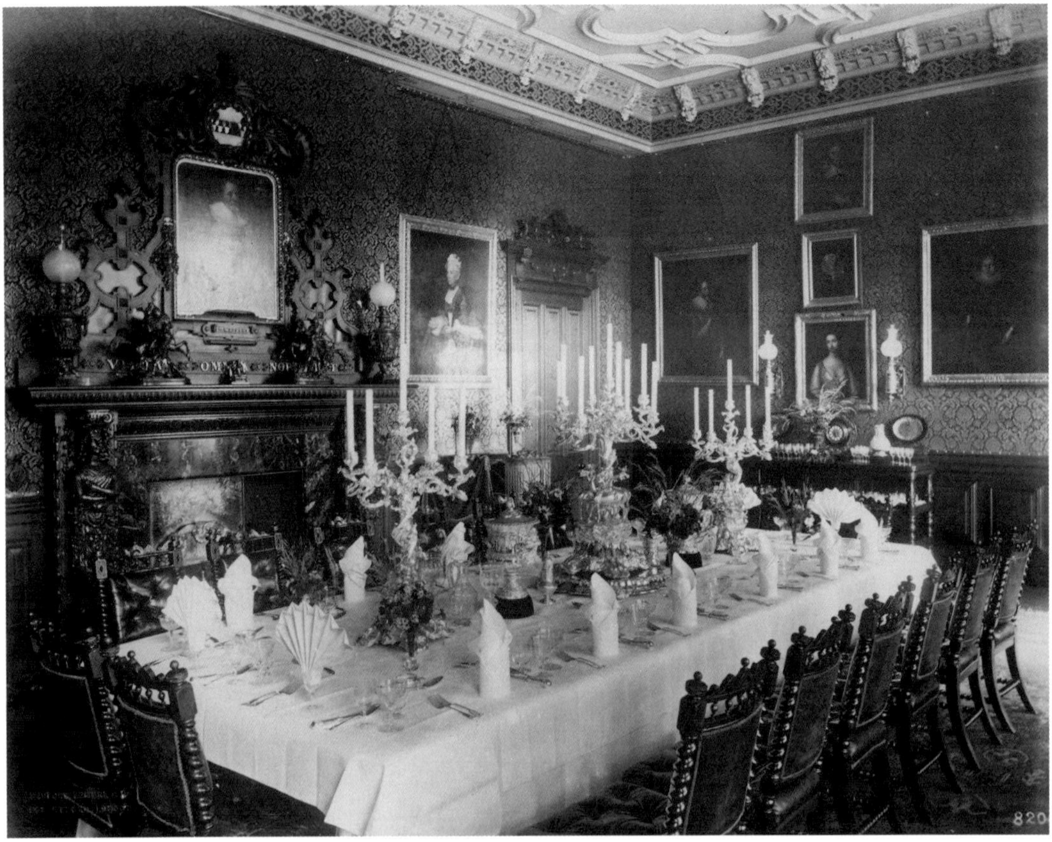

35 Beaumanor Hall in Leicestershire was rebuilt in the 1840s in a neo-Jacobean style, partly a homage by the client – William Perry Herrick – to his ancestors who had first acquired the property. The dining room was able to make use of those ancestors' portraits to create an early Victorian epitome of such a space (photographed in 1887).

of heaviness and mass, not to interrupt it. According to one Edwardian writer spelling out the priorities for this room, 'costly furniture and fine pictures become almost an insult to the guests when offered as an accompaniment to a pretentious but ill-cooked and ill-served repast.'[13] It should be food and company first, the setting second.

It is around the turn of the century that most of the more quotable accounts of the Victorian dining room are to be found, as commentators looked back with eyes changed by the Arts and Crafts movement and Queen Anne Revival style.[14] Thus Arnold Bennett, in one of his stories of life in the Potteries, describes a stolid dining room that smugly ignored anything that William Morris had to teach, and in which the gas-burning chandelier 'cast a dazzling luminance on the tea-table of snow and silver, while leaving the pictures in a gloom so discreet that not Ruskin himself could have decided whether these were by Whistler or Peter Paul Rubens'.[15] In retrospect, the warm dark tones of mahogany, port wine, brown meat and flushed human faces became mingled, and one writer observed in 1913 that the whole arrangement of the conventional dining room of the previous century 'smacks of sirloin of beef'.[16] Already in his reforming *Hints on Household Taste* of the 1860s Eastlake had taken the carcass metaphor to a disturbing level: 'The great solemn dining-room, with its heavy sarcophagus-like sideboards and funereal window curtains, is eminently suggestive of the undertaker's calling.'[17] A French visitor introduced to the Victorian dining room in Mrs Ward's hit novel of 1905, *The Marriage of William Ashe*, agreed: 'I suppose your English dining-rooms are all like this? One might be sitting in a hearse. And the pictures – no! *Quelles horreurs*!'[18] The hold that such conventions had is suggested by the story told by the banker-collector Samuel Rogers, whose elaborate mechanism for manoeuvring the pictures in his drawing room was described in Chapter One. He also had good pictures in his dining room, but, as he recalled of his attempt to entertain the wit and cleric Sydney Smith, displaying them to guests was not a success:

> At one time, when I gave a dinner, I used to have candles placed all round the dining-room, and high up, in order to show off the pictures. I asked Smith how he liked that plan. 'Not at all', he replied; 'above, there is a blaze of light, and below, nothing but darkness and gnashing of teeth.'[19]

The reversal of the standard Rembrandtesque illumination from the centre led to a hellish demotion of the meal to the charnel-house vision conjured by later writers.

The uncertain results of Rogers's experiments with showing his dining-room paintings hints at the larger problem of how to light pictures. Picture galleries, both public and private, were associated with new developments in lighting technologies throughout the nineteenth century. The British Institution, where the first loan exhibitions were held, was sited on Pall Mall, the world's first gas-lit street, and its own galleries were lit by gas from 1819, a couple of years after the huge candelabrum in the Great Room at the Royal Academy's Somerset House premises was converted from oil to gas.[20] These spaces were for temporary displays and therefore not so acutely vulnerable to the deleterious effects that gas fumes were soon seen to be having on books, furniture and pictures in private houses. Many private galleries nevertheless adopted gaslight, especially the grander ones that doubled up in the evening as large reception rooms or ballrooms, but it was not until the 1850s that a museum showing a permanent collection installed gas to allow the extension of opening hours. The newly constructed gallery for modern British pictures at the V&A opened in 1857 with extensive piping letting out naked flames (this is where Mulready's picture was coughed and spluttered at). Although a sub-committee of experts led by Michael Faraday

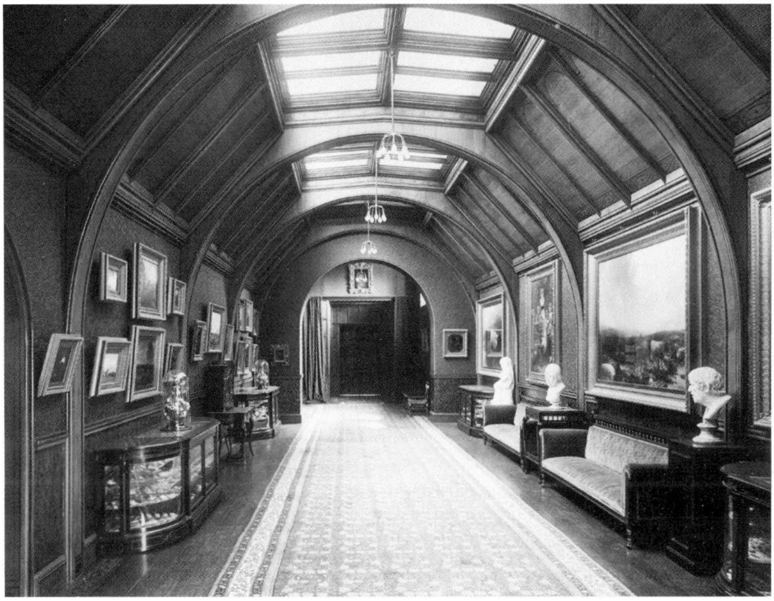

36 The great fantasy castle of Cragside in Northumberland was developed for the engineer William Armstrong by Richard Norman Shaw from the 1860s. The Picture Gallery shown here (at first known as the Museum) has a claim to be the first domestic room in Britain to be lit by electricity, from 1878. The original light fittings and woodwork had already been changed by the time this photograph was taken in 1891.

assured the museum that any risk to the pictures was being mitigated by simply providing egress for the fumes, the V&A moved to electric light as soon as this became feasible. By 1883 all but a couple of the galleries displaying pictures there were lit using the newly marketed incandescent electric light bulbs.[21] Over at the privately run Grosvenor Gallery on Bond Street, home to an Aesthetic mode of British art, the noble proprietors constructed their own generator, which was the germ of the London Electric Supply Corporation, founded in 1887, itself to become a foundation of today's national grid. Among domestic picture galleries, the first to be electrically lit is agreed to have been that at Cragside, the house in Northumberland rebuilt for the wealthy engineer William Armstrong by Richard Norman Shaw from 1869. The pioneering developer of electrical lighting, Joseph Swan of Gateshead, introduced arc lighting into the gallery there as early as 1878, although this seems to have required significant technical competence to operate and was soon superseded by filament bulbs (illus. 36).[22]

Those wealthy enough to have the option seem to have lit their pictures with electricity as soon as possible. The exciting, aristocratic novelty of electric light helps explain the fashion for the dainty fixtures sometimes seen attached to individual pictures. Generally these were fitted to, or near to, the tops of frames, but a few early experimenters fixed uplights to or just under the bottoms of frames. An example can be seen in the scheme carried out in Wimpole Street in 1893 by the architect W. B. Catherwood for the stockbroker Arthur Anderson (illus. 37), in which lamps throw light up to Edwin Long's *The Assyrian Captive* and Luke Fildes's *An Al-Fresco Toilette*. Given that both pictures were glazed, it seems hard to believe that reflection did not make them invisible when lit only by these lamps, and in any case the arrangement shown here was very short-lived: Anderson died less than a year after the photograph was taken and the pictures were immediately dispersed. The idea of a picture having its own light had distant history in devotional contexts and apparently very occasionally in more recent times, such as the elegantly slender-armed sconces for gas once to be found looping over some of the pictures by Reynolds in the Crimson Drawing Room at Holland House in Kensington (illus. 38).[23] But the idea of the electric picture lamp, now often found vulgar in private houses of any age because imagined to be an affectation of *nouveaux riches* picture hoarders, was surely the predecessor of today's system of picture-gallery lighting. Nowadays LED fittings are painstakingly angled along

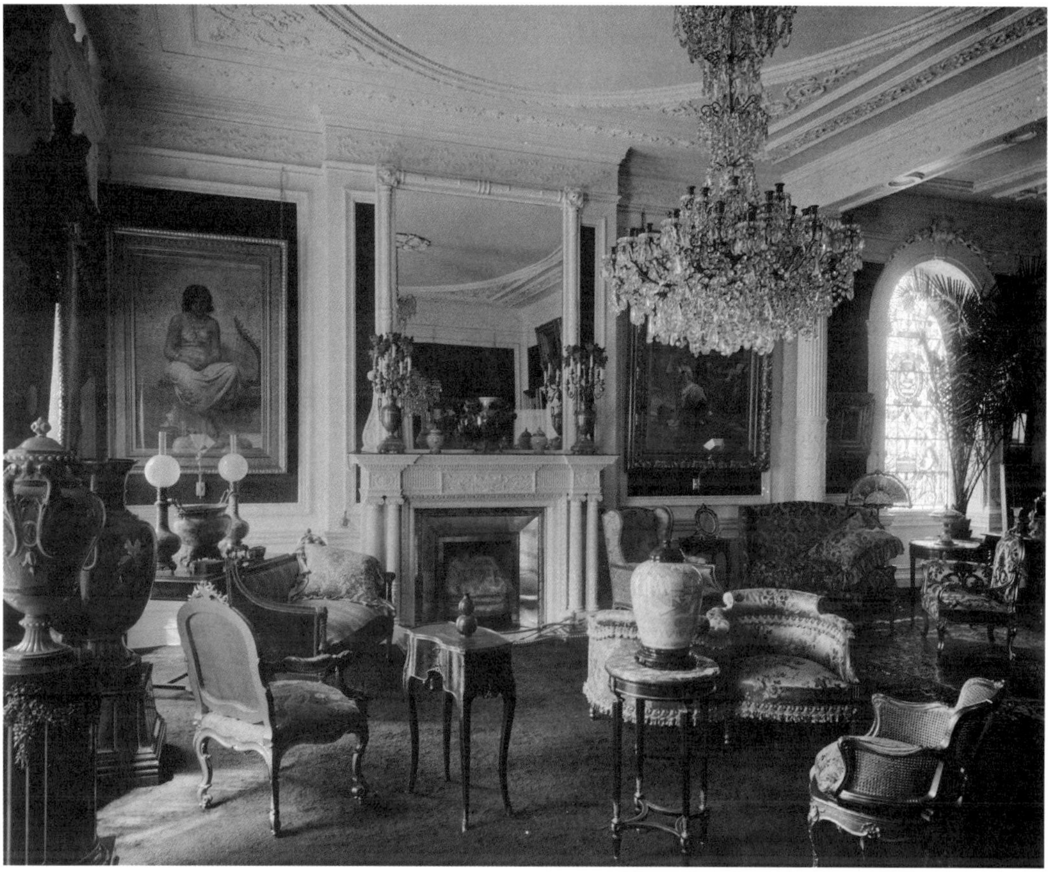

37 As electric lighting became feasible in domestic interiors from the 1880s, those with pictures to show off experimented with running individual lamps to illuminate especially important works. Designers were able to use pictures and pools of light to emphasize one another in schemes such as this of 1893 in which lamps are fitted below two large paintings.

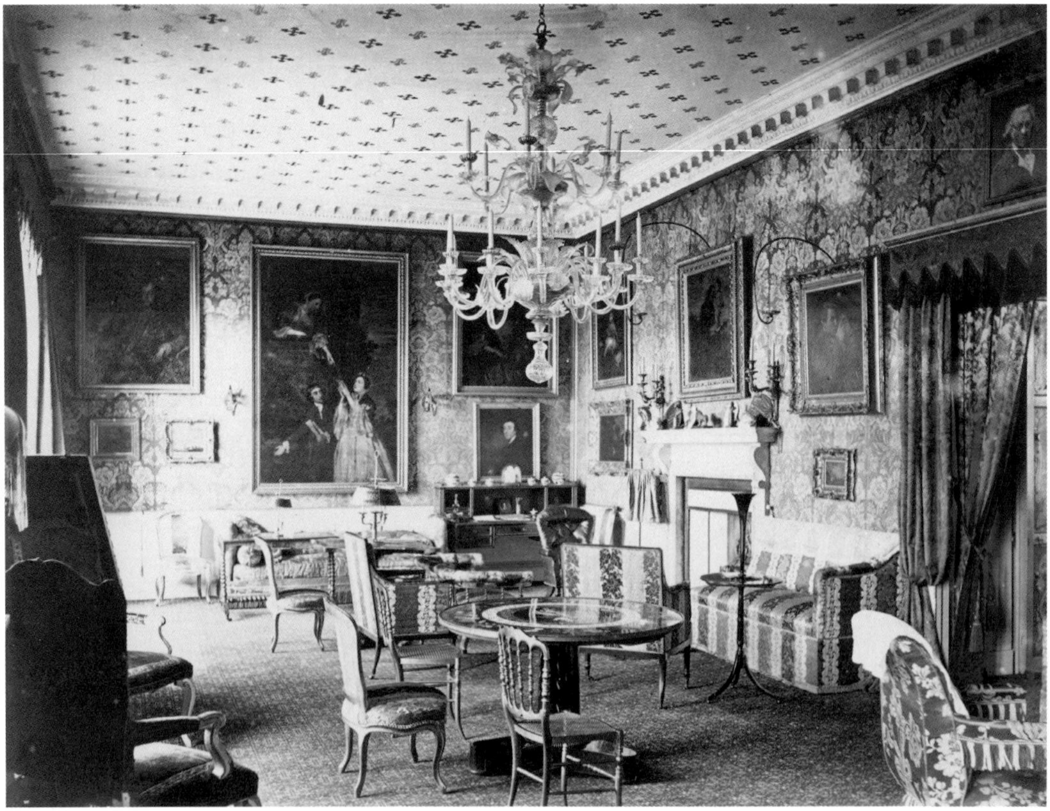

38 Holland House in Kensington was the intellectual headquarters of the Whigs in the eighteenth century, and remained a symbol of that tradition throughout the nineteenth. In this room given over to portraits by Joshua Reynolds, some of the paintings have their own swan-necked gas-burning sconces, most easily visible over the portrait of short-sighted librarian Joseph Baretti on the right.

tracks to spot pictures in rooms that are often entirely deprived of the daylight, which, so collectors were assured through the nineteenth century, was good for their paintings.

In a domestic dining room, as we have seen, such individuation of the pictures was the opposite of the effect required. Here the role of pictures was to add to the sense of solidity and stasis by offering the vague presence of reassuring objects, principally ancestors and still lifes (both categories might be covered by the term used by William Sanderson in the 1650s: 'dead-standing-things').[24] The broad principle that the dining room required pictures which worked in the simplest possible register – easily recognizable subject-matter without narrative or symbolism and shown more or less life-size – appears to have been shared internationally. In France, Henry Havard stressed the theatrical nature of a dinner party, at which the proper focus was towards the centre of the room, with anything on the walls risking becoming a distraction. The pictures must be absorbed into the background and should be 'always of simple subjects, easy to understand; landscapes, still lifes, are the genres which best suit the dining room; above all do not allow an enigmatic composition to raise itself up like a deadly question mark before a gentleman dining'.[25] Von Falke has this intriguing remark: 'Realistic historical paintings are out of place [in the dining room], as they produce a picture within a picture.'[26] His objection is that the things and figures in a narrative picture set in the past or in a mythical age are not just themselves but also signs guiding the viewer through another time and place, whereas the definition of appropriate dining-room art was precisely that representation should operate at its most transparent and immediate level.

We saw in the Introduction that a central plank of Victorian design reform thinking was that nothing in the home should pretend to be something it wasn't. On its strictest interpretation this rule even forbade a picture doing anything beyond its immediate task of offering a two-dimensional facsimile of something real.[27] That the rule be applied strictly in the dining room was considered necessary by reformers because confusion was especially liable to occur here, for example furniture-makers being tempted to add carvings of edible creatures to their buffets and sideboards. The sensible title of Rhoda and Agnes Garrett's 1876 book *Suggestions for House Decoration in Painting, Woodwork, and Furniture* belies its status as one of the most original and readable texts of its genre. Here the authors complain of dining-room furniture that shocks the sense of touch: 'you cannot even open a drawer or a cupboard without having your feelings outraged by coming into contact with the legs or wings of a dead bird or some other ghastly trophy of man's love of slaughter, which frequently takes the place of an ordinary handle.'[28]

So all the furnishings in the dining room needed to keep to their core activities, which for paintings meant that they should deferentially mimic the action in the centre of the room – the food and the family. As Edith Wharton put it in *The Decoration of Houses*, which she published with Ogden Codman in 1897, the convention had been for the walls to be 'hung with fruit or flower-pieces, or with pictures of fish and game: a somewhat obvious form of adornment which it has long been the fashion to ridicule, but which was not without decorative value and appropriateness'.[29] The rule about dining-room furniture being true to its purpose also meant, as we have seen, that a picture should do its work of representation in a single register and, even more basically, that a painting should confidently signal its physical status with a bold gilt frame that would remain discernible even when the image within was obscured. The most beautiful print or watercolour could not hold its place in the darkness of the dining room, and would not go along so well as did oils – as Benjamin Disraeli put it of an aristocratic context – with 'crimson footmen'.[30] Of course, those without footmen, or the budget for paintings, could always fall back upon chromos – coloured lithographic copies – many of which were marketed specially for the dining room.[31]

'It is an old English custom', wrote the younger Eastlake, 'to hang family portraits in the dining-room,' and for once a leading reformer confessed he had found a tradition not needing reform. Family portraits seemed a reasonable custom, he admitted, approving their heavy, substantial presence. Eastlake's rational mission does, however, encourage him to justify their presence in terms of what they offered to the primary function of the room, the dinner party itself: 'it is pleasant on such occasions to be surrounded by mementos of those who once, perhaps, formed members of a social circle which they have long ceased to join.'[32] Illustrating this idea, a touching story was told of the playwright and politician Richard Brinsley Sheridan, who had lost his wife, the beautiful and brilliant musician and bluestocking Elizabeth Linley, some years before he was eventually called into government in 1806. The pretentious painting he had commissioned of her from Reynolds, showing her as St Cecilia accompanying singing angels at her keyboard, had been pawned, but was retrieved from the broker so that for just one night she might again grace their dining room as Sheridan entertained his new, important colleagues.[33] Writing in the seventeenth century, William Sanderson, ever ready with improbable but charming suggestions for justifying the locations of pictures, suggested the habit of portraits in the dining room began with loyally displaying the pictures of the King and Queen, who were subsequently joined by portraits of family members 'to waite upon their princely Persons'.[34]

The cluster of family portraits helped mark the dining room as masculine, for whatever likenesses may been brought into the house by women, 'the family' was of course defined primarily through male lines. The Garretts, distinguished suffrage campaigners as well as pioneering female design professionals, saw the reform of the dining-room picture hang as part and parcel of larger changes in society.[35] '[T]here is no other room in the house where innovations are more grudgingly permitted,' they observed, 'and an Englishman would suspect you of every other revolutionary tendency, if you proposed any radical changes.' Their own opinion was that 'there are wallpapers now made possessing far more artistic merits than many of the family portraits with which dining-room walls are too often disfigured.'[36] There is the true voice of the Victorian domestic reformer, insisting on transparency, rationality, purpose and hygiene, unable to countenance the notion that a picture may have uses other than being looked at for artistic skill and taste. It was the logic of progress, and it was left to reactionaries such as Mrs Ward to defend the owning of bad pictures on moral grounds. In her 1909 novel *Daphne*, the all-too-independent American protagonist of the title marries the son of Lady Barnes, a widow whose mediocre inherited family portraits, extending back to the school of Peter Lely, have been further diminished through the attentions of a local restorer. 'One cannot really live with bad pictures because they happen to be one's ancestors!' exclaims Daphne, and when it is explained to her that it is impossible for them to be separated from the house, she logically concludes, 'Well then, let's move ourselves!' She eventually has her way, and when an old friend of the family sees the improved dining room, he is appalled: 'Where was the portrait of Edward, and of Edward's father by Sir Francis Grant?' They had been moved on to make way for 'the famous Signorelli' (the family's one real Old Master), 'a full-length nude St. Sebastian, bound and pierced – which had replaced them on the dining-room wall. Who on earth ever saw such a picture in a dining-room?'[37] In a rather superior novel on a comparable theme, Henry James's *Portrait of a Lady*, the sickly Ralph Touchett, aware that he is unlikely to live to further his family's line, becomes indifferent to the portraits in the dining room: 'the pictures on the wall, all of them very brown, looked vague and incoherent. There was a ghostly presence as of dinners long since digested, of table-talk that had lost its actuality.'[38]

We have seen enough of the conventions of the dining room to understand that a display of shiny contemporary art there risked being found distinctly brassy. But what could more efficiently show – to a captive, seated audience – that one had made up for a lack of ancestors with wealth and taste? The caste-conscious Disraeli imagined the archetype of such an arrangement in his novel *Coningsby*, set in the 1830s, in which aristocracy and merchant class unite to breed the 'one nation' with which the author's later political career was to be associated. Visiting the home of Millbank, a wealthy Manchester merchant, young Harry Coningsby dines in a chamber proudly displaying the cream of the modern British School – Landseer, Etty, Wilkie and all.[39] The twist is that the collection is so very contemporary as to contain the distracting portrait of the teenage daughter of the house, who of course Harry eventually marries. So this dining-room portrait proves after all to be dynastic but in a prospective rather than a retrospective sense. Published in 1844, *Coningsby* echoed various celebrated real dining rooms of that decade, such as that of the horse contractor Robert Vernon on Pall Mall in London, whose collection of modern British art was donated to the nation in 1847, the year in which the engineer Brunel commissioned a series of largely landscape-based scenes from Shakespeare for his own dining room.[40] Again in this year, the monthly *Art-Union*, ever determined to imagine painting to be an art form invented by the British middle classes in recent decades, recommended 'bright landscapes' to cheer the dining room.[41] When Disraeli himself visited Manchester in 1859, he was able to meet a real-life Millbank, Sir James Watts, the Lord Mayor of the city and an epically wealthy textiles magnate. Disraeli would have dined in the room designed just a few years earlier by Pugin, decorated with modern British pictures, chief among them *Life among the*

Gypsies, in Seville by John Phillip (illus. 39), which must have positively blinged within that gothic interior.

Some who were encumbered with old family portraits used the opportunity provided by a new decorative dining-room scheme to demote them. The versatile writer William John Loftie claimed to know of 'an insolent young gentleman who sent his family portraits to the bedrooms because they did not agree with his new Gothic furniture'. To avoid such enthusiasms Loftie suggested the mixing up of old portraits with watercolours, shields of arms and anything else to avoid visual monotony.[42] Others ran with Eastlake's idea of portraits as a means of effecting a virtual gathering of family and friends in the dining room and proposed expanding this circle. Henry Mogford encouraged

> the portraits of eminent or exalted persons, famous for their achievements in arms or their distinction in the arts, sciences, or literature, looking, as it were, out of their frames upon the company . . . Perhaps it would not be a great stretch of imagination to fancy they are our companions in participating of the hospitality of the table.[43]

But this was potentially dangerous advice, for to be seen to be mixing and matching one's actual family with others bought in was, to anyone who cared to go about policing etiquette, the nadir of *arrivisme*.[44] Some hard-headed people grasped that the best compromise was to commission really good portraits that future generations would wish to retain as artworks. As the aristocratic memoirist Mary Clive observed, with the pragmatism of an upper-class survivor of the twentieth century, 'Portraits have to be very good before grandchildren want to keep them; also quite small.'[45]

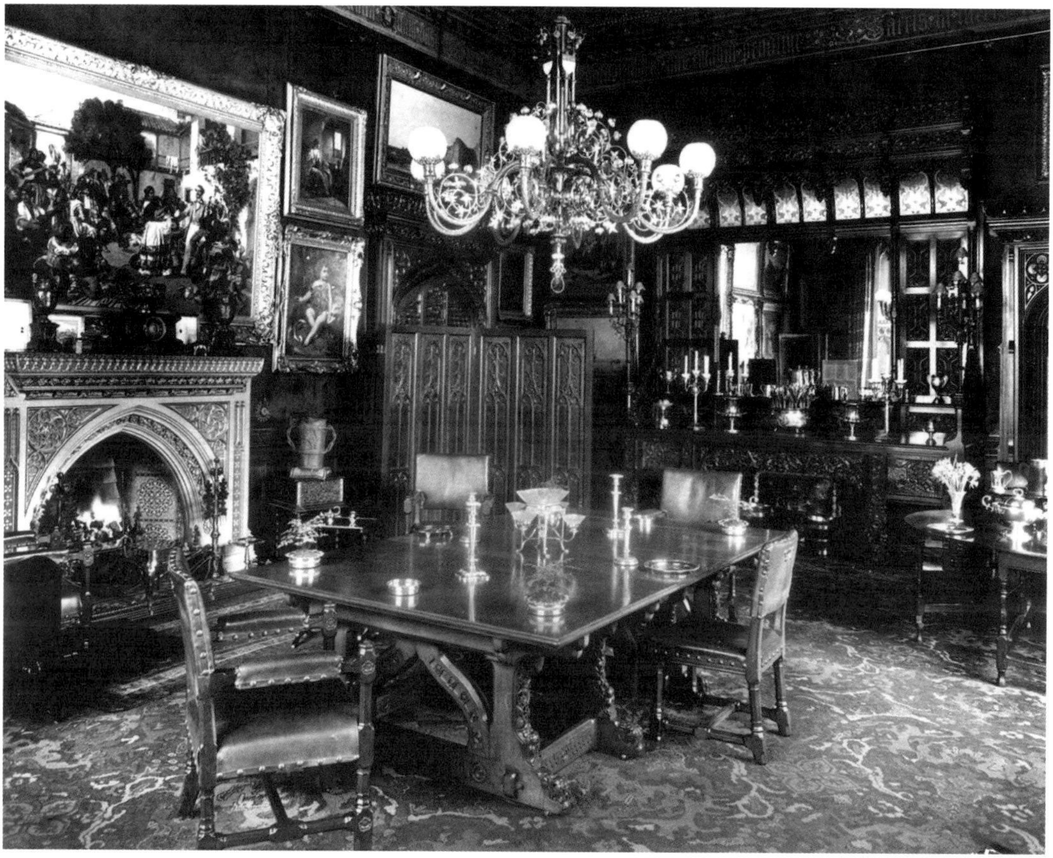

39 Abney Hall in Cheadle was where Prince Albert stayed when visiting Manchester in 1857 to open the vast Art Treasures Exhibition. He must have been entertained by his host James Watts, mayor of Manchester, in this Pugin-designed dining room. The gothic interior is a strange setting for the sunny painting over the fireplace, John Phillip's *Life among the Gypsies, in Seville* (photograph taken 1912).

THE GREAT DESCENT

The conventions that guided the decoration of the dining room depreciated the compositional content of paintings for a very simple reason which we have not yet addressed: people sat down during almost the entirety of their time spent in formal dining rooms and so necessarily looked up at the pictures at angles sharper than assumed to be ideal for close appreciation. This fact helped underwrite the basic division, widely recognized, between the drawing room, where pictures might be inspected, and the dining room, where they offered a cumulative effect. It was the perennial demand of pretty much anyone who wrote about interiors, at any time, that pictures be hung at eye level, and the particular lament of writers in our period, from the early nineteenth century, that pictures were always placed too high.

The American disciple of Ruskin, Clarence Cook, saw the descent of the picture into touching distance as a sign of the diffusion of education and urbanization:

> In remote farm-houses and country taverns we often see pictures, particularly portraits, skyed as high as if their owners had been Academy Hangers, and the painters young rivals of a new school. I suppose the reason is that the simple-hearted owners think a picture such a precious thing, it can't be hung too securely out of the reach of meddling hands. They are often not clear in their minds as to what a picture is meant for, and not finding in it any practical relation to human life and society, they treat it with reverence and put it where it will disturb them as little as possible. But, as people come to enjoy pictures and get some intellectual, spiritual nourishment out of them, they want them, as they want their books, where they can see them and use them.[46]

Lewis Foreman Day in Britain agreed: 'The blunder of hanging pictures too high is as common as that of hanging them too low is rare.'[47] It was a campaign that was ever needing to be renewed, the picture apparently floating upwards again, no matter how often it was ordered down. The novelist, memoirist and well-known writer of domestic advice Jane Ellen Panton warned of leaving workmen to hang pictures unsupervised. She recalled one especially skilful man who nevertheless, 'like all those who have no regular art education, . . . had the usual mania for hanging everything ever so much higher than it ought to be – a mania I most successfully and promptly combated!' As a good evangelical, Mrs Panton searched too for temptation within, castigating herself, or at least the illustration in one of her books representing a cosy corner of her own home, in which the pictures are shown 'as being much higher than they really are'.[48] Indeed by 1919 the only explanation left was that 'An evil genius seems to prompt some people to hang pictures too high.'[49]

Clearly the reformers and advice writers were up against an entrenched habit, a refusal of the population at large to buy into the rational aesthetic (advocated for museums by Ruskin from the 1840s) comprising a single line of pictures at head height. The art historian Ernst Gombrich, intrigued by the evidently long-standing practice of placing pictures counter-intuitively high, conjectured that this related to the panelling of many Early Modern European interiors, which homeowners may have been reluctant to knock nails into. He also noted that, by and large, painters of the sixteenth and seventeenth centuries did not manage their perspective so as to construe a viewer looking upwards.[50] Indeed such adaptive distortion was unnecessary because – so it is now understood – we are well able to read perspectival schemes without needing to act out those optical diagrams where the vanishing point mirrors the eye of the beholder, just as a cheap seat ranged wide of the

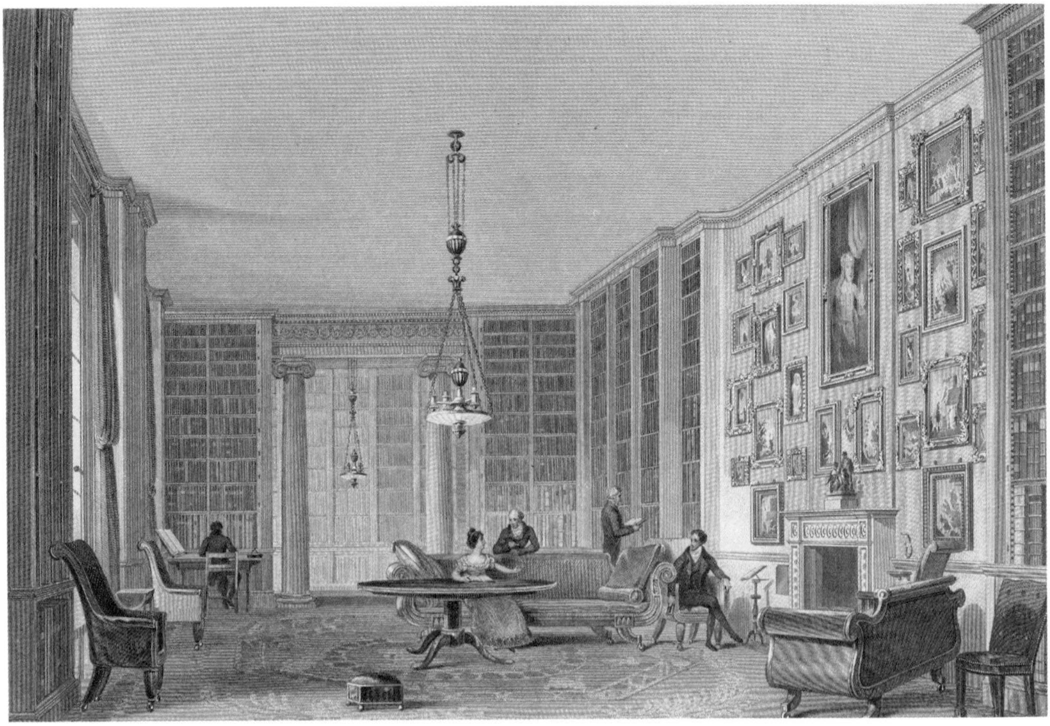

40 The book collection at Althorp, seat of the Spencer family, had few equals in private hands. The Long Library was just one of the spaces needed to contain it, and was used also as the house's principal sitting room. A hang of stacked pictures was used here to help give an enhanced impression of height to this long, low chamber. From a watercolour by Edward Blore, engraved in T. F. Dibdin, *Aedes Althorpianae* (1822).

cinema screen still affords its occupant the full experience of the film.[51] Nevertheless, during the eighteenth century the orthodoxy was firmly established in drawing manuals that there was such a thing as a 'point of sight' from which a picture should ideally be seen, correlating to the supposed relation of the original artist to the place represented. This literary orthodoxy, embedded in the culture of picturesque landscape painting, and naturalism more generally, was amenable to some compromise. Academic picture culture, privileging the human figure in more abstracted settings and imagining an ideal public audience, rather than a lonely student of scenery, was less prescriptive. Some writers even felt able to reassure their readers that, so long as the artist did not insist too rigidly on perspectival space, then viewers could combine, and in each person 'the Eye will overlook little Variations from the strict Appearance the Objects ought to have, and the Imagination will be ready to supply the defect'.[52] On the walls of some of those readers, the grander ones at least, such play of the optical imagination had already long been in effect as pictures were stacked up at uniform intervals, their multiplying spaces amplifying the perceived height of the rooms they decorated. In a print from the 1820s representing the Long Library (but in usage the drawing room) at Althorp, the Spencer family seat in Northamptonshire rebuilt by Henry Holland at the end of the eighteenth century, pictures run up the fireplace wall in measured grades like units in a paternoster lift (illus. 40).

The move of the National Gallery into a new purpose-built home at the end of the 1830s provoked public debates over the best ways to display pictures. The *Art-Union* carried a correspondence on picture-hanging through 1841 which sought to return the problem to first principles (none of the names of the contributors to the discussion were given).[53] The first letter distinguished pictures from photographs, the latter having absolutely fixed points of perspectival reference, the former with greater ambiguity allowing some leeway in hanging. A scene of mountains might not look out of place higher up, nor a lake scene hung lower down. But one respondent insisted absolutely on the eye-level principle: 'The horizon which regulates the painter, ought, likewise, to regulate the spectator.' Arguing from a physiological basis, this writer says that humans are designed to scan around us. To look up deprives us of balance and strength: it is the proper attitude

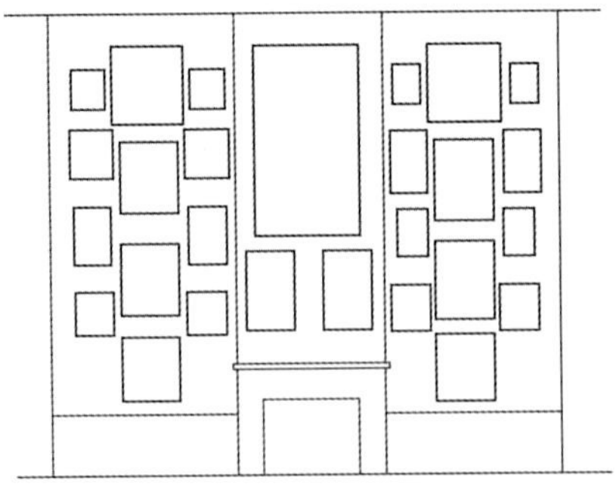

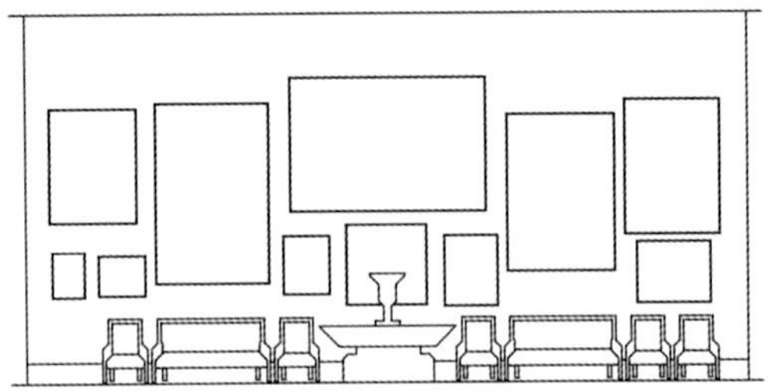

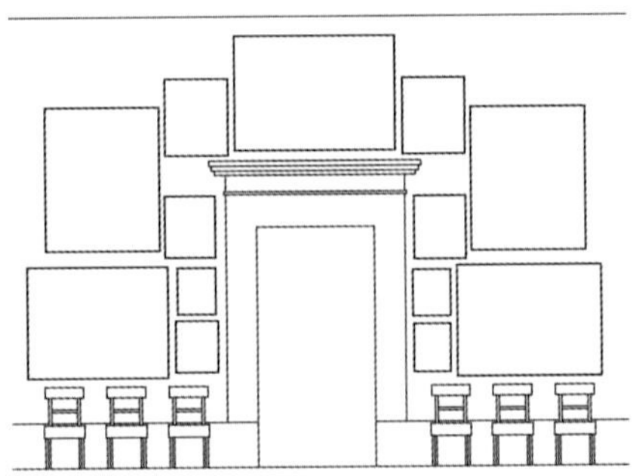

a. If pictures are intended to be looked at directly from eye level, as was always the case in theory, then to stack them up regardless of this principle should, again in theory, create an exaggerated impression of heightened space (the Library at Althorp, 1822: see illus. 40).

b. The New Gallery at Cleveland (later Bridgewater) House, where the Stafford collection was on semi-public view from early in the nineteenth century. A grand room given over entirely to pictures allowed this leisurely lateral flow (from William Young Ottley, *Engravings of the Most Noble the Marquis of Stafford's Collection of Pictures in London*, vol. I, 1818).

c. Patterns such as that at Cleveland House were easily able to absorb symmetrical interruptions from furniture, windows or doorways (from Robert Huskisson, *Lord Northwick's Picture Gallery at Thirlestaine House*, 1847: see illus. 25).

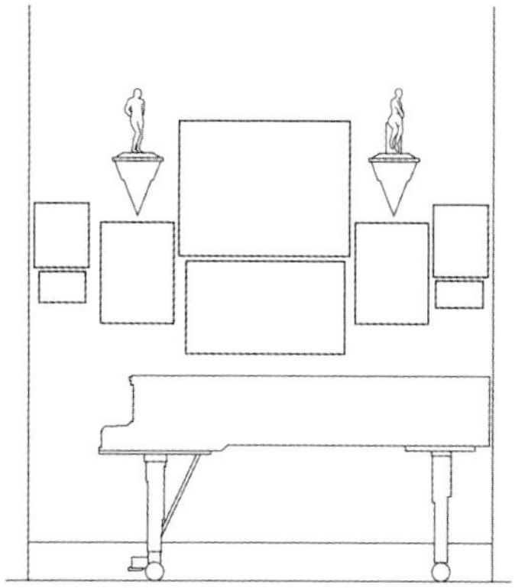

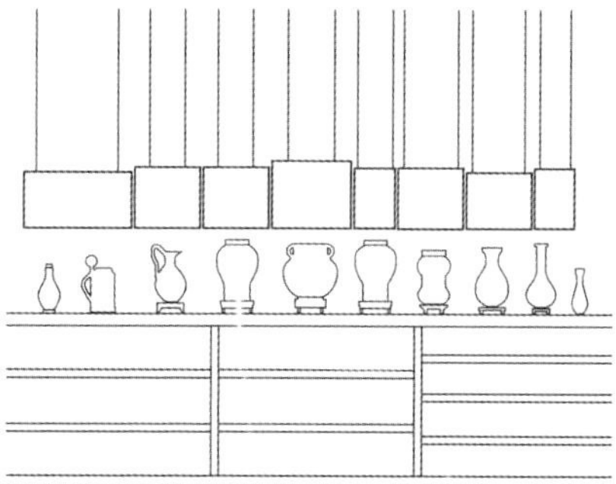

d. A wall with a tidily symmetrical group of pictures might often also involve pairs of wall-decorations such as plates, sconces or – as here – figurines mounted on corbels. So habitual was this practice that in other Victorian arrangements the pictures might be ordered as if to allow for wall fittings that were not in fact present (from George Kilburne, *Poor Relations*, 1875: see illus. 10).

e. The authors of Macmillan's *Art at Home* series of books agreed that pictures should be aligned along their bottom edges, as seen here. The original illustration shows a drawing room wallpapered in a neutral tone with quasi-heraldic mottoes written out in diagonal lines. The pictures (evidently works on paper) and their cords contribute simple rectilinear patterns to the more complex overall design (from W. J. Loftie, *A Plea for Art in the House*, 1877).

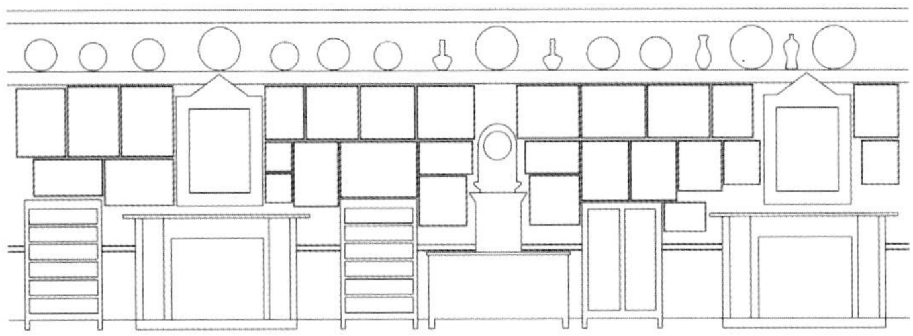

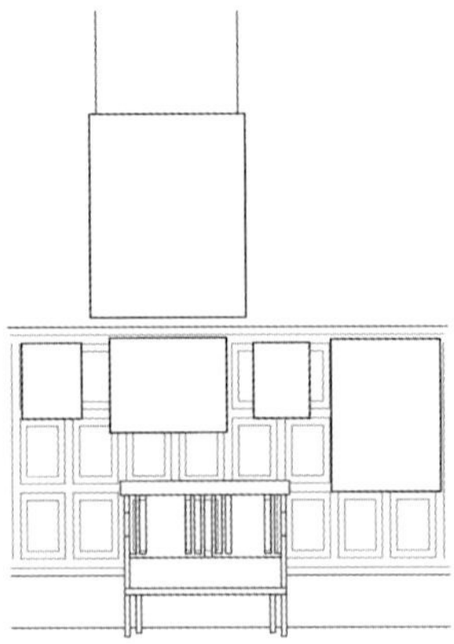

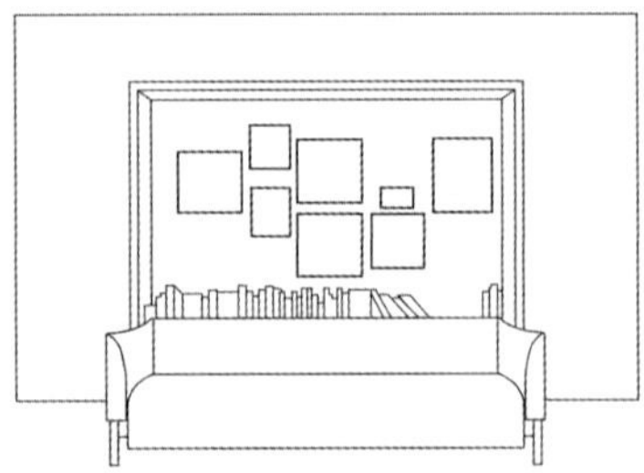

f. The notion of a picture 'band' or 'belt' seemed a solution to the problem of containing the picture within the more articulated wall treatments of the later nineteenth century. Here a veritable gallery of prints remains subordinated to the interior (from a 1950s photograph of 18 Stafford Terrace, Kensington).

g. The tall panelling beloved of Queen Anne Revival and Arts and Crafts architects entailed either the removal of pictures or new forms of presentation. The client of Richard Norman Shaw's 180 Queen's Gate (1883) was a noted collector of pictures and ranged them over two fields, upon and above the woodwork. The hanging space was effectively doubled rather than annulled (from a later photograph showing some pictures not acquired until the twentieth century).

h. High Modernism was generally not willing to offer continuous wall space for picture hangs. One alternative, adopted in Ernö Goldfinger's 2 Willow Road in Hampstead (1939), was a bookcase adapted as a recessed screen on which to mount a changing display of small and lightly framed pictures (from a recent photograph).

of humble prayer, not picture-gazing. An acknowledged case of an exhibition picture painted to shock at Somerset House was Thomas Lawrence's *John Philip Kemble as Hamlet* of 1801, in which the spectator looks up at the looming figure of the actor as if from within Yorick's grave. Our second writer picks this out as an egregious case of offences against perspective, and as emblematic of the whole problematic mode of installing picture exhibitions where a pyramidal form is constructed, all the pictures leaning forwards actually or through sleights of composition. Stacking pictures may give the illusion of added height to a room (as at Althorp), but public exhibitions used this effect fraudulently 'to give vast ideas of the height, length, and breadth of British talent'. This writer's conclusion is worth noting as it encapsulates in brutal logic so much of what was to come in these debates. If there is not space enough to hang pictures properly in a house, they write, then the only solution is to build rooms just for the pictures, where they may have free range and need not adapt themselves to other furniture. So the demand that the picture be looked at directly must ultimately result in its separation from the home.

Given the great middle-class commitment to picture-hanging, the mainstream Victorian writers on furniture and decoration had at least to try to find some compromise between picture and interior. A leading scholar of the Georgian interior has claimed that the growth of picture-owning during the eighteenth century was a key reason for the abandonment of tall wooden panelling and its replacement with lighter papers, fabrics and painted plaster.[54] As walls were increasingly articulated with timber and plaster mouldings, the fields into which the wall was divided were often imagined as emulating the components of a Classical column.[55] The moulding to protect walls from furniture, the chair rail, marked out the dado below, forming a sort of pedestal; just below the ceiling was the more decorative cornice. If a frieze – plain, patterned or figured – ran below the cornice, then this created what became the classic late Victorian tripartite division of the wall, with the 'filling' taking up the register between frieze and dado, in the role of the shaft of the column itself (illus. 41).[56]

Eastlake gave an early basic account of this model in the 1860s, recommending that pictures be hung in a single sequence in the middle part of the wall, centred on the height of the eye of an average adult:

> A row thus formed will make a sort of coloured zone around the room, and though the frames themselves may vary in shape and dimension, they can generally be grouped with something like symmetry of position, the larger ones being kept in the centre, and the smaller ones being ranged on either side in corresponding places along the line.[57]

There indeed is the essential stripped-back recipe for picture-hanging typically adopted thereafter in self-consciously modern galleries, both public and private. It was, moreover, the adoption of this quasi-Classical columnar model that led to the invention of the picture rail in the 1870s. Picture cord could not comfortably be carried up over a frieze to nails in their traditional position along the start of the cornice. Soon the simple expedient was adopted of providing a groove to the moulding marking the bottom of the frieze to form a fixture from which to hang pictures with hook and cord or chain (see illus. 22): the 'frieze rail' became the 'picture rail'.[58] Later the picture rail was retained when the frieze as anything more than a field of defined space was forgotten and the dado long abandoned. Early in the twentieth century the picture rail was even promoted, in the work of architects in the Arts and Crafts tradition such as Banister Fletcher and Parker and Unwin, to become the sole remaining feature articulating the wall, decorative but suggesting lintels extended from the tops of the

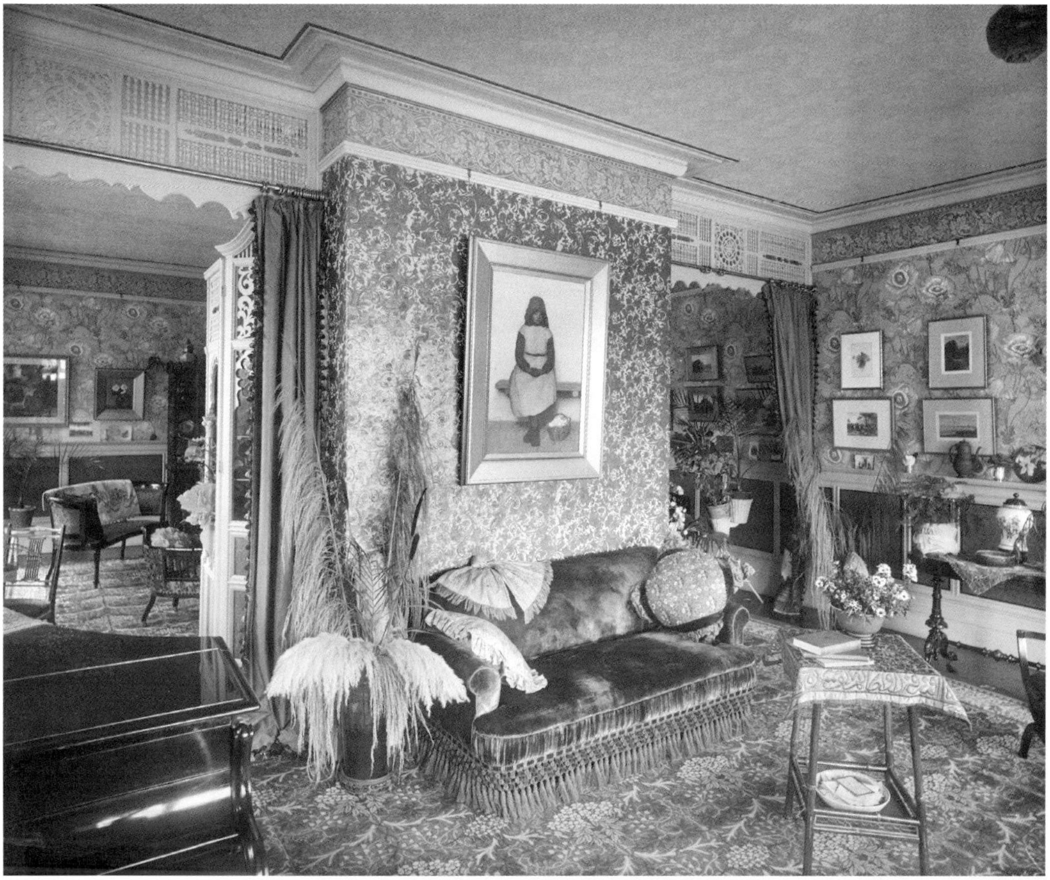

41 The drawing room in the Cheshire house of silk merchant Joseph Boden, shown in 1891. Evidently not someone averse to strong patterns, Boden has a clear three-part wall division in this room with a picture rail in its conventional position at the bottom of the frieze. The hung pictures do battle with the wallpaper while small pictures and photographs are placed upon the dado shelf.

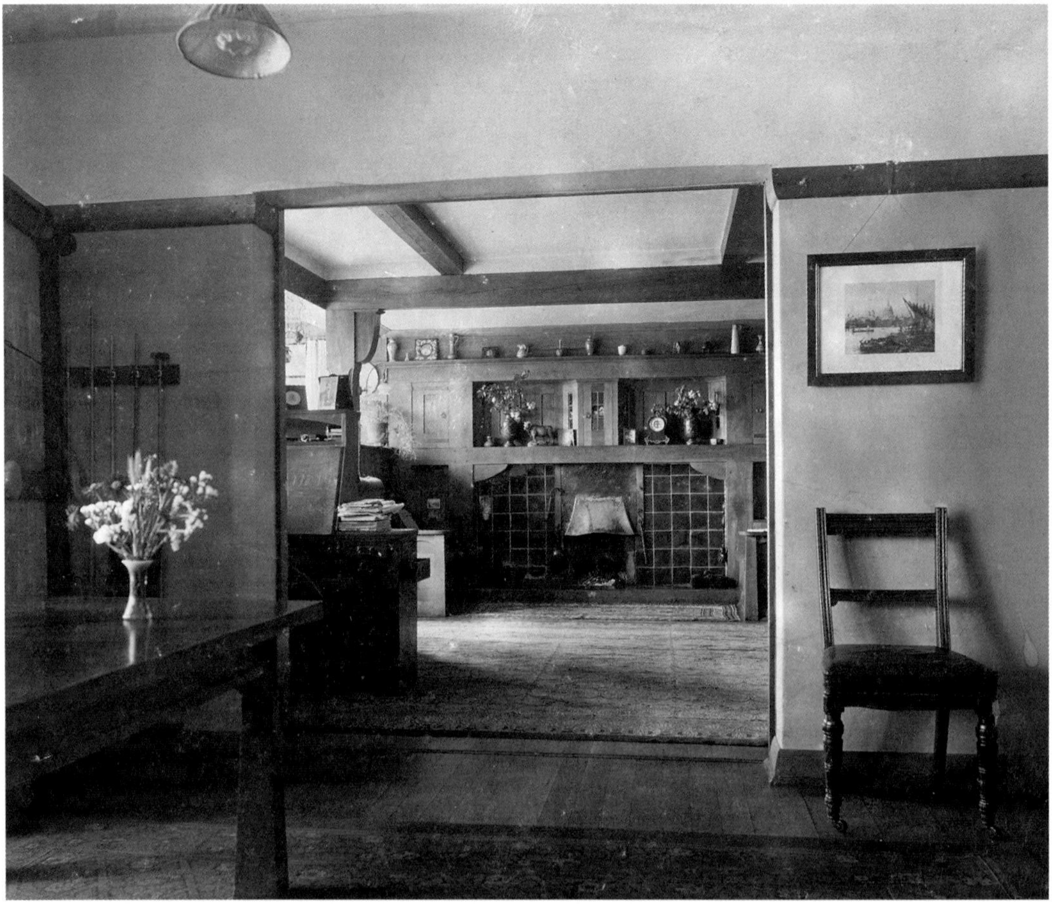

42 In the work of several architects practising in an Arts and Crafts idiom, despite their suspicion of Fine Art elitism, the picture rail took on a new life as a means of dividing a wall into two fields while hinting at traditional timber building techniques. Barry Parker and Raymond Unwin were among those to carry the rail around the room, aligning it with other features along the way, as in this example from one of their houses at Letchworth Garden City (1906).

doors and run on continuously around the room (illus. 42). The picture rail had taken on a life of its own, an element of domestic design that needed to be negotiated. It could easily double as a rack to display plates, or be used to mask electric lighting.[59] Even in the Modernist 1930s homeowners were advised to keep it in use, though painted over to mask its presence.[60] Some designers indeed experimented with its extension by setting out two parallel rails with grooves facing up and down respectively, so that pictures of a standard size might be slotted in between them (an echo of the design Ruskin had imagined for the study room of the Turner collection at the National Gallery).[61]

The resilience of the picture rail did not necessarily mean the settling of the picture into the home. There were a few diplomatic types, certainly, for whom the arrival of the picture rail represented an end-of-history moment at which painter, designer and architect compromised and found common purpose. Through the adoption of the frieze and dado, pictures were allotted a definite berth in the filling: 'the haven in which the artists who produced them would have them rest', according to the designer T. R. Spence. His colleague Lewis Foreman Day agreed that the picture rail was 'decoratively as desirable as it is actually useful', and yet Day spoke of the rail delimiting 'the picture belt', surely something rather narrower than the 'coloured zone' proposed by Eastlake, and we have already seen one of Day's designs (see illus. 17) in which pictures are thoroughly corralled within their own shallow meta-frame.[62] In fact, the picture in the home faced a concerted attack from a generation of newly confident design reformers from the 1870s onwards, inspired by, on the one hand, an economic critique of the picture and, on the other, the popular discovery of the interior as an art form in its own right. To follow this battle for hegemony within the pictorial culture of the home, we must go up to the drawing room.

DRAWING ROOM

The drawing room, to begin with its legendary character, was the antidote to the dining room. The ancestor of the modern living room or lounge, it was the place for more informal talk – the room to which women might withdraw in order to converse among themselves away from the formalized gathering around the dining table, and where family and guests generally might speak more frankly, which might mean more selfishly or more interestingly. Art in the dining room was heavy with the past, its vague gallery of inevitable portraits setting parameters to the identities of those who gathered below them. In the drawing room, identity was in greater flux, so at greater risk. Equally the drawing room was where pictures could expect to be individually interrogated, implying a constant process of sifting of current favourites from items that for one reason or another had started to pall. A story of one of Rossetti's lush pictures of Jane Morris in literary guise illustrates this nicely. His oil of Jane as *Mariana* was completed for his great patron William Graham in 1870 and placed flatteringly over the mantelpiece in the collector's dining room. Yet the artist was not happy – to him it looked 'sadly darkened' there – and so Graham obligingly moved it to the drawing room, which enjoyed 'the very fullest light in the house'. Now, however, Graham concluded that the apparent darkness of the picture was its own fault. It needed brightening a little 'in *feeling* as well as in tone', and he asked whether Rossetti might not take it back to adjust? No, he wouldn't; so Graham suggested he would have to take down the picture and try showing it alone on an easel, as if on a kind of prestigious naughty-step.[63] Again, bringing a picture into sight led to its being kept moving until it came down from the wall altogether. The drawing room was where this process may be seen at its starkest. It was here that the most was expected of pictures – decoratively and emotionally – and so here that they risked causing the most acute disappointment.

One of the most dramatic changes in the understanding of lighting pictures to have occurred since the nineteenth century is the abandonment of the attempt to emulate the light shown in the picture itself. The standard adoption of skylights in public galleries in the nineteenth century, and modern art's insistence on the picture's artificial flatness in the twentieth (reading even the representational image as a pattern), mean that today we see any attempt to light the things shown *in* a picture as a basic category error. But side-lighting for naturalistic pictures, especially landscapes, was considered desirable by the elder Eastlake – when critiquing the National Gallery building in the 1840s – in order to replicate, or at least not contradict, the light source represented in the pictures and to enhance the modelling of the things shown. This was already accepted practice among some private collectors.[64] That light source would, certainly in seventeenth- and eighteenth-century pictures, have usually come from the left, and to light precious smaller pictures from the left was ingrained in picture owners as something they should probably do if possible. When seeking to reassure Rossetti that he was doing all he could for *Mariana*, Graham wrote that the picture was already in 'the best left hand light we have'. Sometimes artists themselves reminded future owners of this requirement through inscriptions. One such was Richard Dadd, who, working in psychiatric hospitals as he did, was even less able to control the placing of his pictures than was Rossetti.[65] The key point here is that, in a picture culture in which images were assumed in almost all cases to be representational, this attitude towards lighting reasserts the virtual presence of the things represented as opposed to the expert marks with which their forms were constructed. (We noted above the literalness of the *Art-Union* contributor who felt it reasonable to hang pictures of mountains high and those of bodies of water low.) How far owners really organized their drawing rooms so as to allow for what we might term analogous lighting we cannot confidently say, but certainly here was something that pictures were understood to expect from their guardians.

When considering the colours against which pictures should be shown, there were again many who sought to base answers on foundational 'natural' arguments. Thus the wall was often compared, as well as to a column, to a landscape, with the dado dark, the frieze and cornice bright and the filling neutral as a fitting ground for pictures.[66] The optimum hue for paintings was frequently said to be what the elder Eastlake described in 1843 as 'the long established rich red, which might be sufficiently allied to purple, to give value to the gold frames and the warm colour of the pictures'.[67] Thus the crimson we so strongly associate with picture galleries established itself through the complementarity of the purple it contained with the gold of the frames, giving a Roman imperial echo to such spaces. One reason why subtle greens were preferred by aesthetes was that greens brought out the reddish grounds traditionally used by European painters and therefore emphasized the composition itself over the frame.[68] Thus the aristocratic artist and connoisseur Ronald Gower cited approvingly the grouse-egg green recommended by Edwin Landseer, and London's pre-eminent fine art auction house, Christie's, standardly used green to display pictures for sale.[69] Such was the fashion for refined greens in the 1870s that Robert Edis (Colonel of the Artists' Rifles and architect to the Prince of Wales at Sandringham) felt moved to warn the public off them, especially in the dining room, where he felt modish apple and sage greens should, when pictures were prominent, cede to 'a good warm brown or chocolate colour, in paint or distemper'.[70] In theory, the compromise between pictures and interior required the pictures to have their own dedicated neutral zone in which to take effect. In practice, however, as we can see from photographs and other representations of interiors, watercolours in drawing rooms were often placed against a lightly patterned wallpaper and sometimes on richer papers such as can be seen at this house in Cheshire (see illus. 41). William Morris papers, because hand-printed, stylized in pattern and strongly associated with an earnestly reformist philosophy of the home, were, for all their complexity and richness, allowed to be a special case and suitable for combination with pictures and indeed anything else (see illus. 44 and 50).[71]

What were considered appropriate subjects for drawing-room pictures? It is tempting to answer: anything in watercolour, although that would be circular, because much of what watercolourists produced was presumably intended for the drawing room and guided by what the artists expected to be welcome there. The Victorian culture of watercolour was resolutely diffident. Even its great proponents, then and since, have it seems felt the need to describe its domestic consumption in almost humiliating terms. Ruskin wrote in 1879 of Samuel Prout and William Henry Hunt – architectural and still-life specialists respectively – that in their early nineteenth-century heyday they had catered precisely to what was meant by the 'bourgeoisie', producing honestly painstaking descriptive works of a 'simple character'. 'There was indeed', says Ruskin, 'no quality in the bright little water-colours, which could not look other than pert in ghostly corridors, and petty in halls of state; but they gave an unquestionable tone of liberalmindedness to a suburban villa.' They will be too quiet, he supposes, for the middle classes of today, who with their great public issues to worry over are distracted by 'far more curious arts'.[72] Ruskin positively defies his sophisticated readership – his text was from a catalogue for a Bond Street exhibition held just down the road from the Grosvenor Gallery – to be able to follow his own aesthetic path back to the kind of suburban drawing room that artistic progress was supposed to have abolished from the collective memory. Specialists of the twentieth century, of course, despised the Victorian drawing room, or their idea of it. Martin Hardie writes in his magisterial history of watercolour painting in Britain of 'the mere traditional and accepted beauty which made the water-colour of the drawing-room'.[73] A wider perspective would surely recognize, with Ruskin, that the value of the watercolour tradition in the home lay exactly in its humility.

Watercolour traditionally was the medium of natural history, of precision, of reporting, and was assistant in that department to the line drawing or print (watercolours were referred to most often as drawings throughout our period). The watercolour had been associated with amateurism, with women, with antiquarianism and with directness of communication. But from early in the nineteenth century the watercolour had sought, through the new opportunities opened by exhibition culture, to 'escape from the album and take command of the wall' as a recent expert has put it, opening a heroic age for the medium, which now vied with oils to achieve not only accuracy but also emotional conviction and even the sublime.[74] When opaque bodycolour (gouache) was added to its repertoire, as it was especially from the 1830s, there seemed to be little left that the watercolour could not do in the hands of artists such as the Orientalist John Frederick Lewis or Edward Burne-Jones. Yet the older format of the watercolour, which can perhaps best be thought of as defined by its singularity of motif, lived on happily in the habitat of the drawing room. Here it proposed visual statements with which none could disagree, that were inclusive in a way in which a set of family portraits was rigidly exclusive. There we can see a mountain, a lake, a bunch of grapes, a portico, a street musician. With its rhetoric of amateur science, the watercolour simply announced that such a thing really existed and had been found interesting. To wish to share such images in one's drawing room was to welcome conversation on an equal footing, perhaps simply starting with the weather, recent journeys undertaken, a strange but inoffensive sight seen – conversation anyone could begin without needing any special privilege. Hence the 'liberalmindedness' that Ruskin provocatively associated with Prout and Hunt.

The work of such masters of the prosaic did in fact continue to attract buyers throughout the century, many of them financially well beyond the suburban bourgeoisie imagined by Ruskin. The colliery owner John Grant Morris had Alfred Waterhouse build him a thoroughgoing modern Gothic pile, Allerton Priory, outside Liverpool, in the 1860s. A photograph of the drawing room there taken a few years later (see illus. 9) shows a typical William Henry Hunt still life on the right and other no-nonsense watercolours hung two or three deep against a restrained paper. They are suspended very securely with pairs of rods descending from decorated nails just below the frieze. A work by Prout is among the rather more expensive watercolours to be seen in the lavish drawing room of John Edward Taylor at 20 Kensington Palace Gardens (illus. 43). Taylor was the proprietor of the *Manchester Guardian* and a serious collector of watercolours. In 1892, the year before this photograph was taken, he made a substantial donation of drawings to the newly established Whitworth Art Gallery. The style of the room does not exactly shout about progressive politics. It is a full-blown re-enactment of eighteenth-century French designs supplied by the elite London firm of Charles Mellier & Co. But it is a measure of how ubiquitous the humble picture rail had become by the 1890s that it is in use even in so grand an interior as this, with double chains to steady the uniformly framed watercolours against the silk damask wall fabrics. In both of these highly stylistically determined drawing rooms we sense that the watercolour itself has a steadying role. The wealthy owners have allowed their celebrity architects and designers free rein, yet their pictures, even the expensive ones sported by Taylor, imply basic, shared human values, suggesting that if anything could make a

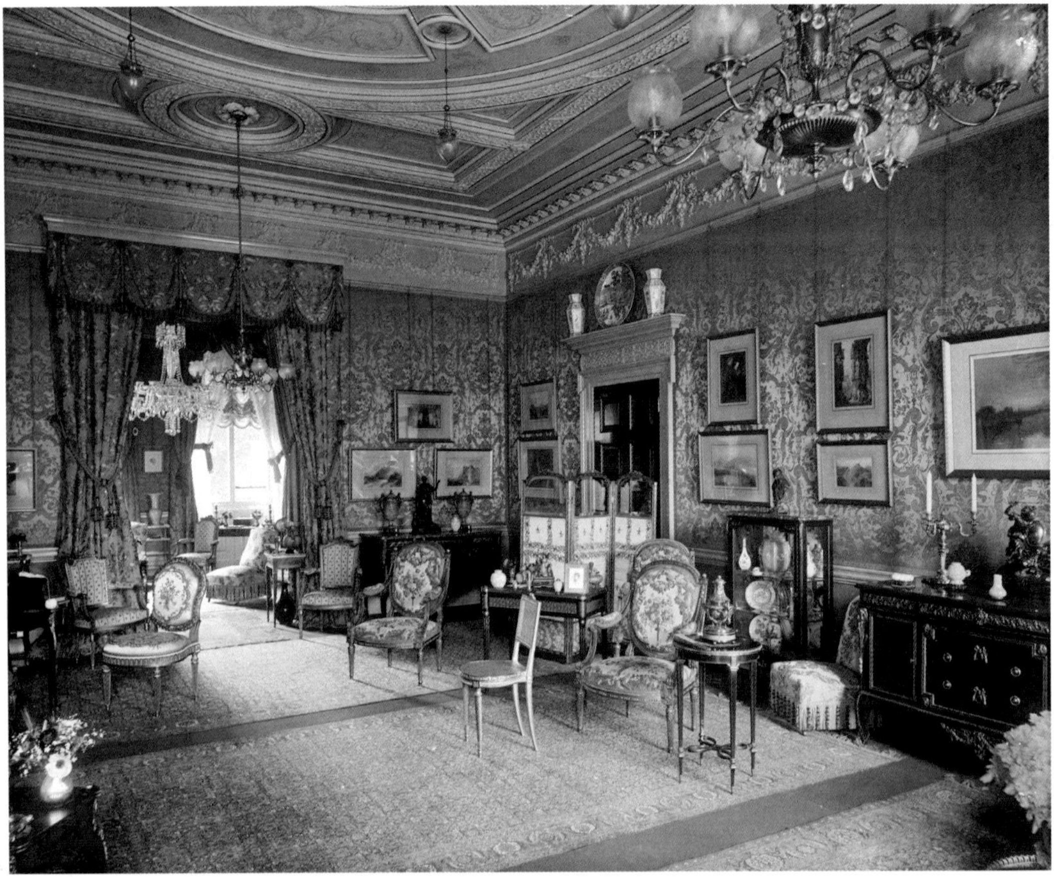

43 The style of this very finely appointed drawing room in Kensington Palace Gardens is firmly rooted in *ancien régime* opulence, but the pictures are British watercolours. This was the home of the owner of both the *Manchester Guardian* and the *Manchester Evening News*, J. E. Taylor, who donated hundreds of watercolours to the Whitworth Art Gallery in that city (photograph 1893).

visitor feel at home in such self-conscious environments, it would be these pictures of immediately recognizable, sympathetic and unchanging things.

We can well see how offering up these tokens of common experience might help set any conversation, however awkward, off on a more comfortable footing. But therein might lie their disingenuousness for those suspicious of the whole ideal of the drawing room as a place where truth is politely negotiated. In George Eliot's *Middlemarch* (1871–2) the heroine, Dorothea Brooke, is upright to the point of narrowness. Her landowning uncle and former guardian complains that 'young ladies are a little ardent, you know – a little one-sided, my dear', a lament prompted by her not approving of his pastoral pictures, which her literal mind cannot help contrasting with the reality around them:

> That is one reason I did not like the pictures here, dear uncle – which you think me stupid about. I used to come from the village with all that dirt and coarse ugliness like a pain within me, and the simpering pictures in the drawing-room seemed to me like a wicked attempt to find delight in what is false, while we don't mind how hard the truth is for the neighbours outside our walls.[75]

The suggestion that the drawing room was corrupt must have been especially painful to Dorothea because in terms of theoretical etiquette it was a space over which she had herself presided until she left the house upon her marriage. The uncle is a bachelor, so she had been the lady of the house: the lies told there were her responsibility.

The socialists Lucy Crane and William Morris later addressed the question from an industrial point of view, angered at capitalists' evasion of the provisions of the 1875 Public Health Act, among which were restrictions on air pollution. Crane lamented:

> I am told that the Smoke Act is in many places a dead letter; so it is impossible not to ask how the rich men of these places can really care for beautiful pictures while they allow their chimneys to blot out and spoil the natural beauty of the hills, and vales, and garden around them.[76]

Speaking in Birmingham in 1880, Morris agreed, denouncing those who 'burn a deal of coal': 'I say that their love of art is a mere pretence: how can you care about the image of a landscape when you show by your deeds that you don't care for the landscape itself?'[77] Crane's designer brother Walter asked rhetorically why, given the tendencies towards realism in contemporary art, British painters did 'not give us pictures of the actualities of modern industry. Weird scenes from the "black country" – those desolate regions that bloom but in furnace flames; scenes in the mines; at iron works; nail and chain makers.' The answer must lie in what people were prepared to hang in their homes. The 'man who makes a fortune in business generally thinks it well to spend something in pictures', yet we do not see such subjects in his home.

> Our attention is called to the finished product of civilisation, and it is thought desirable to draw a veil over some of the intermediate processes. But few have the hardihood to invite the skeleton to the feast.[78]

By 'finished product' Walter Crane seems to be referring to elegant oil portraits in private picture galleries and dining rooms, self-congratulatory pictures that naturalize the status that has been bought at others' expense. But here, as I have been arguing, is the genius of the drawing-room watercolour, which precisely eschews such self-congratulation and sticks instead to the facts as agreed by all (with the exception of such ardent sticklers as

Dorothea Brooke). The houses of Messrs Morris and Taylor were full of ostentation, yet in their drawing rooms the pictures were reassurances of modest common values that presumed nothing over their guests.

Part of the definition of the archetypal drawing room *vis-à-vis* the dining room was that it allowed for movement. The much derided skill of knowing how to behave in a drawing room involved linking and separating at opportune moments within the company, challenging because it had to be done elegantly and meaningfully. There were different opinions as to the role of pictures in this choreography, but there was a rough consensus around two notions. The first was that the drawing-room picture was one 'that will bear looking into, that actually invites close study'.[79] Before the development of a domestic advice literature that prided itself on sober practicality, this might be imagined to mean important paintings on a modest scale. Loudon's *Encyclopaedia* of the 1830s, in its description of the *beau idéal* of an English villa, recommends 'A small Claude, a curious portrait or historical subject, or rare cabinet picture; indeed, any beautiful picture of moderate dimensions'.[80] The elder Eastlake too felt 'the best specimens of painting' suited the principal drawing room, specifically commending Poussin (like Claude, a Frenchman working in seventeenth-century Italy), who had adapted grand themes and styles 'to domestic conditions'.[81] When more realistic advice became the norm, the drawing-room picture came to be understood as something with precise detail, typically a water-colour. The second consensus of the later advice literature was, contradictorily, that the drawing-room picture, while certainly alluring to the gaze, should only be looked at within the constraints of broader drawing-room etiquette.

Thomas Sheraton, the great furniture designer, was also a rather puritanical Baptist minister. His *beau idéal* of the modern drawing room naturally required 'the highest display of richness of furniture', but anything that risked pulling the company away from one another was to be avoided, so

> the walls should be free of pictures . . . The grandeur then introduced into the drawing-room is not to be considered, as the ostentatious parade of its proprietor, but the respect he pays to the rank of his visitants.[82]

Sheraton's chair-rich but picture-poor vision of the drawing room was on the face of it an extreme one, with little to offer the nineteenth century. Yet we have seen that the idea of drawing-room décor as having a duty to flatter the visitor lived on in the format of the Victorian watercolour, and more generally Sheraton's notion that pictures risked dissipating the social energy of the room persisted. Florence Hartley, in *The Ladies' Book of Etiquette and Manual of Politeness*, published in Boston in 1860, gives precise guidance. When paying a morning call, and being kept waiting by the lady of the house, do not wander about the drawing room (Hartley calls it the 'parlor') 'examining the ornaments and pictures', as this is 'ill-bred': that is, nosey. But if invited for dinner and kept waiting in the same room for the company to gather, then one must 'look over the books and pictures with an air of interest', thereby neither risking seeming bored nor wasting your best conversation ahead of being seated.[83] This was more of a problem for men than for women, as the former were much more likely to arrive alone and find themselves in a room of strangers to whom they had not yet been introduced. Another American etiquette book, this one for gentlemen (Philadelphia, 1847), acknowledged the horrible possibility that such a lone man 'would look much like a zany if you walk about in silence, staring at the pictures; therefore request the mistress of the house to present you to any lady present whom she pleases'.[84] Only once the dinner is over and the company briefly reassembled in the drawing room may one really stroll about without ceremony 'conversing or admiring the pictures, articles of *vertu*, and whatever else may invite notice', to follow the advice of Lydia E. White in her rather later *Success in Society*.[85]

This complex set of rules relates in part to the problem of turning one's back on other people, one of those few questions of etiquette not to have lost its capacity to worry. Slights and fights still follow from real or imagined insults offered by the positioning of one's torso. For example, there was some stigma about looking out of a window when in company, and one objection raised against any kind of ceiling painting was that admiring it from the optimum angle might require one to take up an uncivilized attitude such as standing with one's back close to the fire, which would be 'very awkward, as the rules of society do not allow us to stand in this position before company'.[86] But more seems to have been at stake with pictures. Ruskin never forgot being chastised, when a boy, for gazing about at pictures in a room of adults whose conversation he should have been trying to follow.[87] In Virginia Woolf's short story 'The New Dress', the painfully self-conscious Mabel Waring finds herself simply unable to cope on entering Mrs Dalloway's drawing room, her confidence collapsed, so that she

> slouched across the room, positively slinking, as if she were a beaten mongrel, and looked at a picture, an engraving. As if one went to a party to look at a picture! Everybody knew why she did it – it was from shame, from humiliation.[88]

Others better practised at the modes of the drawing room were able to work around the rules, as in Henry James, where characters use the pretext of examining a picture to grasp the briefest respite from exhausting mutual social examination before returning to the circle.[89]

The drawing-room picture was in theory supposed to be looked at closely, and to reassure visitors of their equal status, and yet at the same time that act of looking was hazardously restricted. It was precisely the picture's capacity for the absorption of the individual's gaze, in this most social of domestic spaces, that produced the tension. So, as in the dining room, the picture in the drawing room cannot after all be said to exist simply to fulfil its ostensible purpose of being looked at, let alone for straightforward aesthetic appreciation. This left the picture highly vulnerable to anyone minded to apply strict economic logic to the home. Of course, all writers on the home always had their own logic. Some of the most fantastical advice about pictures in the home, such as that of William Sanderson in the seventeenth century, was also the most internally consistent. Thomas Sheraton was also true to his own nonconformist logic of artisanal pride and suspicion of images in his advice to remove all pictures from the drawing room. His domestic aesthetic was informed by larger commitments to society and to God. So when we talk about a ruthless new economy of design, from the 1860s, that found the picture wanting, it is important to name its novel qualities. The reforming authors of the Arts and Crafts era took egalitarianism seriously, seeking to remove much of the anxiety surrounding the negotiation of social hierarchy; they took up Henry Cole's plea of the 1850s to create things that looked like what they were, not something else; and they addressed – if only as a rhetorical fiction in some cases – a homemaker of ambiguous gender who was prepared to take full responsibility for the beauty of the interiors they inhabited. The reader was understood to be on an economic, moral and aesthetic adventure, their path littered with intimidating old prejudices and expectations which it would require courage to pass beyond. The picture gradually came into focus as one of the most formidable of these obstacles.

THE PROBLEM WITH PICTURES

This chapter has scrolled up and down the timeline of our period in pursuit of the picture in the reception rooms of our imaginary house (see illus. 11). We have also followed a couple of digressions, into lighting and around the question of the height at which pictures were hung. In this section we will focus on a specific historical phase in which we can see the domestic picture at the centre of a public debate. From the 1860s, and acutely around 1900, the interior's impatience with the picture reached a point at which a divorce seemed the only way forward.

We have seen that the picture could be very demanding of its fellow furniture, understood by Victorian designers to require its own space in which to operate – its dedicated zone or band. All experts agreed on the principle that nothing other than the picture should attempt naturalistic representation, which risked appointing the picture to the role of enforcer. 'Where there is pictorial art, there can be no imitations of it by mechanical means,' as Henry Mogford put it in the 1850s, while others felt the picture was incompatible with any strong pattern: 'the richer forms of decoration must be reserved for rooms in which we do not intend to hang pictures,' says Von Falke.[90] But we have also seen that homeowners, whether wealthy picture collectors or otherwise, voted with their wallpapers against this orthodoxy, and that Morris papers in particular were seen as acceptable companions to pictures. Robert Edis, in his book of 1881, *Decoration and Furniture of Town Houses*, describes his own drawing room in what he modestly terms 'an ordinary London house' in Fitzroy Square, the interiors of which had been established some ten years earlier (illus. 44). Dominating the dado-less room is a very tall frieze with a flatly figurative design by Henry Stacy Marks, below which the 'general wall surface is covered with Morris's pomegranate pattern paper of bluish grey ground'.[91] As the room

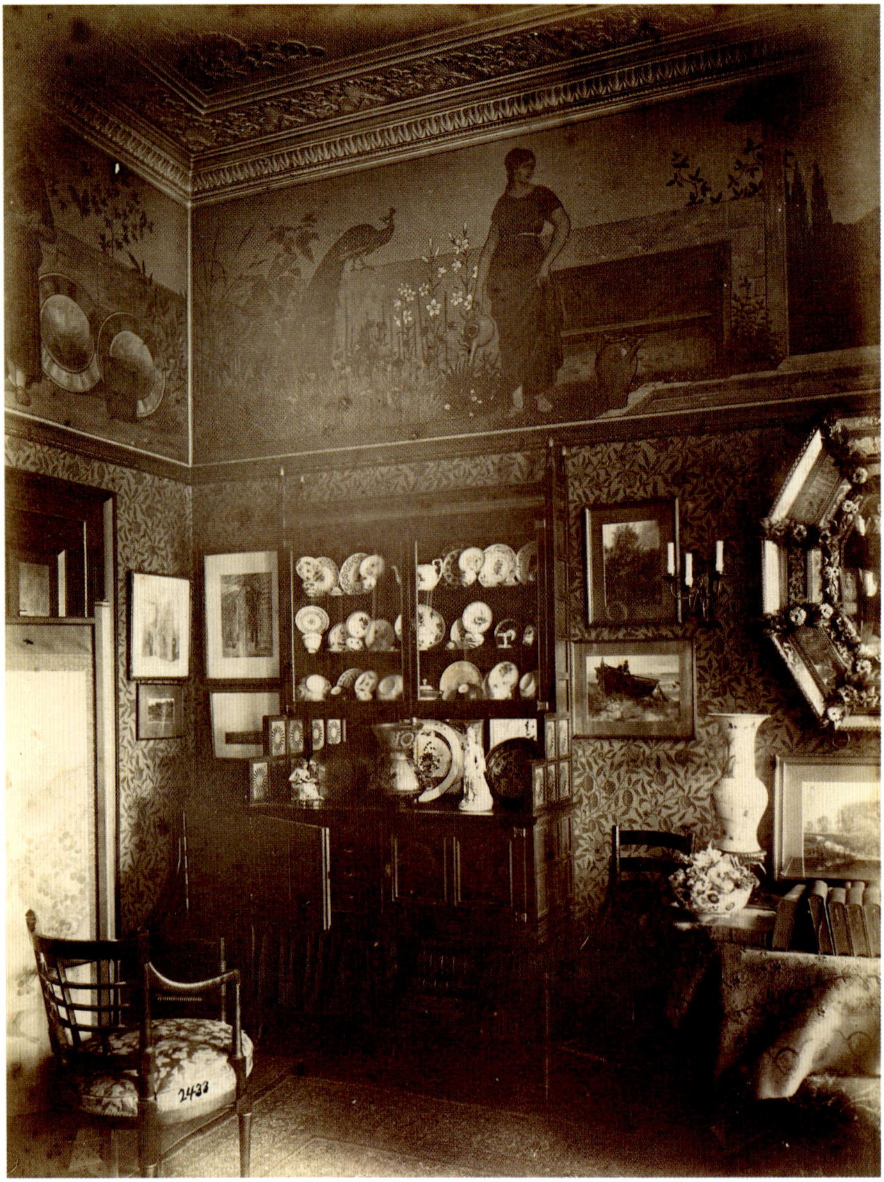

44 Robert Edis was a well-connected architect now best remembered for his 1881 book *Decoration and Furniture of Town Houses*. The frontispiece to the book was an engraving after this photograph of Edis's own house on Fitzroy Square, showing a massive frieze by Stacy Marks, and the pictures – against a Morris paper – left to plug gaps between the furniture.

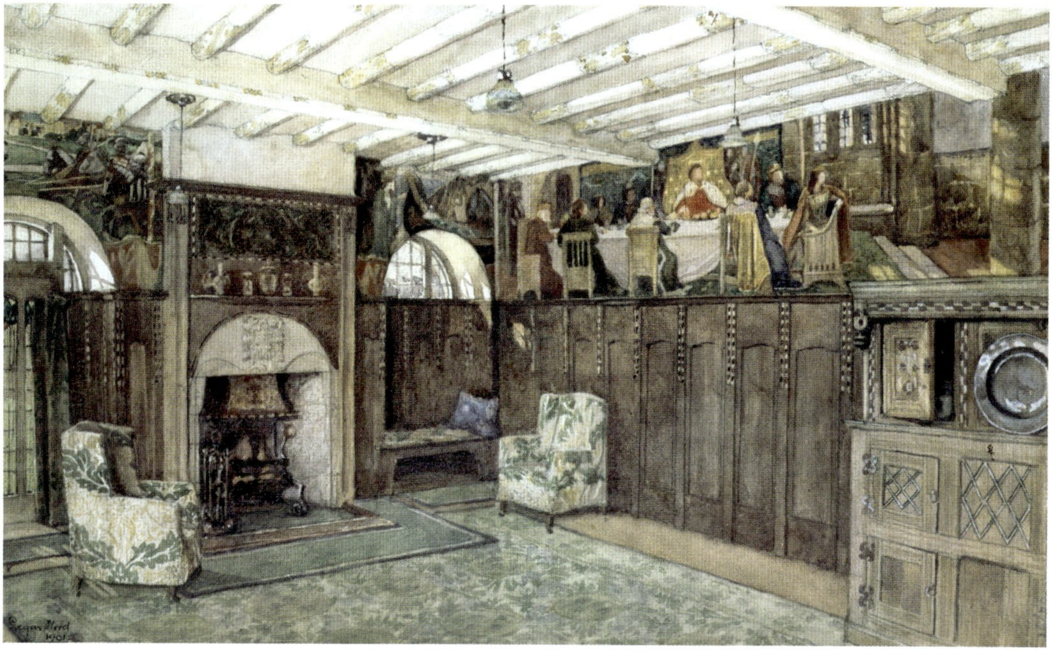

45 The dining room of Birkby Lodge in Huddersfield, 1901, the work of Yorkshire architect Edgar Wood, who himself painted this watercolour. Wood brought in his friend Frederick Jackson to paint the medievalizing frieze. This marks the nadir of the picture, absolutely banished from interiors which had rediscovered alternative modes of imagery.

slightly pre-dates the invention of the picture rail, the pictures are hung from a gilt '½ inch gas pipe' recruited as a picture rod. Edis was one of those establishment authorities seeking peace between the increasingly fractious elements of the interior, but his own drawing room speaks for itself: the pictures (watercolours) have clearly been demoted, without any proper space of their own. The dominant pictorial imagery of the room is in the frieze, where, of course, Classical precedent had always suggested it should be. The pictorial potential of the frieze was part of the broader rediscovery of the Early Modern interior that we associate with Morris, the Arts and Crafts and indeed the Aesthetic Movement (illus. 45). In such a richly furnished interior, pictures may have to renounce their own zone to play a secondary role to a frieze or fabric, and cannot take for granted an unimpeded gaze – that is, *objets d'art* might be placed in front of them. They may even have to give up their right to movement in order to be fitted into panelling, effectively ceasing to be pictures at all.

Treating an easel painting as a panel to be inserted into a timber wall covering, or fitting it into a field defined by decorative plaster surrounds, were common features of seventeenth- and eighteenth-century rooms, and such solutions were readily available to those later Victorian designers keen to put an end to the problems generated by the peripatetic, high-maintenance picture. Edward Gladstone-Lingham, in his 1879 book *The Science of Taste*, proposed that pictures be fixed within a decorative moulding in the wall continuing the cornice design (illus. 46), and bans tilting, which 'savours too forcibly of temporary suspension in an auctioneer's mart'.[92] Day, ever ready to offer compromises, had suggested, as we saw, a 'picture belt'. This, he imagined, would feature pictures fixed semi-permanently in place, with rich surface decoration added only in the interstices between and around them.[93] There is, in fact, a surviving example of precisely this approach at the Kensington house of the *Punch* cartoonist Linley Sambourne. When his original Morris paper was replaced with an expensive *faux*-Spanish-leather paper, this was cut sparingly and inserted only between and around the pictures.[94] It is, however, not easy to imagine such make-do solutions appealing to the leading architects and designers of the period, and indeed when Edward William Godwin had the opportunity to create the famous interiors of Oscar Wilde's house in Tite Street in Chelsea, Whistler etchings were fitted into the panelling of the walls in the white drawing room.[95] A few years later Wilde opined that fabrics and furniture produced 'a far more decorative and far more artistic effect than can be gained from our somewhat wearisome English practice of covering the walls with pictures and engravings'.[96] William Morris himself perhaps demonstrated the clearest possible sign of an alternative order when he appropriated picture rails to hang fabrics rather than pictures.

Where did things go wrong for the domestic picture? The art market boomed, artists were raised to the peerage, exhibitions and journals flourished, and picture galleries and art schools proliferated throughout the nation. If ever anyone had doubted it, most occasional writers on the subject of pictures continued to maintain that they were for looking at and that they should be

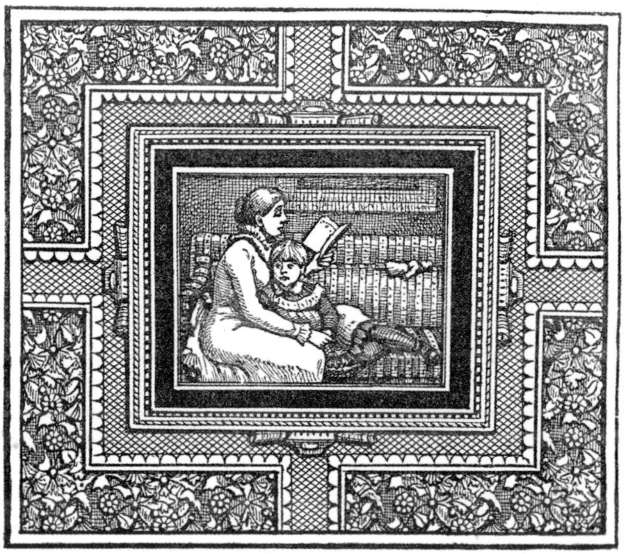

46 The urge to fix the picture more permanently in its place within the interior, found so commonly among writers and designers from the 1870s, was given philosophical support by Edward Gladstone-Lingham in his *The Science of Taste* (1879). He advocates frames which recede into the wall and decoration fully embracing the picture. The illustration uses for an example the recently exhibited *Alice in Wonderland* by G. D. Leslie.

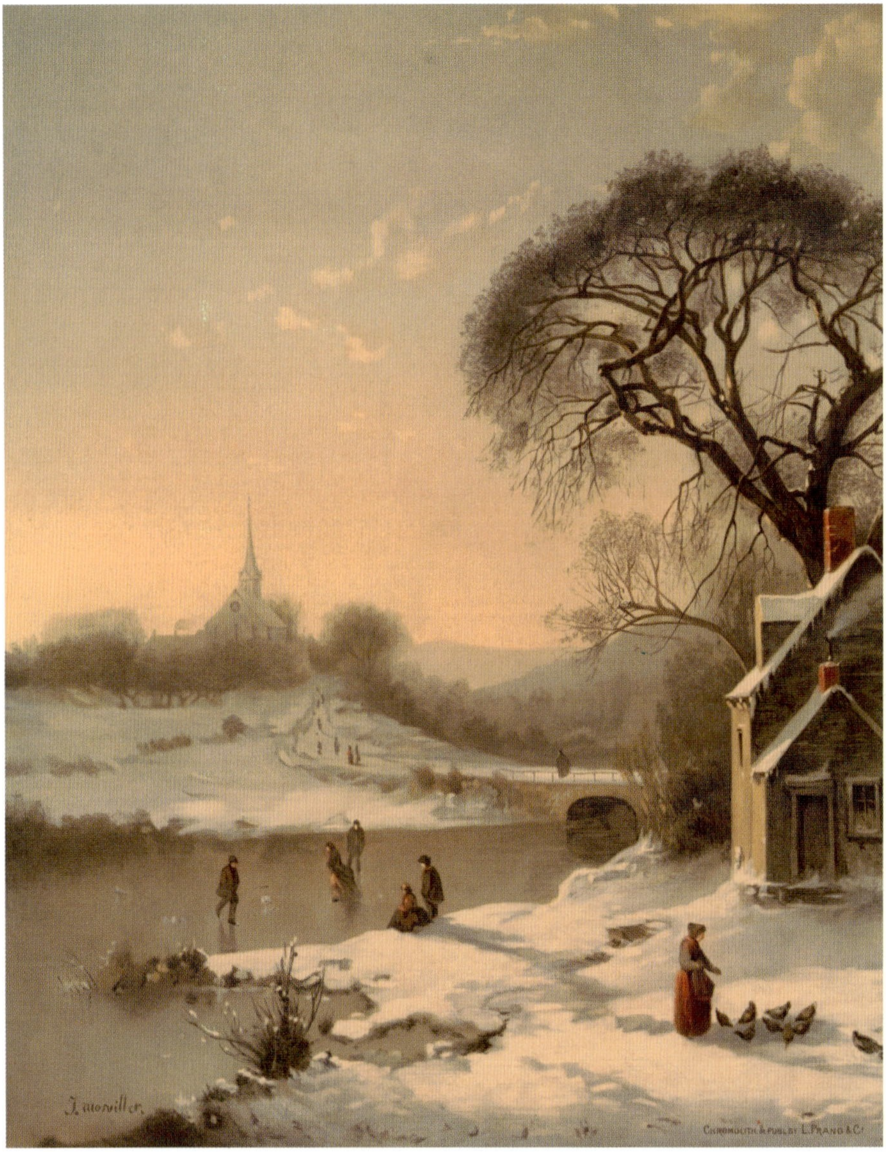

47 The French landscape painter Joseph Morviller is not to be found in many books on art history, but his was a name to start arguments in America, where he settled in the 1850s. His landscapes, especially snow scenes, were vigorously promoted by Louis Prang, who published hugely popular colour lithographic reproductions of them, to the disgust of high-brow critics (chromolithograph, 1869).

hung in the home at eye level. Yet we have seen that this commonsense view of the matter did not tell the real story, which was of a domestic object requiring complex negotiation in different rooms at different times. Those writers who consistently devoted their thought to managing the modern home in the later nineteenth century sensed this sufficiently to wish to give the picture a more narrowly defined and less troublesome role, and in this they were encouraged by the disapproval met by the picture when considered from the viewpoint of domestic economy.

In the United States advice writers often championed thrift and simplicity as American virtues in their own right. Harriet Beecher Stowe is best remembered as the author of *Uncle Tom's Cabin*, the great anti-slavery novel of its age, but she was also a prolific writer in many other genres, including domestic advice. In her article 'The Economy of the Beautiful', collected in *House and Home Papers* (1865), Stowe imagines a dialogue between a couple of newlyweds. The wife relies on her own innate good sense, taste and ingenuity to create a beautiful home at very little cost, having been productively thrown back on her own resources because her husband has spent all their money – not on drink or horses but on a bona fide original specimen of American landscape painting by the popular Joseph Morviller.[97] A lesson in the complementary value of separate spheres. In fact, much more often American authors assumed oil paintings were out of the reach of their readers, and that it was in the creative exploration of alternatives that their guidance was required. Art was arriving in the average American home, reported the *New York Times* in 1879, but rather than paintings, 'engravings, chromo-lithographs, and decalcomanie [transfer prints for decorative objects] prove the growing taste for beauty of form and color'.[98] Chromolithographs, cheap colour prints after oil paintings, were recommended more than they were in Britain, not least by Stowe, and indeed it is notable that she imagines her young couple acquiring a Morviller as this was an artist championed by Louis Prang, the great chromolithographic entrepreneur (illus. 47). Sending a chromo after Morviller to the distinctly highbrow critic Clarence Cook, Prang received a less than complimentary review, Cook trashing both the original design and the process, and pessimistically concluding that 'we are not surprised to see that its excessive popularity is ruining the art of this country.'[99]

Stowe soon joined the fray, with one of the sharpest broadsides against snobbish art critics of the period. She imagines a poor man who would dearly love a chromo of a farmyard but who has been convinced by the critics that it is his duty to purchase and hang a fine engraving of the Sistine Madonna. When in need of a consolatory image he hangs a print after Fra Angelico rather than the raw modern emblem of a baby being taken to heaven that his wife prefers.[100] Great art, says Stowe, does not make for a good 'home picture', which should express 'not the tyrannical dicta of some art-critic' but rather 'represent our own tastes and preferences, and not those of others'. Thankfully a 'host of such simple, inexpensive ornaments are given by Prang in his lithography' – flowers, children, American landscapes and other things from the real world known to her readers. Such thing-based iconography formed, as we have seen, the British notion of drawing-room watercolours, but Stowe would not have a true home picture wasted in a 'fashionable parlor', where it would be 'about as thoroughly hidden and smothered as if it were behind an altar in a European cathedral, chiefly useful in being smoked with incense'. Her idea of healthy everyday art was in conflict with the very notion of such a polite and sedentary space. Prang was delighted, of course, reprinting most of Stowe's 'iconoclastic' paper in his own house journal while she further deliberately ignored elite taste by recommending in one of her books that readers make, to go cheaply with their chromos, their own rustic frames decorated with acorns, moss or shells.[101]

Stowe's championing of the chromo united a folksy wisdom with an almost sentimental attachment to bulk producers of household wares – a combination perhaps still seen today in popular home improvement advice. A self-confident, practical person could do without the upmarket brands, which depended on lazy, wealthy types ready to pay to be reassured their taste was sound. Her special animus against austerely black-and-white reproductions of Old Masters is a well-aimed barb at the European intellectuals we met in Chapter One, who liked nothing better. Even the picture-shy William Morris allowed himself an autotype of Botticelli's *Primavera*.[102] But both Stowe's anti-professional polemics and the highbrow preference for cultural icons transposed into monochrome took their primary impetus from a simple economic conclusion: modern paintings were over-valued. Stowe was ready to recommend saving up for an example by someone like the humble Morviller, but not for anything grander. In Britain, earlier in the nineteenth century, no sooner had the idea of a flourishing British school of artists become an accepted phenomenon than complaints began that painting was getting above itself, appropriating the prestige previously shared more widely among the arts of design and seducing too many young aspirants who would have done better as designers, house painters and the like.[103] It looked like an irrational economic bubble but showed no sign of bursting as an elite of artists such as Millais and Leighton became very rich indeed, and others, including Rossetti and Watts, became the first British artists to be treated as major intellectuals. By the 1880s and '90s anyone working in design was ready with a complaint along the lines of this entirely typical passage from Edward Prior's contribution to *Arts and Crafts Essays* (1893):

> Painting remained to us, arrogating to herself the rôle which hitherto the whole company had combined to make

> successful. In her struggle to fill the giant's robe, she has run unresistingly into the ruts of the age. She has crowded her portable canvases, side by side, into exhibitions and galleries, and claimed the title of art for literary rather than artistic suggestions. The minor coquetries of craftsmanship, from which once was nourished the burly strength of art, have felt out of place in such illustrious company. So we have the forced art of public display, but it has ceased to be the habit in which our common rooms and homely walls could be dressed.[104]

The confused gendering of the terms of this argument seems to imply the disruption of a properly ordered home as well as of an appropriately organized system of Fine Arts.

To help put the picture back in its place, as just one among many contributions to the interior, was now an economic, indeed a moral duty for reformers. Lewis Foreman Day, again trying to see both sides of any argument, acknowledged the excessive price of paintings but suggested that, because a true lover of pictures knows that the very best of them are extremely rare and completely beyond their budget, it follows that they will allow few or no paintings in their home.[105] Walter Benjamin, so often cited as the pioneering scholar of the bourgeois interior, proposed that such spaces were dominated by fetishized objects that had been taken out of circulation, any labour value inherent in them overwritten by the self-directed work of collecting them.[106] But in Britain, at least, the interior as an independent art form remained an economic unit, answerable both to what it had cost its creator and to the greater world of human relations. The self-consciousness with which, say, Whistler neglected this ethos in creating his notoriously profligate Peacock Room for his unsuspecting client Frederick Leyland only helps define the norm against which he rebelled. This ethical consumerism is what fundamentally defined the Victorian interior for those contemporaries embedded within its discourse, such as the Revd W. J. Loftie, for pioneer enthusiast Hermann Muthesius and for modern scholars such as Judith Neiswander.

As the interior as a thing in itself sharpened into focus as an idea from the 1870s, the painting was revealed as hopelessly uneconomic, its value determined by the polite randomness of success at an Academy exhibition or Christie's auction. A cliché of journalism and fiction was the picture collection comprising works by dependable Academicians, lovingly put together over many years, suddenly liquidated from the rostrum for next to nothing upon the collector's demise.[107] The Irish novelist and Francophile George Moore was a resolutely socially superior aesthete, but he too felt something needed to be done urgently about the artificially inflated status of painting. His essay 'Art for the Villa', published in the *Magazine of Art* in 1889, is an important moment for the demise of the domestic Old Master. A self-consciously exasperated Moore would consign all important old paintings to public museums, leaving the inhabitant of suburban villas with properly domestic pictures, a category he describes as 'at once *biblot* [*sic*] and a work of art', which he claims is familiar from Japanese culture 'and will soon become a natural product of English life'. As for the artist, once a proud artisan, 'to the artisan he shall return'. This ideal of paintings being replaced by Japanese woodcuts (or equivalently craftsmanlike pictures) was realized, if not in suburban London, then at least in the rigorous Arts and Crafts idyll of the Gloucestershire cottage of the architect Sidney Barnsley (illus. 48).[108]

Once the emperor's clothes of the painting's money value were openly called out, there were those whose confidence was strengthened to question the very existence of the picture – of any portable kind – in the home. Even the lukewarm reformer Day accepted there was 'something approaching to superstition' in

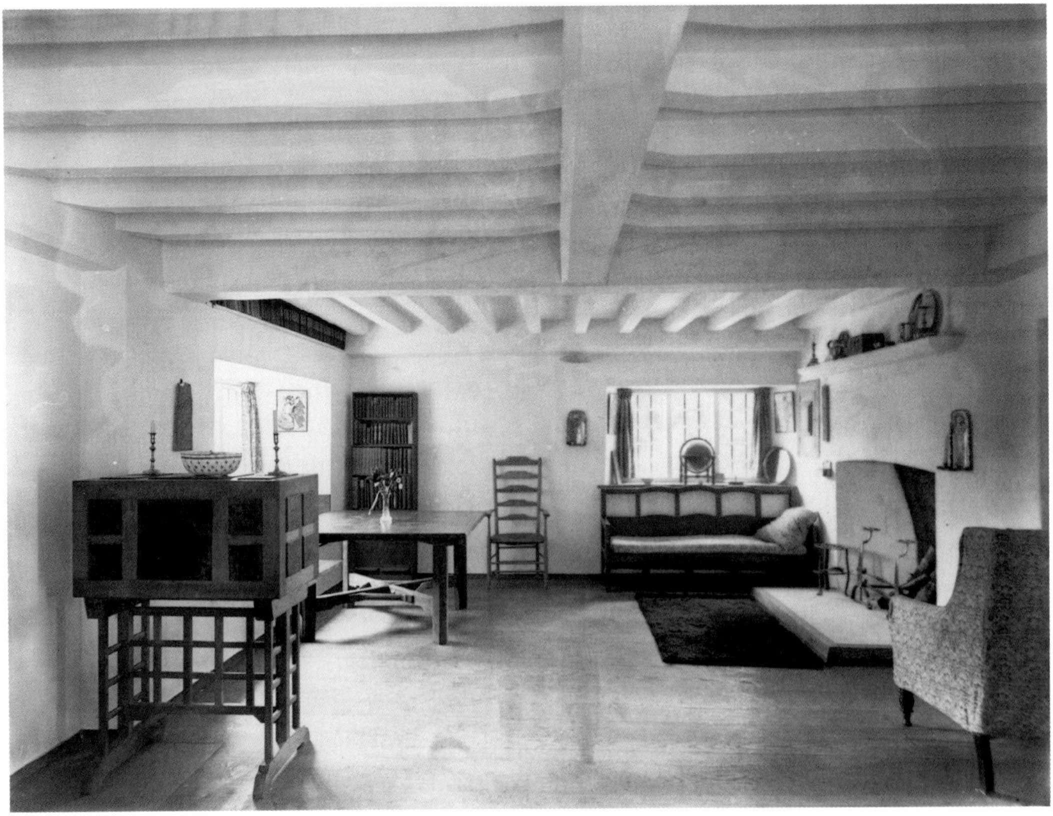

48 This is what an Arts and Crafts architect came up with when building from scratch a house for his own family in an idyllic spot in the Cotswolds. The main living room of Sidney Barnsley's cottage, Beechanger in Sapperton, is part William Morris, part Greek monastery and almost entirely picture-free other than the Japanese prints just visible in the window recesses. Photograph of *c.* 1905.

our 'reverence for a painting in oil', and by and large wanted rid of them, with the exception of family portraits.[109] As he frustratedly put it, 'very frequently all choice lies between pictures and decorative oneness, the two being incompatible.'[110] If the picture would not commit to where it wanted to sit, and carried within itself its own vagabond three-dimensional imaginary space, then how indeed could it be compatible with an interior itself imagined as a composition in its own right, and which, because experienced dynamically from within, was itself mobile? This was spelt out by Mary Eliza Haweis in her *Art of Decoration*, of 1881. 'After all', she exclaims at the beginning of a section titled 'Misuse of Pictures', 'when we shake off the fetters of association – what a ridiculous object is a "picture", hanging on a wall by a string!' A room is itself like a picture, she says, in so far as it is 'composed with equal skill and forethought; but unlike a picture, the arrangement must revolve around to a point which is never stationary, always in motion'.[111] A room only becomes harmonious – only becomes an interior, properly speaking – once set in motion by the bodily and optical presence of its human occupant.

Haweis was herself no political radical, but how differently this reads from the comparison made a dozen years earlier in the Tory *Blackwood's Edinburgh Magazine*, according to which the interior must emulate the academic ideal of the picture. The model of the interior proposed here is a static, unitary composition of abstracted forms with a clear hierarchy and no trivial detailing: 'In a house, as in a picture, above all things shun crowded medleys or common forms as you would the unkempt rabble of democracy.'[112] On Haweis's kinetic understanding of the interior, the picture deserved no such deference; indeed its demand for the disciplined attention of its viewer appears an embarrassing domestic tantrum. 'Only those who know the intellectual and aesthetic slums of suburbia', intoned Charles Holme of the *Studio*, in 1901, 'and the degradation of craft and ornament in which they are sunk, understand how tenaciously the misconception of "art" as "pictures" . . . clings yet to the average English mind.'[113]

That the picture risked becoming excluded from the spaces of modern architecture was acknowledged across the art and design professions in the first years of the twentieth century. The architect Richard Norman Shaw imagined in 1904 an artist visiting a newly finished house only to be astonished to find that '"There is not a single good place in this house for a picture." And it is true. The architect has worked for his own ends, without giving even a half-thought to the painter.'[114] The architectural partners Barry Parker and Raymond Unwin quoted what a picture dealer allegedly said upon looking over their designs:

> You, and those who follow your teaching are the worst enemies I have. I want people to have houses of the ordinary type, that they may always be trying in vain to make something of them . . . Each of these rooms is in itself a complete and satisfactory whole: there is no temptation to add anything.[115]

Hermann Muthesius singled out the architect Mackay Baillie Scott, one of the most prolific of the Arts and Crafts generation, as the first to have realized the interior 'as an autonomous work of art'.[116] That claim is of course debatable, but the novelty that Muthesius perceived in Scott's interiors must have been in part due to their open antagonism towards the picture, which Scott labelled as nothing other than 'an alien in the decorative community' in his 1906 book *Houses and Gardens*.[117] The plates in that book, illustrating Scott's own work (illus. 49), prompted a rather morose paper in the *Burlington Magazine* on 'The Modern House and the Modern Picture'.[118] The anonymous writer lamented that a deeper appreciation of art had not kept pace with the spread of domestic design reform through the towns and suburbs.

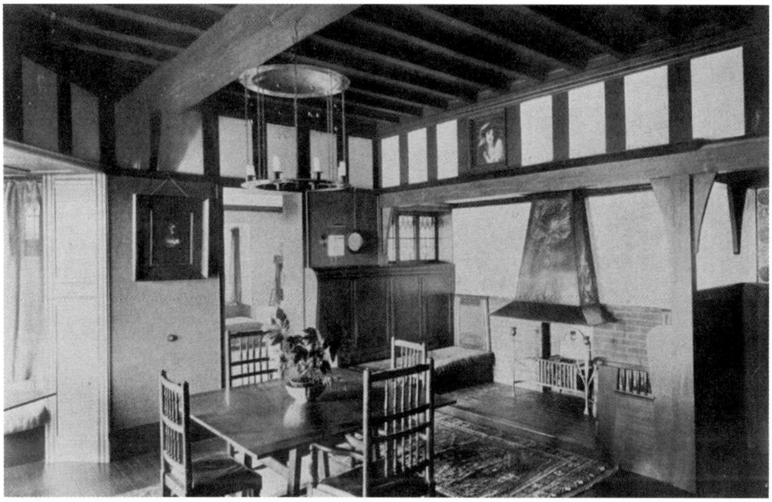

49 M. H. Baillie Scott's 1906 book *Houses and Gardens* provoked a debate over the disappearance of pictures from new domestic architecture. This plate from the book shows the dining room of Scott's White House at Helensburgh near Glasgow, where the two modest pictures appear deliberately inconsequential.

The beautiful idea of the artistic home swept all before it during the 1890s, one result being that there was no wall space left for pictures, as evidenced by the illustrations in Scott's book, where the only pictures visible are 'perched on the high mantelpiece or hung upon the frieze' and are the kind of thing – 'small reproductions of heads by Greuze!' – almost chosen deliberately to annoy an old-fashioned British picture lover. Our writer, maddened by the richly decorated wall of the Arts and Crafts architects, 'which makes the collection of pictures ridiculous, if not impossible', does their own case no favours by insisting that 'A picture is its own place, its own world; and the sole concern of those who hang the picture should be to see that that world is not obliterated or nullified by its temporary surroundings.' This is of course precisely why the picture had to be excluded from the house beautiful.

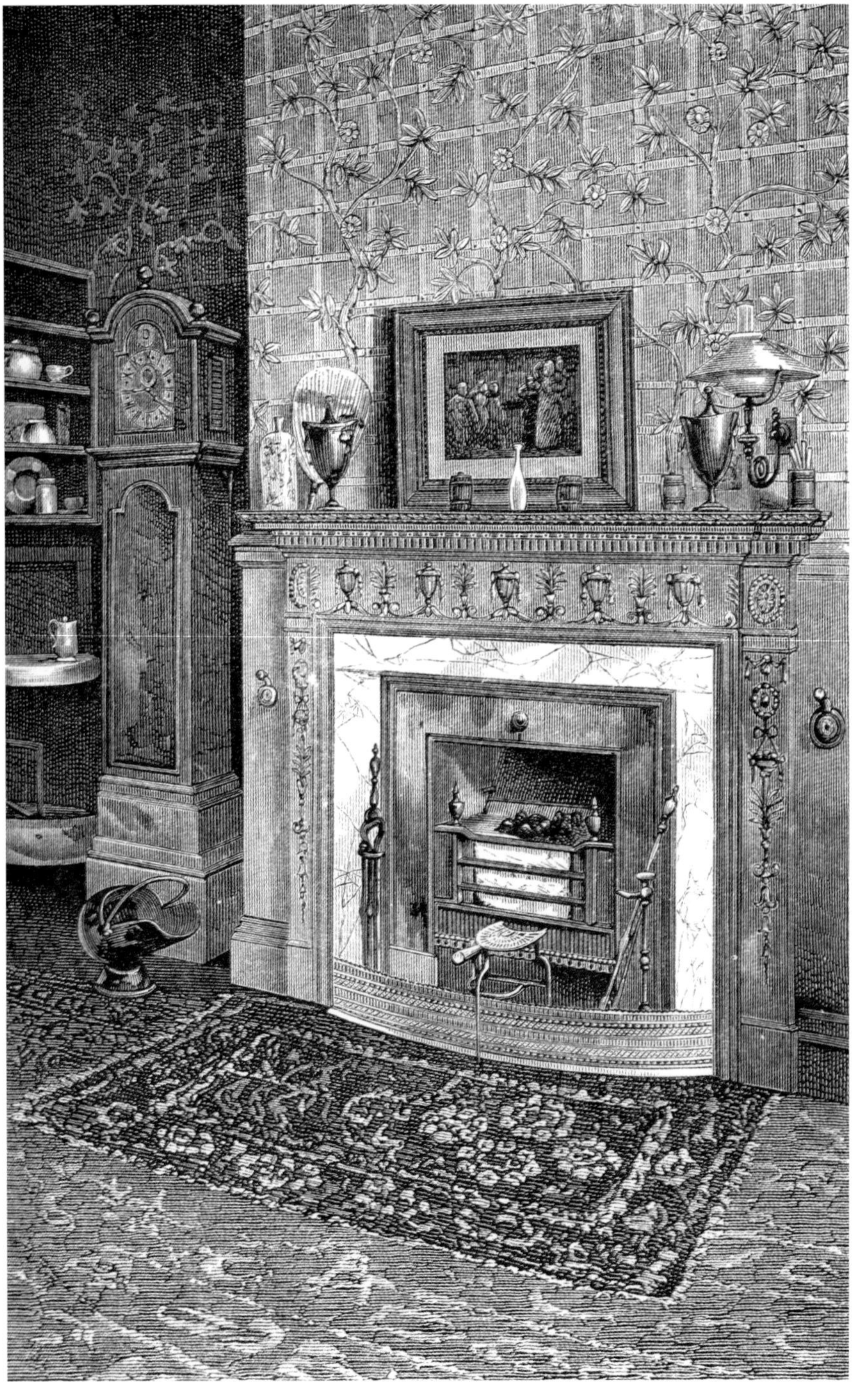

The solution, proposed the critic Arthur Clutton-Brock in reply, was that modern painters should renounce their obsession with 'so complete an illusion of reality', cease seeking after envelopes of space and instead focus on *things*, motifs, with which will come an acceptance of the picture's decorative, ornamental role in the home.[119] It was a remarkably prescient prognosis.

OFF THE WALL

Some earlier reformers and experts on the interior, while not presuming to pontificate on the philosophical questions around the picture, had already quietly relegated it, either simply by saying less about it or by showing how to use pictures decoratively without all the rigmarole that went with hanging and properly respecting their space. We have already referenced Rhoda and Agnes Garrett as quietly radical in their attitude towards the pictures of the dining room. In their book they include illustrations derived from photographs of their own house in Gower Street (illus. 50), which show pictures over the fireplaces in both the dining and drawing rooms. But in each case the pictures are *placed* rather than hung, inserted as decorative objects whose flatness is used to help articulate a larger pattern within the garniture of objects with which they interact. In the dining room, the genre painting on the mantelpiece is made to feel its sedentary position all the more acutely by contrast with the paper against which it is seen – a Morris trellis pattern with its confidently climbing tendrils.[120] I do not wish to claim that no one thought of placing a picture on

50 Cousins Rhoda and Agnes Garrett published their *Suggestions for House Decoration* in 1876, two years after launching their interior design business, probably the first in Britain to be run by women. The book was illustrated from photographs of their own house on Gower Street. In the dining room, a solitary painting humbly forms part of a mantelpiece display without being hung.

a horizontal surface before the Garretts. Indeed this was something of an Aesthetic fashion in the 1870s, and other writers of this period suggest that small pictures might be placed on the surbase of the dado, if made sufficiently deep (see illus. 41).[121] But the Garretts' few illustrations were intended to summarize an interior design aesthetic on which their pioneering business depended, and as such we are entitled to read much into them. In their scheme, cheaper pictures are retained but with reduced scope, to the extent that it is questionable whether they remain pictures at all by our definition. They are now just another class of object, ready to be picked up and examined, a long-standing way of thinking about smaller pictures that had become obscured by the haptic restrictions of museum and exhibition culture, a tactile mode that Edmund Gosse championed in the 1890s in the case of domestic sculpture.[122]

When the picture became problematic, one solution we have already noted was to take it down and examine it in isolation on an easel: William Graham threatened to do this with Rossetti's difficult *Mariana*. The idea suggests an owner close to their artist friends, someone able to appreciate the processes of painting. An easel with an unfinished picture was a feature of Oscar Wilde's rooms at Oxford, while others who were certainly not aesthetes might sport a new purchase on an easel in their domestic picture gallery (illus. 51).[123] For ambitious picture-painters who had no intention of downsizing their operations to comply with the decorative needs of suburban interiors, a kind of mirror image of this process was suggested by creating elaborate, bespoke frames which had no conceivable life other than to shout the presence of the painting they escorted. Far from providing a link to an ensemble, as *ancien-régime*-pattern frames were traditionally said to, these noisily idiosyncratic creations firmly reasserted the primacy of the individual picture. A good example is provided by William Holman Hunt, whose single-picture touring exhibitions

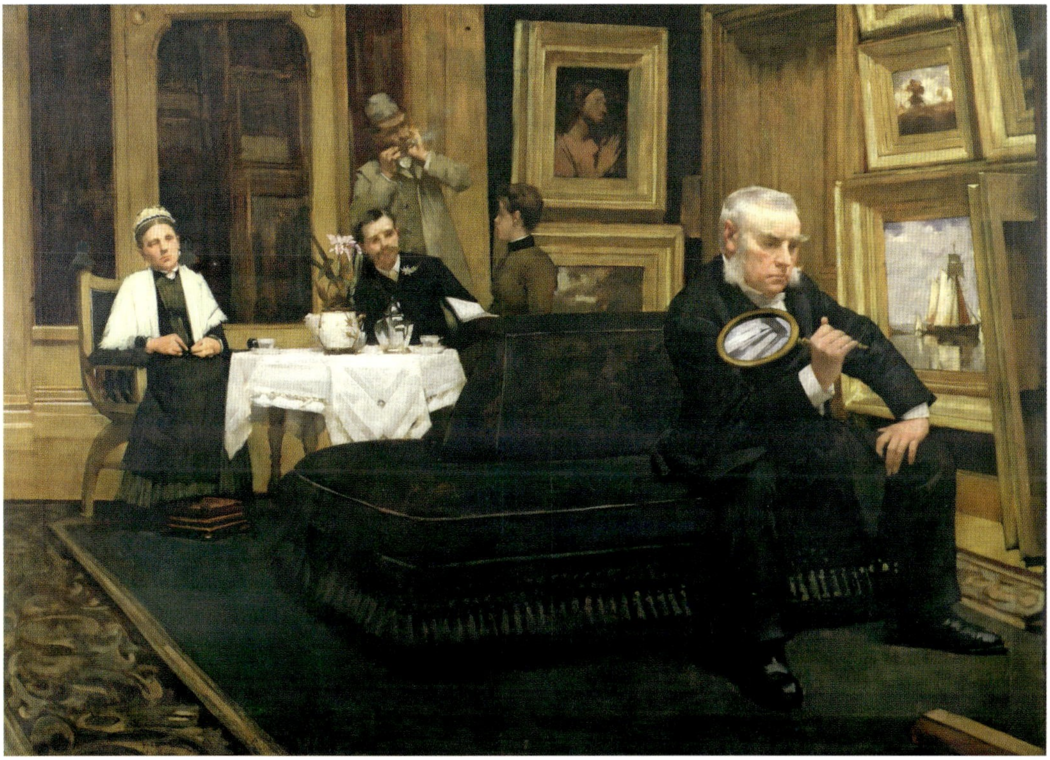

51 Abraham Mitchell, Bradford mohair spinner and art collector, sits in his picture gallery with his back to his family who are assembled for tea. His son Tom, a dedicated amateur artist himself, has just come in but waits with the others for his father to complete his inspection of the painting on the easel (Henry Herbert La Thangue, *The Connoisseur*, 1887).

of religious works were major events of the Victorian scene that viewers found hard to categorize. Gosse remembered Hunt's *Finding of the Saviour in the Temple* as a kind of wonder of natural history, like seeing a comet or a whale, while William Graham wrote to Rossetti of seeing *The Shadow of Death* '"lying in state" in a silent room draped with black with slippered attendants and reflected gas light and gaping spectators'.[124] These pictures were framed in ways that suited a work intended to be seen in complete isolation, with appropriately allegorical still-life carvings, 'oriental' decoration and attached text panels.

Finding means to allow homeowners to examine pictures one at a time became a popular idea among early Modernist designers who accepted the hung picture's demotion but who continued to believe in the Fine Art tradition. The logic of such sequencing supposed an excess of pictures. In Paris in 1860 the art historian Elizabeth Eastlake visited the great collection of the unspeakably wealthy founder of the Wallace Collection, the Marquess of Hertford, of whom it was later said that 'He was the Napoleon of collectors, but unlike Napoleon, directly the victory was won, he apparently ceased to care for the spoils.'[125] Lady Eastlake was shown into 'an entresol of the tiniest dimensions', where, at least so she was told, 'Lord Hertford lived for thirty-six years, thinking it a bore to move into his present gorgeous apartments'. She was then invited to sit before an easel on which were placed 'a succession of small pictures, of great value, which were piled on the floor'.[126] What may have seemed a charming eccentricity to Eastlake was taken entirely seriously in the early twentieth century.

That alternatives to the Western wall-show were possible was demonstrated by reports brought back by travellers to Japan of the *tokonoma*, or picture niche. This is from the American scholar Edward Morse's 1886 book on *Japanese Homes*:

> A Japanese may have a famous collection of pictures, yet these are stowed away in his *kura* [storehouse for precious items], with the exception of the one exposed in the *tokonoma*. If he is a man of taste, he changes the picture from time to time according to the season, the character of his guests, or for special occasions.[127]

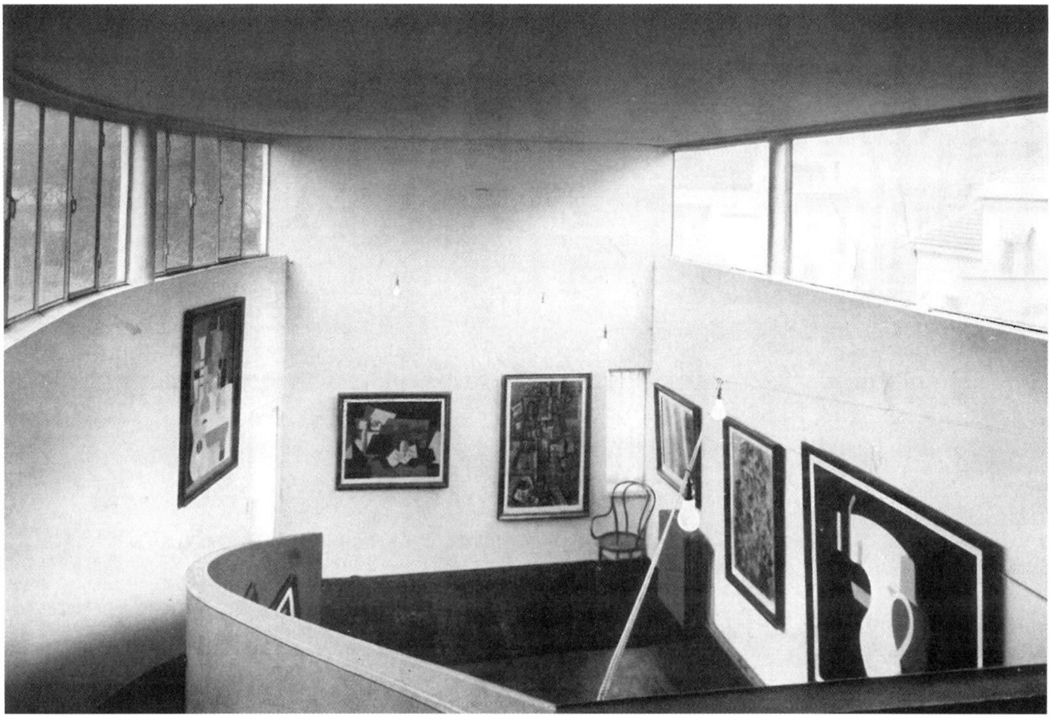

52 Le Corbusier's Maison La Roche (Paris, 1923–5) was intended as a domestic showcase for a modern art collection, but the architect found the pictures risked spoiling his dynamic interiors, which emphasized the movement of bodies within them. Eventually a compromise was reached following a redesign led by Charlotte Perriand, as illustrated here in Dorothy Todd and Raymond Mortimer, *The New Interior Decoration* (1929).

Here was surely a lesson for Westerners unable to resist the compulsion to place all one's possessions on display simultaneously, the one aspect of the English house that Muthesius could not comprehend. Why, he asked, did people not see that it was obvious common sense to have an 'art cabinet' for all the decorative objects they owned but which were not currently required?[128] In the 1920s Le Corbusier made it one of the axioms of *Towards a New Architecture* that 'The true collector of pictures arranges them in a cabinet and hangs on the wall the particular painting he wants to look at.'[129] The prophet of Modernism in architecture had the chance to work with a 'true collector' soon after the first publication of his manifesto when he was commissioned by the Swiss banker Raoul La Roche to create a house in Paris in which to show off his pictures, which were principally examples of Cubism and Le Corbusier's own painterly '-ism', Purism (illus. 52). (Indeed the collection included several pictures painted by Le Corbusier himself.) The architect, however, eventually concluded that the pictures got in the way of the beautiful lines of his interiors. 'I commissioned from you a "frame for my collection"', complained La Roche; 'You provided me with a "poem of walls".'[130] In 1924 Le Corbusier sought a solution in the form of a large cupboard or *bibliothèque à tableaux* that would sit in the principal picture room and from which works would be taken out singly for inspection like volumes from a bookcase. The suggestion was declined, and Le Corbusier handed the problem over to his collaborator Charlotte Perriand. But the idea was maintained by, perhaps not predictably, D. H. Lawrence, writing in 1929 in, again not obviously, *Vanity Fair*.

In 'Dead Pictures on the Wall' Lawrence, himself an artist of racy paintings, follows through with harsh logic the proposition – apparently so simple yet, as we have seen, in fact so elusive – of hanging a picture on a domestic wall and looking at it.[131] He refers to the Arts and Crafts ideal of building the picture into the wall – a fallacy, he says, for a good picture is not architecture, and has an entirely different purpose, namely to offer 'fragrance' and 'subtle rejoicing' to the mind. Neither is he convinced by Le Corbusier and his followers,

> the young school which thinks pictures should be kept in stacks like books in a library, and looked at for half an hour

> or so at a time, as we turn over the leaves of a book of reproductions. But this again entirely disregards the real psychology of pictures.

Pictures are meant to be lived with, but we get bored of them and cannot throw them out because they have become, not an effervescent scent, but on the contrary 'looked on as solid property'. The brutal solution: 'Burn them!' Once the thrill is gone, throw the picture away like stale flowers or a tattered paperback. Lawrence returns to Le Corbusier's idea of the *bibliothèque à tableaux* but prefers an actual lending library – 'a great "pictuary", where we can go and choose a picture' to keep 'till we have got all the joy out of them, and want a change'. The flaw in this sternly democratic and modern idea, Lawrence admitted, was economic: the picture refused to bend to the healthy basic laws of supply and demand, hanging around the house unproductively, useless once enjoyed, yet declining to go back into the circulation its nature seemed so suited to. 'If only we could get rid of the idea of "property" in the arts!'

The idea of the disposable picture hung around some Modernist circles. Woolf's 1930s vision of a futuristic women's college, on an anti-Oxbridge theme, rejected anything that might 'hoard dust and perpetuate traditions': 'Let the pictures and the books be new and always changing.'[132] But the picture could not keep its prestige and lose its price: it remained a stubbornly unreformable, special kind of commodity. This was, after all, a golden age for the art dealer, as the old London exhibiting societies grew stale, wars and depressions churned up countless collections, waves of new styles seeking interpreters and sympathizers emerged from Europe, and with the auction houses yet to realize their own market-making potential (as they did only from the 1950s). Modernist culture exalted the avant-garde picture ever higher. To be sure, there were those who maintained the Arts

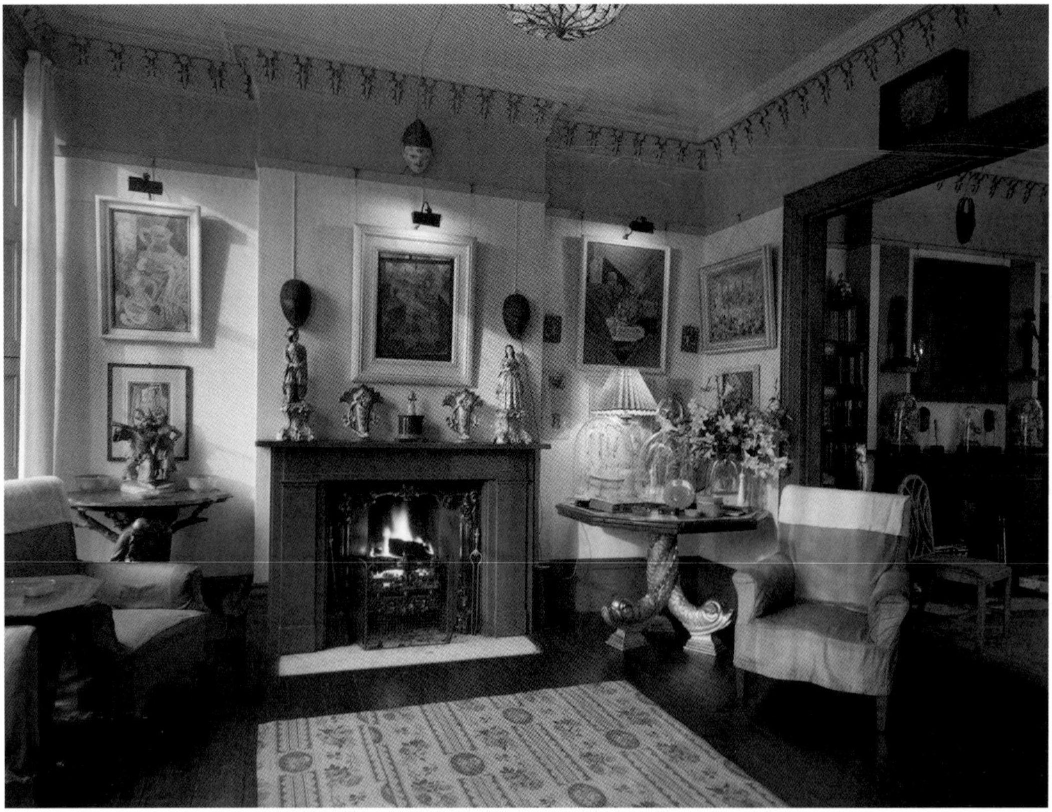

53 The house of the novelist and aesthete Osbert Sitwell in Chelsea, photographed in 1937. These rooms were written up in *Vogue* in 1924 as exemplifying the wit of their proprietor through their combination of such very disparate elements (cutting-edge sculpture, Chelsea porcelain, Victorian shell-work) to achieve unity. The pictures are more obviously coherent, being more or less Futurist or Cubist, with homely subjects – domestic objects and a London cityscape by C.R.W. Nevinson over the fire.

and Crafts talk of dialling down the picture's demands and of the unity of the arts, and certainly many innovative and sincere projects were carried out both in domestic and non-gallery public spaces on these lines.[133] But the picture in its traditional format survived, if now the focus of much worry over the decorative qualities it was supposed to manifest. For everyday journalists the decoratively abstracting picture meant something that went with a strict Modernist interior and that made no reference to the things of the past. For art-world insiders, the modern picture decorated *itself*, completing a finished scheme within its own borders.[134] Now more self-involved than ever, it was better able to suit interiors of any style because it paid none of them any attention whatsoever. As Clutton-Brock had foreseen in 1907, in response to jeremiads on the demise of the picture at the hands of the modern interior, the salvation of the domestic picture lay in its renunciation of conventional spatial representation (the ingredient the interior could never digest) and renewed focus on concrete motifs (think Cézanne). This attitude allowed for the strange possibility of the sympathetic integration of the traditional drawing room with avant-garde modern painting, for all that the run of commentators felt that the estrangement of modern homes and modern pictures was complete.[135]

An example can be seen in one of the most renowned literary homes of the 1920s, that of the aristocratic avant-garde brothers, Osbert and Sacheverell Sitwell (illus. 53). In this house there were even Modernist pictures in the kitchen, although these were put up by the cook, Mrs Powell, who greatly resented any suggestion that they did not reflect her own choice and taste.[136] The self-consciously whimsical sitting room shown here was the subject of a 1924 feature in *Vogue*, whose author was shocked (in an amused way) by its use of pink paint and bibelots created by nameless Victorian ladies.[137] These and other eclectic decorative features, however, played a secondary role to the pictures, mainly by the Italian Futurist Gino Severini, although the London landscape over the fire is by C.R.W. Nevinson. These pictures work with an essentially Cubist idiom to analyse their selected subject-matter, a quasi-scientific approach to the motif which for all its self-conscious *avant-gardisme* meant the paintings work as conventional drawing-room pictures. The still lifes and workaday views-out-of-the-window in essence conform to the requirements for this kind of room that we have seen in earlier decades: careful descriptions of actually observed things and scenes that offer a base of shared common experience against which it was safe to set off a pageant of charismatic individualism.

3
Picture Galleries of the Memory

mon souvenir n'est plus que la gravure.

Stendhal[1]

STAIRS AND CORRIDORS

Where would you hide a picture? If it was absolutely horrific, literally cursed, like the portrait of Dorian Gray, then in a silent attic entirely out of sight. If it was just rather dull, out of fashion or in poor condition, then perhaps in a gloomy corridor or on the unlit staircase. These were parts of the home where one did not dawdle – transitory and functional spaces which, because one could never settle there, might be unsettling.[2] Moving between rooms and floors via the stairs, when in company, also entailed some potentially awkward etiquette. For example, women should precede men when descending, but follow when ascending. All kinds of reasons were offered for the origins of this custom, but it was left to a plain-speaking American writer of the 1850s to note the most likely one, that a woman might feel more comfortable if able 'to protect her lower extremities from observation'.[3] With such worries in mind, and considering the irregular wall spaces created by a flight of stairs, it became conventionally understood that no picture of any aesthetic or financial worth should be hung here. Even in so magnificent a place as Stourhead, the owner, Richard Colt Hoare, frankly advised in his own privately printed guidebook that 'In the hall and stair-case, there is not much worthy of remark: the walls being allotted to pictures of the second class.'[4] Once accepted as a principle, it followed that one risked seeming to care little for whatever was represented on the way up and down the house. Charles Eastlake (the elder) cautioned against placing family portraits up staircases, which he implied was not uncommon, for fear of giving the impression 'that there is no room for the pictures in better situations' – that is, that the current generation have little interest in their ancestors.[5]

At least a sequence of ancestors implied the momentum of a blood line, a range of images in some sympathy with the vertical sense of the architecture of a staircase. Otherwise an irregular set of rectangles is virtually impossible to arrange comfortably above a rising dado, especially if there is a wallpaper reasserting clear vertical lines, in which circumstance adding pictures only seems to lead to a chaos of competing patterns. There was the no-nonsense solution of simply tiling over these complex fields with small prints, as a sturdily Aesthetic acquaintance of Virginia Woolf's had done in her London house, which was

> furnished on the great South Kensington principle of being on the safe side & doing the thing handsomely. Good Mrs Samuel Bruce went to the Autotype Company & ordered the entire Dutch school to be sent round framed in fumed oak. And so they were; & just covered the staircase walls, leaving an inch or two's margin in between.[6]

At the other extreme, single, massive pictures might be installed wherever the horizontal resumed, on a half-landing or at the top of the wall rising over the staircase. Beyond these options there

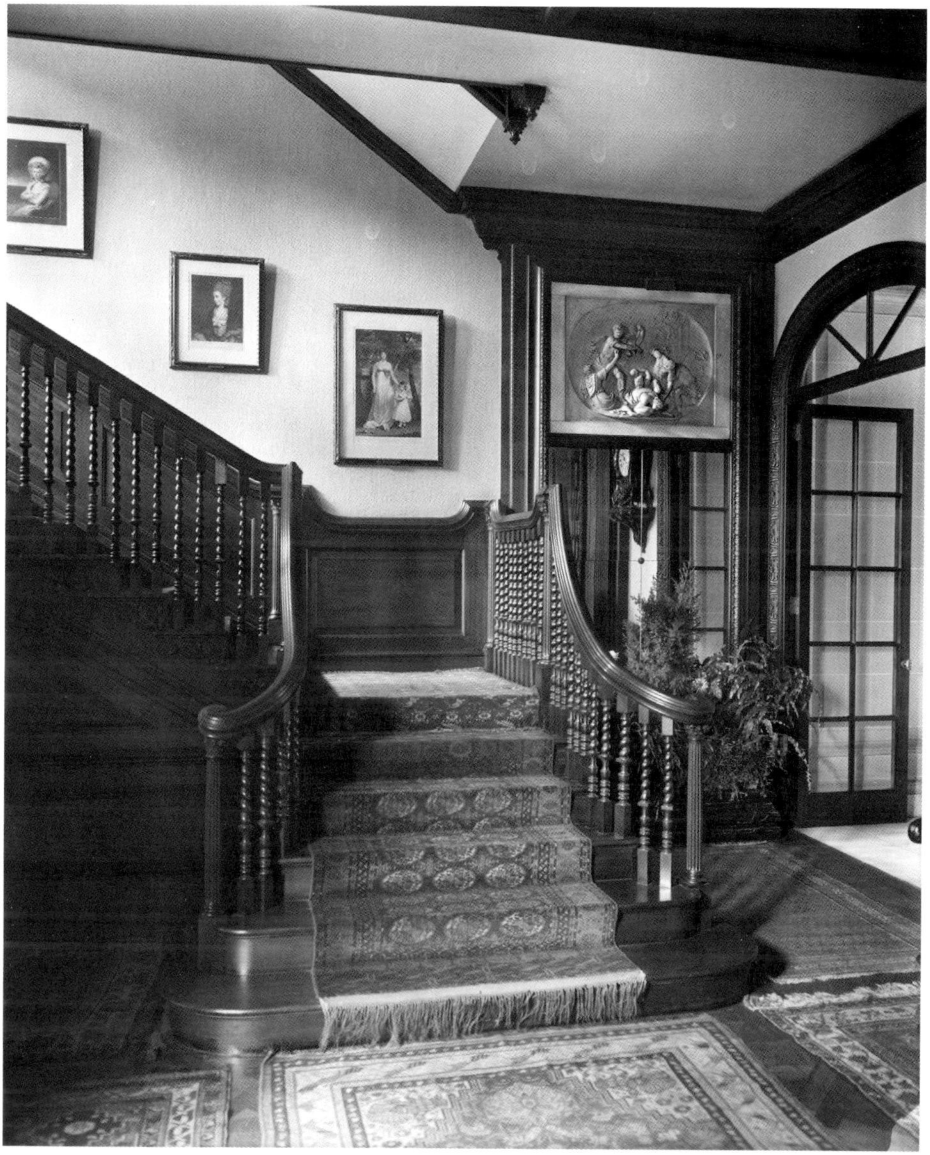

54 This modern house in Bayswater was photographed in 1918 to record the rooms decorated for John Mangos, a member of a Greek shipping dynasty who managed the family's coalmining concerns in Britain. The staircase is hung with mezzotints after eighteenth-century portraits while to the right is a Neoclassical relief plaque of the *Massacre of the Innocents*, scarcely a comfortable domestic subject but a period-fit with the prints.

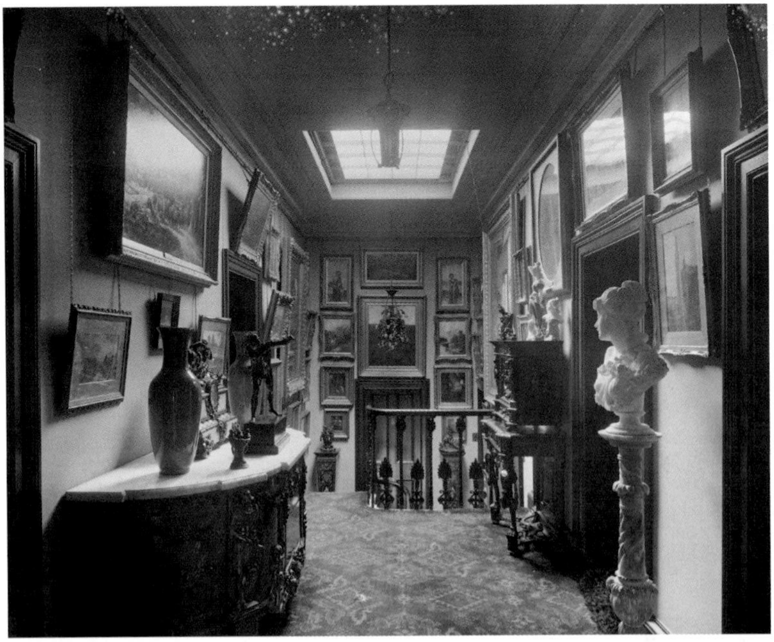

55 The landing at Park Lea, the Sefton Park home of Richard Blackler, founder of the Liverpool department store of that name, showing a dense arrangement of pictures throughout the available wall space. The pictures are cheap and cheerful by the standards of oil paintings, as suited a location where they were unlikely to be examined carefully. Photograph taken in 1916 to record work undertaken by the furniture-makers and decorators Waring & Gillow.

was little choice but to anchor a portrait-format picture at standard height at the foot of the stairs or at a half-landing and to run off from it a regular line of small pictures following the diagonal of the stairs (illus. 54). The example shown here uses prints after eighteenth-century portraits of the kind much in vogue in the decades around 1900. The portraits were all familiar and did not need to be looked at individually, which they were not intended to be, as this would have been both inconvenient and even dangerous further up the stairs: another piece of staircase etiquette dictated

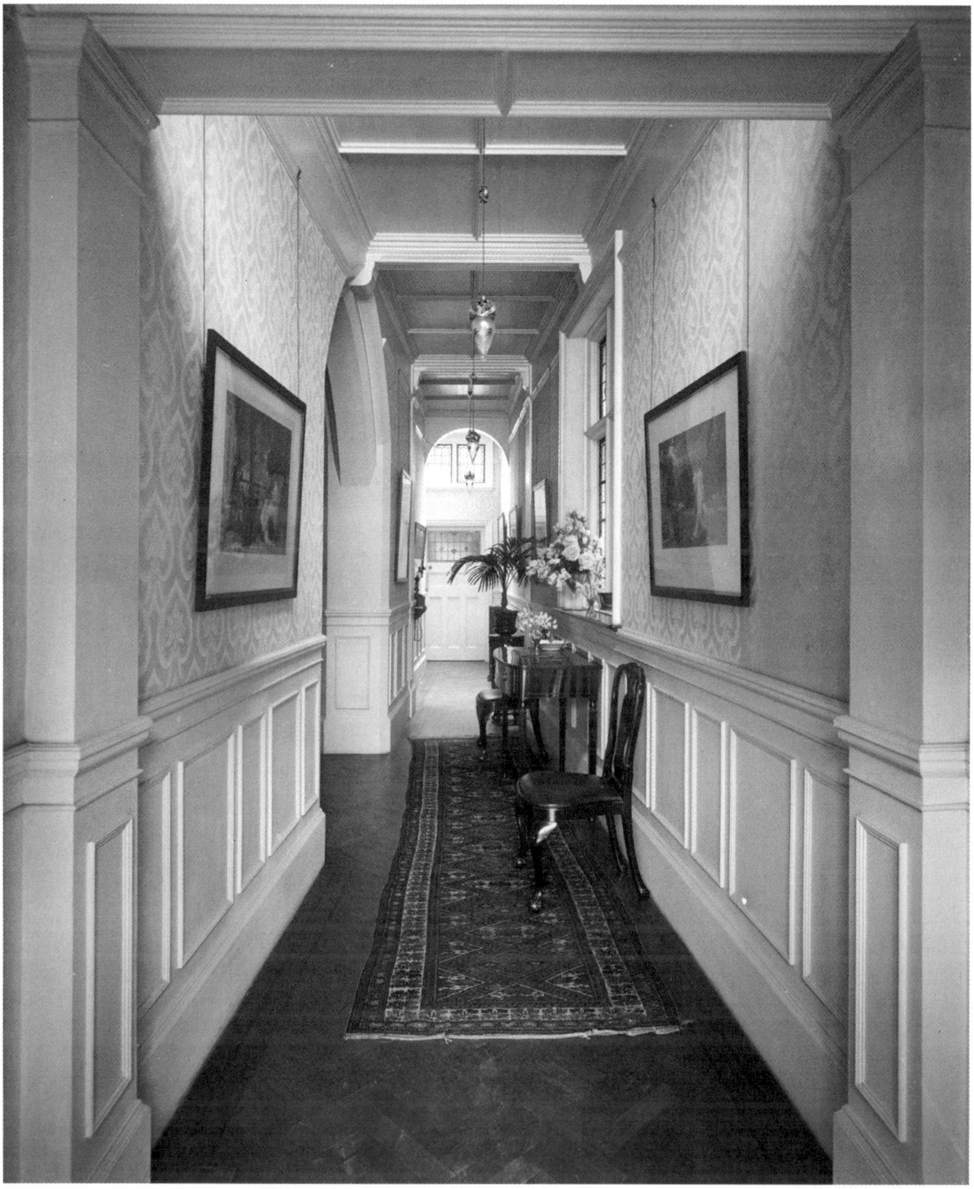

56 A corridor in an unidentified building in Dean's Yard, Westminster, with a telephone at the far end. Much effort has been made to lighten the space, with white paint and pale paper, flowers and large, wide-margined prints. The two nearest pictures are both after romantic costume paintings of the 1880s by Marcus Stone – *In Love* and *The Peacemaker* (photograph of 1908).

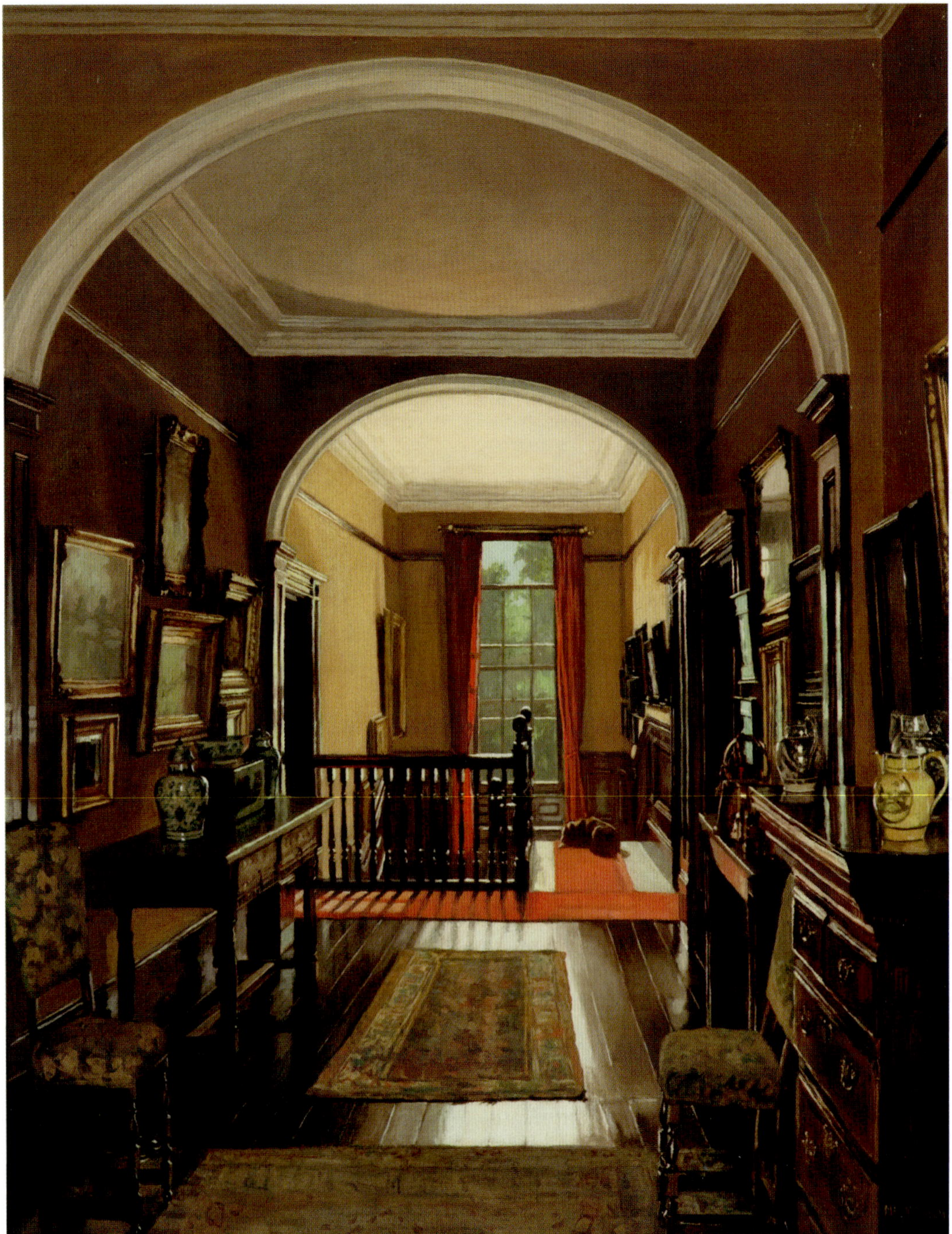

that, when coming downstairs in mixed couples for dinner, the lady kept to the wall to avoid any chance of her being squeezed over the banister rail.

The view of such pictures as there were around the staircase would be sharply oblique until, if ascending, one paused for breath on the landing to look back, as in this view of the Liverpool home of the co-founder of Blacklers department store (illus. 55). Placing pictures in transitional spaces such as stairwells, landings, corridors and passages will have made the theoretically optimum viewpoint on them impossible. But we have already seen elsewhere in the house that such a manner of focused, analytic viewing cannot, in fact, have been standard. How much, for instance, of the interest of the pair of Marcus Stone romantic subjects shown here (illus. 56) could have been made out by someone moving through this tight corridor to or from the telephone? Surely the uncomfortable proximity of the images would have added to the impetus of that movement, encouraging onwards anyone minded to linger. These tightly angled lines of vision could, however, unify a disparate group of pictures precisely by obscuring their images, if enough light was available for them to join any neighbouring polished furniture in contributing to a scattered pattern of reflections from their surfaces and frames (illus. 57). Here was a way of using pictures to articulate and link open-ended spaces that needed rescuing in some way from becoming leftovers from the named apartments of the house. To be sure, any number of decorative objects might play a role in such space-marking, but the picture was especially well suited to sign routes along the

57 *The Landing in Summer*, 1930, by the Yorkshire artist Mary Dawson Elwell, offers a rare and thoughtful consideration of the appeal of pictures seen obliquely. The frames take their places within a satisfying medley of woodwork while the painted imagery itself functions abstractly. An unused picture rail runs throughout the space.

spaces in-between by virtue of itself taking up the minimum of the restricted space available and being fundamentally of a single format, allowing an easily achieved flow of pattern.

Where light was restricted, as it must have been in most corridors, passages, halls and vestibules, advice writers traditionally recommended black-and-white art – engravings and then, from the 1870s, specifically the autotypes with which Woolf's friend got carried away. Not much happens in a hall, if understood as a liminal room between outside and in, other than greeting and parting, although many were eager to stress the emotional significance of these moments. The Irish writer Katharine Tynan recalled treasured girlhood visits in the 1880s to the home of the historian and philanthropist Sarah Atkinson, where a print of

> the beautiful Visitation – of Luini, is it? – met you when you entered the house. The meeting of the two Holy Women at their mysterious hour in that setting of a white loggia, with the ultramarine sky of Italy beyond the pillars, seemed to give a keynote to the feeling within those doors.[7]

Because so near to the dirt of the road or street outside, and because it was a space in which bodies moved haphazardly, swirling off coats and capes, the hall was not suited to bulky or fragile decorative objects. Pictures, less susceptible to dust and collisions, were the ideal furniture here, and the poignancy of the first impression of a house even led Candace Wheeler, one of the great gurus of American interior design, to claim that 'If there is one place more than another where a picture performs its full work of suggestion and decoration, it is in a hall which is otherwise bare of ornament'. Here framed images may function as 'indications of the tastes and experiences of the family'.[8] But this idea of a snapshot montage of family values in the hall became one of the reformers' targets. Cassell's *Household Guide* of 1869 cautioned that

> It is certainly bad taste to crowd into what is generally a narrow space the furniture fitting only for a larger one; but how often are seen pictures crowded on to the walls as if it were the entrance to a photographer's studio.[9]

Reason soon suggested the right arrangement, namely, restricted numbers of black-and-white pictures of little monetary value announcing good taste without ostentation, requiring no interruption in the already complex negotiations of coming and going, and ideally forming a sequence gently accelerating ingress and egress. Thus Edith Wharton, in her book of 1897 (while always insisting on imagining an audience with aspirations to own a Renaissance palazzo) spoke for her generation on both sides of the Atlantic in asking for a hall hung with just a few prints, preferably with clear, firm lines in the noble tradition of copperplate engraving, the ideal being 'some frieze-like procession, such as Mantegna's *Triumph of Julius Caesar*'.[10]

Historians of interior design observe a darkening of the ideal room in the later nineteenth century.[11] In a period of rapidly changing lighting technology, much of it cumbersome and smelly, there was the beginning of a nostalgia for candlelight that is still with us. More broadly, the entire historicist mood – from picturesque abbeys to the Arts and Crafts – precluded bright light, while the notion that an interior was composed like a painting implied a dark field from which lights emerged.[12] Those eager to learn from Japanese tradition, meanwhile, pondered the *tokonoma*, with its picture placed deliberately in shadow – indeed, according to later nostalgics at least, with the principal purpose of setting off the play of those shadows.[13] But while this aesthetic can clearly be seen in traditions of furnishing the dining room (see Chapter Two above), in the kinds of communicating spaces that concern us here, light was at a premium, which added further cause for enthusiasm for the autotype.

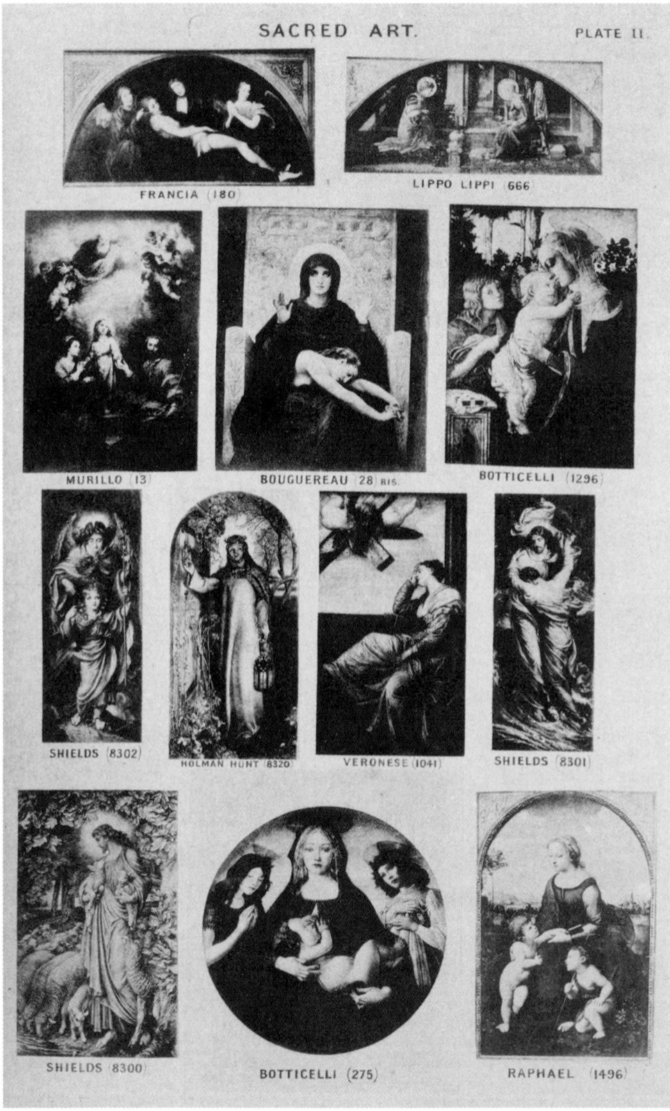

58 A selection of religious imagery offered by the Autotype Company in their 1907 catalogue. Classic favourites by Raphael, Botticelli and Murillo rub shoulders with modern Christian art in the Pre-Raphaelite tradition by William Holman Hunt and Frederic Shields. The latter's *Good Shepherd* (bottom left) was the picture Christina Rossetti was most attached to in her final days.

The autotype was a photomechanical printmaking process using light-sensitive gelatine to reproduce the intermediary tones of a transparency of an initial photograph. Developed on paper, its fundamental appeal lay in its accuracy, permanence and cheapness. The autotype was nothing less than the first photographic process to generate mass-produced pictures on our definition of that term: images intended for wall display.[14] The key technological breakthrough was made in the 1860s by none other than the same Joseph Swan who was soon afterwards to become the inventor of the electric light bulb and who installed a very early electric lighting system in the picture gallery at Cragside (see illus. 36). Swan took his invention into production for a few years before a series of buy-outs and mergers gave rise to the Autotype Company, whose Fine Art Gallery on New Oxford Street was the go-to address for affordable, entirely respectable art reproductions for several decades (illus. 58).[15] The company's stylized rising-sun logo, and its motto, from *King John* – 'The glorious sun/ Stays in his course, and plays the alchemist' – suggested a parallel miracle to the switched electricity also pioneered by Swan. The autotype was an illuminating picture. We saw in Chapter One how intellectuals enthusiastically took up the idea of this very modern process, which made redundant the interpreting hand of the engraver in favour of chemical ingenuity, bringing the very strokes of the artist into one's rooms (the autotype was seen as being especially well suited to reproduce Old Master drawings). The new art was regularly contrasted favourably with the chromo, a reproduction effected by teams of hack copyists (see illus. 47), whose ultimate abominable product was the oleograph, a chromo that had been varnished or otherwise treated in ever more desperate methods to counterfeit the original oil painting.[16] Thus George Gissing opens one of his novels, *In the Year of Jubilee* (1894), with an account of his protagonist's pictures that is characteristically credible in its mix of the good, bad and ugly: 'The pictures were a strange medley – autotypes of some artistic value hanging side by side with hideous oleographs framed in ponderous gilding.'[17]

For those with taste but limited funds, the autotype was the passport to authentic art in the home. To the great champion of artistic life in the suburbs Jane Ellen Panton it was more or less the last word required in pictures. Her aesthetics, as they emerge from her many books, were naturally suited to her readership, to whom she espoused an intriguing kind of snobbish anarchism, suggesting that people of good taste should step forward to lead new suburban communities without deference to traditional elites. The autotype was cheap, clean, modern, honest and respectable, and Mrs Panton lavished her approval on it for just about every room in the home, as if she were receiving a commission (a not unconscionable idea, given the mutual puffing that has been observed between the author and some of the tradesmen she recommended). If only those who hankered after unobtainably expensive paintings by household names would realize that 'their lives and houses would have been brightened at once had they spent 20*l.* on autotypes'.[18] Upstairs, the autotype suited the servants' bedrooms ('this will discourage the maids from hanging up ugly pictures or glazed oleographs or other horrors'), the lady's bedroom (over the bed itself 'should be two good-sized autotypes') and even the nursery.[19] Above all, they suited passages, of which 'the walls shall only be decorated with good autotypes repeating the *motif* set forth in the front entrance'. So affordable are these endlessly useful things that Panton suggests regularly refreshing their selection with the latest Paris Salon reproductions offered each year at the Autotype Gallery. Such images should, she stresses, be 'carefully and lovingly chosen', turning the corridors of her suburban utopia into a personalized art gallery of bright new productions, without reference to portraits of ancestors, let alone the monarchs and grandees whose authority she rejected.

The modern corridor may be a primarily functional architectural feature, yet it has noble kin: the picture gallery began life as a corridor. The 'long gallery' evolved in the late Middle Ages and, in Britain at least, comes clearly into focus in the great houses of the Elizabethan and Jacobean periods, such as Hardwick Hall in Derbyshire or Ham House on the Thames near Richmond.[20] The archetypal gallery in this sense was (with the usual caveat attaching to any attribution of fixed custom to any species of room) essentially an indoor cloister, a walkway offering views from one long side and decorated with perhaps tapestries, and later pictures, on the other. The gallery was (again, at least conceptually) the resort of a rainy day, somewhere for genteel ball games or to allow children to let off some energy. In the eighteenth century, at picture exhibitions, the gallery-as-corridor model was overlooked in favour of top-lit rooms maximizing wall space and allowing for circulation rather than linear traversal. The meaning of 'gallery' changed, the indoor-cloister sense now being retained as a flattering euphemism for the long wards of hospitals and asylums, while to consign pictures to old corridors came to seem unenlightened. For example, there were regular complaints regarding the fate of the engravings exhibited at the Royal Academy at Somerset House, relegated as they were on some occasions to 'a dark passage leading from the library to the Antique Academy', where they 'cannot be surveyed for a moment by any curious visitor.'[21] In public galleries, such as the National Gallery, which moved into its purpose-built spaces in the late 1830s, lighting pictures from above in expansive chambers was accepted as the common-sense approach to display, clearly signalling a modern civic solution. Such democratic transparency, however, left some aesthetes hankering after shadows, such as this design authority writing in 1907:

> Many priceless old masters appear to small advantage in the National Gallery because they have been taken from

> panels over a reredos or dark corners in chapels, and having been executed to appear at their best under those particular conditions of lighting or position, they look strange and bizarre in their present surroundings.[22]

Memories of the gallery-corridor or cloister were also retained by those who – so complained National Gallery reports – brought their toddlers to the Gallery as an ideal place for them to learn to walk, with the inevitably concomitant bumps and puddles.[23]

During the glory days of British picture-buying early in the nineteenth century some architects were still offering side-lit long galleries to house important private collections, such as that designed by Charles Heathcote Tatham at Castle Howard. John Nash's picture gallery for Lord Berwick at Attingham Park, in Shropshire, of 1807 – cast-iron-roofed and with restrained screens of paired columns at either end (illus. 59) – established a strong precedent for modern private picture galleries to be top-lit, as in the public sector, and to have more of the character of a long room than a corridor. But the lure of the past continued to draw some architects back to the idea of the ambulatory long gallery. John Claudius Loudon, in his fantasy of the ideal English villa of the 1830s, includes a gallery that would be 'a sort of promenade, and place of recreation for the children and young people in wet weather, and would be an ornamental appendage to the house . . . ornamented with the inferior pictures, and family portraits, and a few glazed prints'.[24] Loudon's fellow Scot, Robert Kerr, author of *The Gentleman's House* (1864), which vied in voluminous detail with Loudon's *Encyclopaedia*, sought to reapply some historical rigour to the category of the domestic gallery when designing Bearwood, a vast country house in Berkshire, for the owner of *The Times*. A room set aside for pictures, attached to a house 'as a mere show-place', says Kerr, is simply an undomestic idea. Yet there remained good sense in gathering any valuable collection

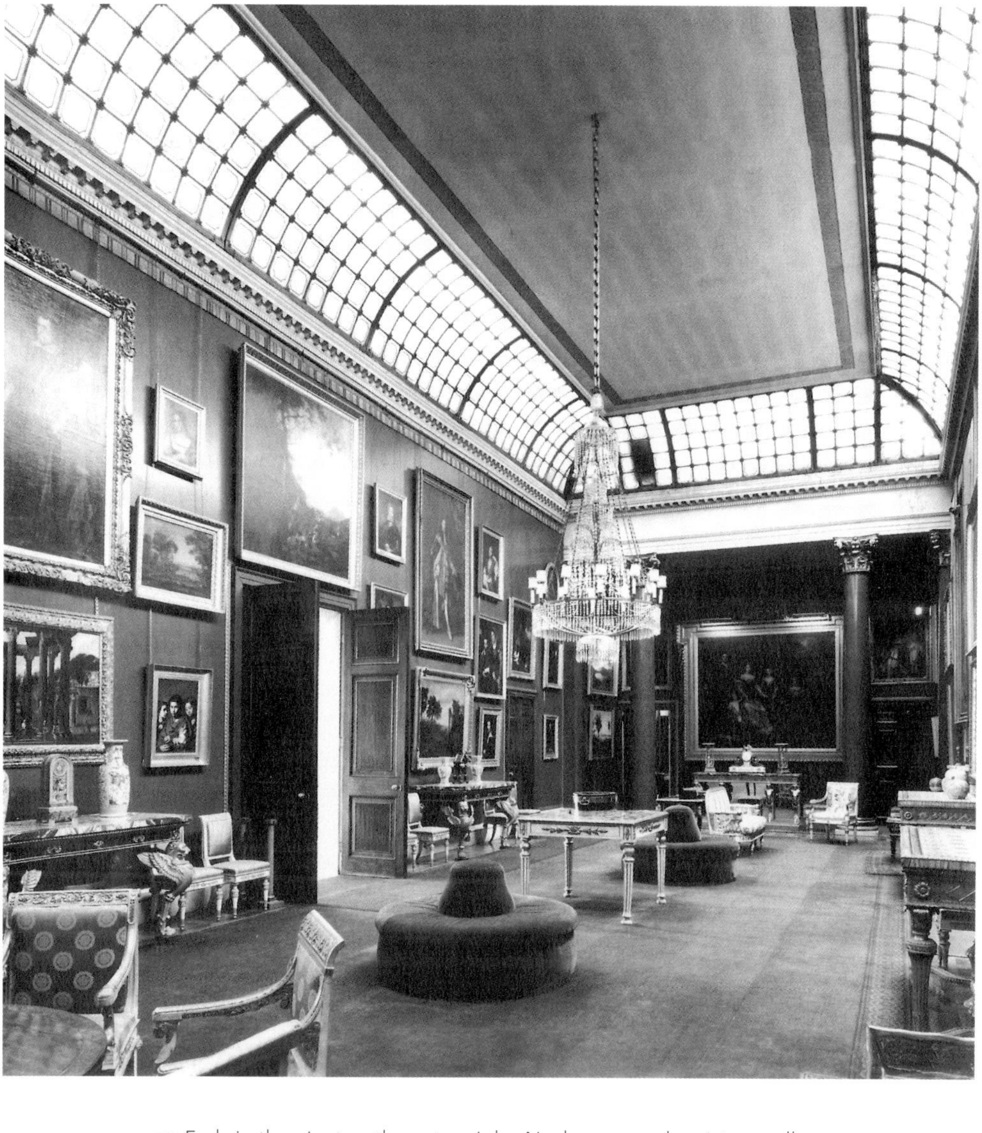

59 Early in the nineteenth century John Nash squeezed a picture gallery into Lord Berwick's Attingham Park in Shropshire. Requiring toplighting, cast iron ribs were used to mount the windows in the coving, a new idea in a domestic setting. It was therefore possible to give over all the wall space to the pictures, as at public exhibition venues such as Somerset House where the Royal Academy held its picture shows from 1780.

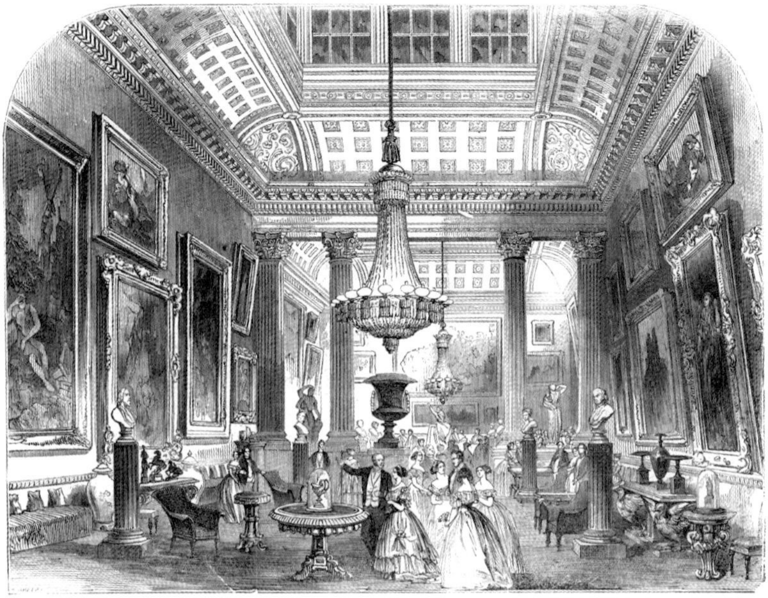

60 A new picture gallery was added to the side of Lord Grosvenor's London mansion on Park Lane in 1819 (the ceiling shown here was installed in 1827). The magnificent collection of pictures at Grosvenor House had been available to a very limited public from soon after the family's acquisition of the property in 1806. But the new gallery's majestic space – housing relatively few very large paintings – now also lent itself to grand receptions. Here Queen Victoria and Prince Albert are being given a tour (*Illustrated London News*, 30 June 1849).

together rather than distributing it haphazardly through the family rooms of the house.[25] His solution was to revive the 'Gallery-Corridor' but now as 'a chief Thoroughfare' in the very centre of the enormous house, 'scientifically' top-lit and so without external views. Kerr's gallery at Bearwood had pairs of doors at each end, which the architect took as a fundamental element of 'a Thoroughfare-Gallery'.[26] With only one end clearly opened, a gallery became enclosed with the character of a kind of drawing room, as indeed might be said of many of the grandest of the great London aristocratic private collections, such as the gallery at Bridgewater House (formerly Cleveland House) remodelled for the Earl of Ellesmere by Charles Barry around 1850.[27] Naturally such spectacular chambers were indeed used as reception rooms, for dinners and balls (illus. 60). The German art historian Gustav Waagen attended an evening reception at Bridgewater House in the 1830s and was thankful when the company's attention was drawn away to a group of Tyrolese singers with their 'sharp, shrieking' notes, for this allowed him some time alone with the pictures.[28]

It is worth reflecting on what was lost with the decline of the walk-through gallery model: most notably, children, for whom the open-ended long gallery was potentially a play space alongside pictures. When galleries became public, children were assumed to be unwelcome, although they had apparently sometimes been taken along to the early Royal Academy shows to judge from engravings of these. When there was a great public interest in the exhibition of designs for frescoes for the new Houses of Parliament in 1843, small children were barred yet were 'nevertheless carried in with the throng'. The police in attendance gathered them up and walked them out again 'in droves, and packed [them] up for a time in the vestibule' until collected.[29] At the National Gallery there seems to have been a tradition among some easy-going relatives of depositing children there, knowing that the attendants would keep an eye on them. The artist Gwen Raverat recalled being 'parked' there in the 1890s.[30] Debates over whether the Gallery was a suitable place for nursing babies have remained perennial right up to the present day. It was only when the picture became a key weapon in the hands of late Victorian cultural missionaries such as G. F. Watts that children were actively welcomed back. Speaking at the new South London Art Gallery in Camberwell in 1893, Watts gave his opinion 'that even very young children might be conscious of the influence of beautiful art'.[31]

The domestic long gallery model also provided for adults a particular style of looking – allowing walking, talking and glancing sideways at pictures simultaneously. To be sure, such a mode remained possible in public galleries, not least along the massive extent of the Grande Galerie of the Musée du Louvre. That great museum had, of course, been the Palais du Louvre prior to its Revolutionary re-branding, so fundamentally processional rather than explicatory in its spatial rhetoric.[32] But a purpose-built national gallery was indisputably supposed to facilitate the viewing of pictures, whereas the long gallery was for walking-cum-talking. In the seventeenth century William Sanderson, as ever too logical to be entirely credible as a historical witness, noted that galleries were where you 'Walk, Judge, Examine, Censure' and that therefore these were the places for '*Graver* stories; *Histories*', containing the 'best figures, and rarest worke' – pictures as cues for highbrow conversation.[33] Yet long galleries were in practice more often associated with portraits illustrating family lines whose evolution well suited the strolling viewer and whose quality (that is, of the portraits) did not demand more than cursory inspection. Thus at Lord Arlington's East Anglian seat, Euston Hall, the indefatigable tourist Celia Fiennes found in 1698:

> A Long gallery hung wth pictures at Length, on ye one side the Royal family from K[ing] Henry ye 7th by ye Scottish race, his eldest daughter down to ye present King William and his queen Mary. The other side are forreign princes from ye Emperour of Moroccoe, ye Northern and Southern princes and Emperour of Germany. There is a square in ye middle where stands a billiard table, hung with outlandish pictures of Heroes.[34]

Notwithstanding that last detail being rather hard to visualize, Fiennes gives an intriguing account of the long gallery's pictures as structured through a mix of myth, history and play which the Enlightenment would seek to segregate.

A few years after Fiennes's visit, in one of the *Spectator* papers narrating the doings of the amiably simple squire Roger de Coverley, Richard Steele uses a guided tour of Sir Roger's gallery of ancestors to comically illustrate his host's 'way of saying things as they occur to his imagination, without regular introduction or care to preserve the appearance of chain of thought'. So, for all the nominally well-ordered sequence of de Coverley forebears, the walk involves an anecdotal stream of consciousness scarcely amounting to a history of anything.[35] Later in the eighteenth century, Horace Walpole at Strawberry Hill filled his gallery with a rich company of portraits of his own relations, royalty and plenty of other 'remarkable persons', while that other gothic wonder-house, Fonthill Abbey, included a gallery of portraits of the purported noble ancestors of the owner, William Beckford, which few seem to have accepted as authentic genealogy.[36]

With the decline of the gallery through which one walked, talked and picture-spotted – with no one of these activities presuming to be more important than another – came the etiquette of the public picture gallery in which, in strict contrast, it became considered vulgar to talk because pictures were now associated with a professionalized expertise which virtually no one possessed. By the end of the nineteenth century more was expected of pictures than to line a promenade, and, in an age of racial obsession, more was expected of ancestors and relations. Lady Dorothy Nevill, a Victorian kinswoman of Horace Walpole's, regretted the selling off of royal portraits from an old Walpole house, and scared herself with the idea that these 'are now serving as ancestresses to some American or Semitic millionaire!'[37] Borrowed or fantastical ancestry was no longer acceptable when degeneration was a looming threat. In Henry James's *Portrait of a Lady*, which addresses exactly the awkward encounters of the waning English upper classes and new American money, the picture gallery makes one of its last stands in its old format, as a prompt to formal conversation and a refuge from the elements. 'Ah yes,' says Ralph Touchett, the owner, 'pictures are very convenient', to which one of his guests eagerly agrees: 'They're so very pleasant when it rains.'[38]

In the private house the long gallery traditions proved hard to replace. The idea of a room – a destination rather than a route – with only pictures in it seemed, as Robert Kerr had objected, just not very homely. The logic of a carefully selected collection of pictures seemed to demand a dedicated environment, so that 'justice may be done to them all'.[39] But we have seen already that, when the picture was imagined to dictate terms to architecture, the latter ended being spun into impossible shapes. Ruskin was led to imagine a mythically labyrinthine sequence of rooms for an ideal national picture gallery, while a contributor to the *Art-Union* in 1841 concluded that, if a private collector were to lay out serious money for good pictures, then architecture must give in to their requirements, meaning rejecting the idea of a gallery in favour of 'many rooms, each [with just] one light, and, in many instances, one picture'.[40] Certainly many rather more sober private galleries were built onto the houses of the newly wealthy, as we see in Henry La Thangue's portrait of Abraham Mitchell (see illus. 51). But it is remarkable how little private galleries were much noticed by contemporaries or remembered later, other than when a room was given over to a single celebrity artist – Reynolds, Turner or Rossetti – to create a unique curated space. An artist's own home was again a special case, where the unity of conception could give rise to a sense of a living company of figures. One of Rossetti's friends recalled feeling that the women in his pictures at the artist's Cheyne Walk house were enjoying a poetry recital by Swinburne, while the wife of G. F. Watts wrote of her love of spending evenings in his darkened studio, where 'The pictures are like spirits silently standing all about.'[41] In contrast to such magical environments, a

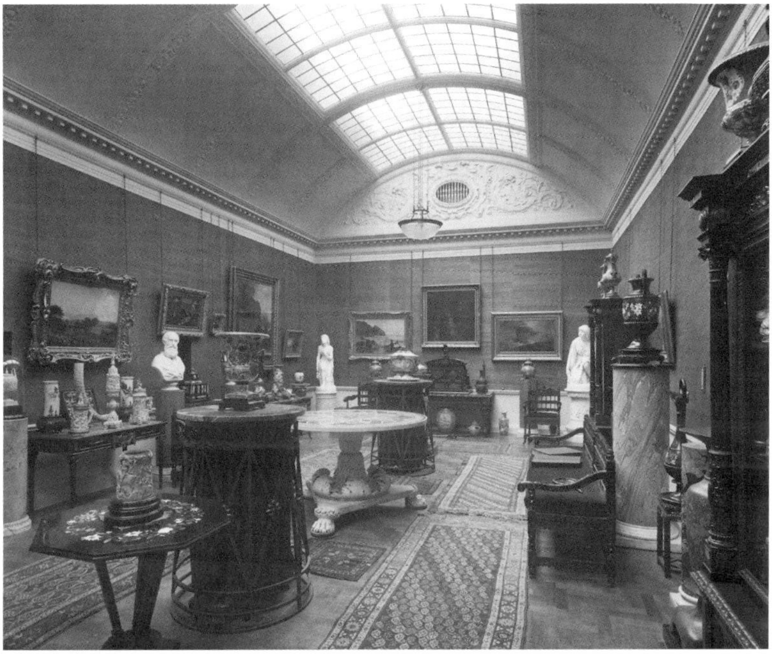

61 The gallery of the chemical industrialist Holbrook Gaskell at his house Erindale in Cheshire, photographed in 1910. This is the kind of apparently joyless art-barn that gave private picture galleries a bad name. The Gaskells were active in nonconformist religious work and promoted temperance among their workers. The imagery of the pictures here sticks safely to rather austere landscape.

rich man's gallery could seem rather sad, as Mitchell's does in his portrait, showing the collector separated from his family to stare at a picture that seems to have exhausted him.

On hand to warn of such masculine self-indulgence was the admonitory tradition of the myopic or masturbatory connoisseur locked away in his picture cabinet – an image that extends at least from the seventeenth century via the caricatures of Rowlandson down to the picture-mad Soames Forsyte in John Galsworthy's Edwardian novel cycle *The Forsyte Saga*. In his provocative essay on 'Art for the Villa' of 1889, George Moore proclaims the end of the private picture gallery altogether. This absurd excrescence he declares to be 'a monstrous and ridiculous anomaly which no one would build but a retired cheesemonger, and which no one could at all bear with except a duke who spent the greater part of his time abroad'.[42] Such places remind him of hotel sitting-rooms, a harsh but perhaps not entirely unfair criticism given the coldly unappealing aspect of some private galleries as they are recorded in photographs (illus. 61). 'A great picture is out of place in a private house,' says Moore: it 'demands the soul, the entire soul, and in return it gives absolute annihilation of past and future, creating a momentary but ecstatic present' – something incompatible with things seen vaguely over the heads of guests at a ball in an aristocratic house. The picture's relationship with the home at this point risks breaking down entirely: an alien in the modern interior, unaffordable in more modest homes and – if a masterpiece – with a duty to carry itself off promptly to the nearest museum.[43] The literary treatment of the picture in the home in the years around 1900 reflects this sense of dislocation and unwelcomeness through a new life being breathed into traditions of the magic, haunted or ghostly picture, which, as often as not, was likely to be found in an old-fashioned location such as a gallery-corridor. Its demands on the soul no longer satisfiable in the home, any picture left behind there risked spilling out of its frame into the excesses of the gothic.

A GOTHIC GALLERY

The Victorians embraced gothic architecture and design, and a picturesque version of their own pre-Reformation history. Yet they held this in tension with a continued prejudice against Catholicism, imagined as the emotional European other, not least in matters of art. For centuries the picture, especially the portrait, takes a regular role in English drama and literature as a portal into the irrational, as *doppelgänger*, premonitory virtual ancestor, surrogate companion or voyeur.[44] Hidden behind such texts were surely all kinds of actual unorthodox emotional experiences with pictures that went unrecorded, not least out of fear of being suspected of Catholic practices. No picture lover was more scholarly in their literary approach than art historian Elizabeth Eastlake, yet even she, after the death of her husband, Charles Eastlake (the elder), was in the habit of keeping one of his pictures in his old chair alongside her at the fireside for company.[45] The picture's presence in such real and fictional stories suggests that the modern, mercantile Protestant life of the picture cannot be the whole story, that there was a pictorial surplus of which public British culture was in denial.[46]

The case of Horace Walpole shows that a fascination with the larger possibilities of the picture was perfectly compatible with conventional expressions of anti-Catholicism. Indeed, perhaps a willingness to dwell on theological difference precisely opened up the question of what more a picture might be able to do.[47] In his preface to *The Castle of Otranto* (1764; soon subtitled 'A Gothic Story') Walpole takes us through his novel's framing device. The tale is a translation of a book printed in Naples in 1529, using a copy 'found in the library of an ancient Catholic family in the north of England'. Walpole surmises the work was written by a priest, at the very moment of the Reformation, 'to confirm the populace in their ancient errors and superstitions' and to encourage belief in the 'Miracles, visions, necromancy, dreams, and other preternatural events' which in modern Britain are 'exploded now even from romances'.[48] Early in the narrative occurs the iconic scene in which the tyrant Manfred makes advances, in a gallery, to the fiancée of his lately deceased son. As if in protest, Manfred's grandfather steps down out of his portrait and, summoning the reprobate to follow him, 'marched sedately, but dejected, to the

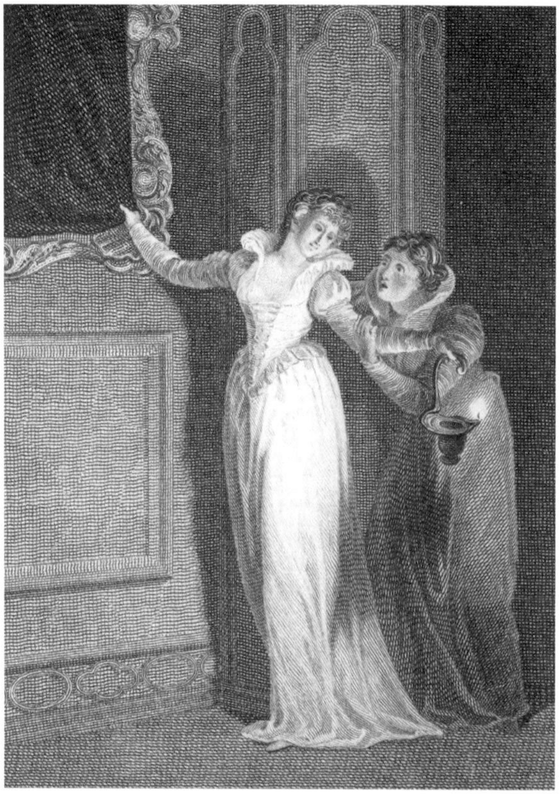

62 Ann Radcliffe's classic gothic novel *The Mysteries of Udolpho* was pirated in 1802 in drastically reduced form as *The Veiled Picture*. The frontispiece, after a design by William Marshall Craig, shows the heroine Emily St Aubert about to look behind the curtain which covers an extravagantly framed painting (if it *is* a painting . . .).

end of the gallery', a ghostly demonstration that seems a lesson in the proper use of a gallery for walking past a respectably ordered line of relatives.[49] The motif of ancestors being disappointed to the point of enchantment was so lucid as to spawn endless reworkings, such as the scene in Gilbert and Sullivan's *Ruddigore* (1887) in which the shades of the hero's ferocious forebears descend from their pictures to chastise their faint-hearted Victorian descendant: 'It is our duty to see that our successors commit their daily crimes in a conscientious and workmanlike fashion.'

The gothic picture might become animated, like those in some medieval hagiographies, or might be curtained, a practice that was the emblematic antithesis of all that the modern British picture represented by the later eighteenth century – a commodity to be judged openly and *en masse* at exhibitions. Thus the crucial motif in Ann Radcliffe's *Mysteries of Udolpho* (1794) is a large picture draped in black with 'something very dreadful belonging to it' (illus. 62). The reveal, when it comes, is in the form of a homily against 'monkish superstition'. The veil hides not a picture but a kind of *memento mori* sculpture, a waxwork of a decayed corpse which an arrogant earlier owner of the castle had been sentenced by the church to contemplate as penance for his sins. Such gothic motifs as those of Walpole and Radcliffe can be found in literature throughout the nineteenth century, alongside other stories in which the picture precipitates drama and tragedy through its capacity to confuse identities and contaminate characters with the sins of the past.[50] There is a shift, however, from making use of theological difference to a focus on tainted ancestry, and towards the end of the century we have the sense that any picture in the house will have become in some degree uncanny, resulting from the falling out we have described between picture and interior. The old sense of Protestant superiority over Catholicism *vis-à-vis* the responsible use of pictures was no longer, for the Victorians, strong enough to provide in itself the impetus for striking narratives.[51]

That notion of difference was dealt various intellectual blows during the century, not least by the single most controversial theological text of the age, John Henry Newman's *Remarks on Certain Passages in the Thirty-Nine Articles* (*Tracts for the Times* no. 90, 1841). Here the leader of the Oxford Movement argued that the Catholic Church had in fact condemned all idolatry in the sixteenth century, and so technically there was no doctrinal difference between the Anglican and Roman churches over pictures. In the furore that ensued regarding Newman's larger claims for the catholicity of the Church of England, orthodox Protestant iconoscepticism was reasserted, but the question had implicitly been put: if Italian devotion to images, and faith in their agency, were based on instinctive emotional response, not official Catholic teaching, then why would not or should not the British respond in similar ways?[52] This controversy is one overlooked context for the quasi-devotional manner in which Rossetti's pictures were displayed in the homes of aesthetically inclined collectors who occasionally gave his *spirituel* art a place apart. One such, George Rae, wrote to Rossetti of the effect on his wife of the arrival in their home of the artist's *The Beloved* in 1866: 'It is my belief that she spends half the day before the picture as certain devout Catholic ladies had used to do before their favourite shrines in the days of old.'[53] Here were modern pictures that, in George Moore's terms, demanded the entire soul and were granted it. Yet Rossetti's own decline into drug dependency and poor mental health suggested, after all, another gothic tale of the terrible price of supplying them.

By the last years of the nineteenth century the sense of the picture being an 'alien' in the home promoted a late flowering of the gothic picture tale. As we saw in Chapter Two, plenty of advice writers were ready to suppress ancestral portraits, but now the continued presence of such pictures threatened their owners not only with *dépassé* interiors but also with degeneracy. Katharine Tynan and Vernon Lee (the pseudonym of Violet Paget, a British writer living in Italy) both wrote of women brought down, in different ways, by madness inflicted by portraits of their ancestors (illus. 63).[54] Was it safe to have pictures in the house any longer, given the curses and temptations that they seemed to embody? All roads in this field of enquiry lead to *The Picture of Dorian*

Gray, which surely answers 'no' to that question. Wilde's story of a curtained portrait, which ages on vicarious behalf of its decadent subject, powerfully distils the entire tradition of gothic and magic picture tropes. Dorian subsumes all into the cult of his own beauty. He adores the Catholic Church – yet only as a beautiful image. He loved 'to stroll through the gaunt cold picture-gallery of his country house and look at the various portraits of those whose blood flowed in his veins' – yet these were now mere spectacles of

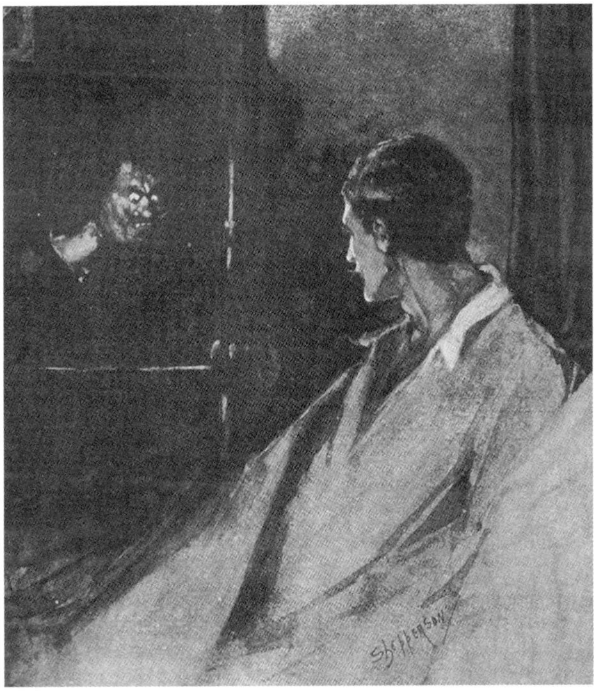

63 In Katharine Tynan's short story 'The Picture on the Wall' a young couple's romance is ended by an encounter with a portrait of one of the lady's ancestors. A Van Dyck cavalier on one side of the canvas is belied by the same sitter, raving mad, appearing on the reverse. The picture comes alive, forcing the lady to confess the terrible secret of inherited madness which at any moment might strike her down: the match is off (illustration by Claude Shepperson in the *English Illustrated Magazine*, 1895).

debauchery to whom he owed nothing, for his actual self had been reconceived on the basis of his literary hero, Des Esseintes in J.-K. Huysmans' *À rebours*, a self in any case now possessed by another picture kept safely locked up in Dorian's London attic. Only the portrait of his mother, in the guise of a Bacchante, seemed vital: 'the eyes were still wonderful in their depth and brilliancy of colour. They seemed to follow him wherever he went.'

This last motif is another of the standard properties of the gothic portrait whose eyes, even if the picture stays put, can still track a visitor. The idea has a very long history, not least in Christian tradition. The German theologian Nicholas of Cusa, for instance, in his *De visione Dei* (*c.* 1453), describes a sacred picture keeping its eyes on a community of Bavarian monks however much they might move around the room in which it is placed, a metaphor of God's ability to see us all individually and simultaneously.[55] In the gothic mode the watchful picture survives as an instance of religious culture of which modern theology could not approve, and yet which demanded recognition as a psychological fact. One of Wilde's models for Dorian Gray was *Melmoth the Wanderer*, published by his great-uncle Charles Maturin in 1820. Here the narrator encounters the seventeenth-century portrait of a man, the titular Melmoth, who horribly turns out to be still alive, having sold his soul to the Devil: 'He started, turned away; but, as he turned away, he thought he saw the eyes of the portrait, on which his own was fixed, *move*.'[56] As Walter Scott observed in his 1811 essay on *The Castle of Otranto*, this gothic motif was effective precisely because it was credible: 'There are few who have not felt, at some period of their childhood, a sort of terror from the manner in which the eye of an ancient portrait appears to fix that of the spectator from every point of view.'[57]

That this perception was not in fact merely a childish weakness was signalled by the paper read to the Royal Society in 1824 by William Hyde Wollaston, 'On the Apparent Direction of Eyes

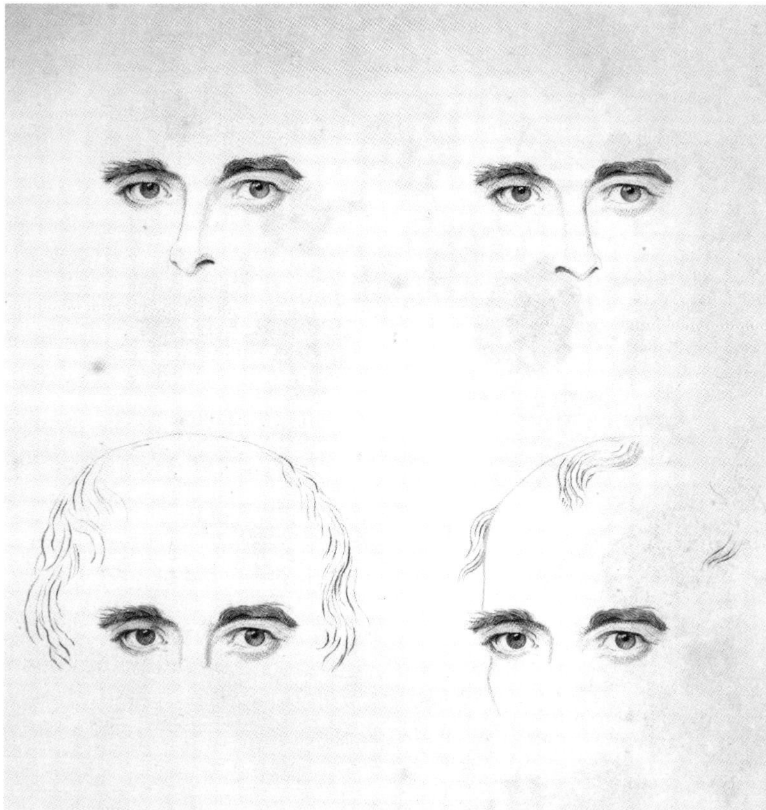

64 The gothic novel encouraged serious consideration of the long-attested suspicion that the eyes of portraits followed the viewer around the room. In 1824 William Hyde Wollaston addressed the Royal Society 'On the Apparent Direction of Eyes in a Portrait'.

in a Portrait', illustrated with help from no less an artist than the President of the Royal Academy, Thomas Lawrence (illus. 64). Wollaston thought it was all about the nose failing to move as we track past it, producing a compensating illusion in the eyes of the portrait. Ernst Gombrich, in the twentieth century, worried over the problem for decades, sensing that it was not quite solved, and indeed modern neuroscience suspects that the brain is hard-wired to look out for being looked at, so that the illusion may turn out to have little to do with perspective or geometry, and everything to do with the fundamental physiology of self-preservation.[58] That primeval fear was tapped by the writers of ghost stories, but also recognized by Victorian scientists. Neil Arnott's standard textbook *The Elements of Physics* notes that 'It is related of a murderer, that he was impelled to commit suicide by observing that the eyes of the portrait of his victim were always fixed upon him,' a story echoed in various picture tales, including Tom Hood's 'The Shadow of a Shade', in which a portrait gives various signs, just barely rationally explicable, of the fate of the sitter, driving his assassin to self-destruction.[59]

The idea of the eyes of a portrait meeting and moving with those of its viewer suits, above all, the long gallery of ancient ancestral portraits. Walking past one stiff figure after another, the visitor is eventually rewarded with some living spark. The effect can only transpire if the viewer keeps moving, and so is a form of aesthetic engagement especially associated with the corridor-type space. I say 'aesthetic' because this *frisson* of the uncanny in itself entails little other than moderate fright – sublime-light, so to speak. The movement of the portrait's eyes is also perceived in relation to the otherwise stationary head and body of the sitter, which remain unthreateningly stable (*pace* Otranto and cases of the descendants of the portrait there). After all, the eyes are paying us attention, at least confirming our sense of our own importance. More frightening are those cases where the picture changes *unnoticed*, morphing beyond our presence or our control.

The masterpiece of this version of the picture story is M. R. James's 'The Mezzotint', published in his 1904 collection *Ghost Stories of an Antiquary*.[60] As Freud was to point out, the uncanny is most effective when experienced within the sanest, most enlightened context, and James's characters are scholarly data-miners, largely unimpressed by life: if they are spooked, we are terrified. The mezzotint of the title is sent to the curator at a university museum, who takes it into his private college rooms. It is a very ordinary topographic scene, other impressions of which were to be found 'in the passages of undisturbed country mansions'. But this particular print reveals a slightly different composition each time it is looked at, its successive states narrating a terrible historical crime, although the image – like the picture of Dorian Gray – never changes while being looked at. The story may be read as an allegory of the danger of leaving pictures unregarded. More or less anyone in our period who put pen to paper to consider pictures in the home could only repeat the inevitable mantra that a picture was for looking at. Yet we have also seen that the home had become a less and less congenial place for pictures, its presence there a 'superstition' according to one sober reformer. This resulted in a tension resolvable only through hauntings. The picture, designated an alien in the home, delegated its natural instinct to move about to the figures it contained. An ignored picture was now haunted by its own image, which auto-developed in the dark room to which it was confined.[61] When he realizes his portrait is starting to evolve in secret, Dorian Gray takes to spending all morning staring at its beauty, which now threatens to depart, as if pausing the metamorphosis at a point of equilibrium between picture and sitter: 'Once, in boyish mockery of Narcissus, he had kissed, or feigned to kiss, those painted lips that now smiled so cruelly at him.'

THE NURSERY AND PICTURES OF CHILDHOOD

Having wandered the corridors and passages of our imaginary house, which we may perhaps be glad to leave behind, we continue up the building (see illus. 11). Here are the bedrooms, into which we will in due course invite ourselves. But first, the nursery:

how are pictures put to use here? Children were credited, in regard to pictures as with many other things, with a naive insight into the essence of things. Leigh Hunt, in his article encouraging everyone to put up a picture, defines a picture 'in the child's sense, meaning any kind of graphic representation', that is, without reference to media: what counts is the presentation of an image. Children, along with any other category of person conventionally believed not to be in the know, were also assumed to make less of a distinction than was appropriate between image and reality.

If lucky enough to have illustrated books as a toddler, a child may have grown to find something strange about pictures being expanded to become wall fixtures. Surely one key difference between their books and wall pictures would have been the relative absence of children from the latter. In books children would have met with resolved tales, pointing a moral and with relatable characters, yet what were they to make of the kinds of iconography available elsewhere in the house? As regards biblical imagery, a couple of examples from literature suggest a frustration at the lack of closure to be found there. In *The Mill on the Floss*, set in the 1830s, George Eliot has little Maggie Tulliver stand on a chair to examine a series of prints telling the story of the Prodigal Son absurdly costumed in the fashions of the previous century. Maggie had been a precocious devourer of pictures in books, making up her own stories to go with them, but she found the parable unsettling because the history of the young man following his return to his family had been 'left a blank'.[62] Relating the Victorian childhood of Ernest Pontifex in his semi-autobiographical *The Way of All Flesh*, the novelist Samuel Butler describes a painting in the family home, attributed optimistically to Salvator Rosa, that represented Elijah being fed by ravens in the desert:

> When Ernest was a very small boy it had been a constant matter of regret to him that the food which the ravens

> carried never actually reached the prophet; he did not understand the limitation of the painter's art, and wanted the meat and the prophet to be brought into direct contact. One day, with the help of some steps which had been left in the room, he had clambered up to the picture and with a piece of bread and butter traced a greasy line right across it from the ravens to Elisha's [*sic*] mouth, after which he had felt more comfortable.[63]

Both stories remind us that the height of a picture on a wall was supposed to be convenient for an average adult, not for a child, and that the focus of Western art on transcendent moments often invited the question: but what happened *then*?

We have mentioned the romantic painter Benjamin Robert Haydon several times in this book, the friend of Wordsworth, Keats and Leigh Hunt's whole literary set, the bombastic creator of vast dark canvases of momentous action. He had few champions, especially after his suicide in 1846, but it is a pleasure to recall that one was none other than Henry James, who, as a teenager in the 1850s (along with his brother, the future psychologist William James) greatly admired the pictures by Haydon on show at the Pantheon in London's Oxford Street, where the artist's family were still trying to sell them. James recalls that the appeal of a picture such as *The Banishment of Aristides* lay in its rejuvenating the florid rhetoric of baroque art to celebrate romantic heroes such as this noble Greek, who nonchalantly accepted his unjust ostracism from Athens:

> the grand manner, the heroic and the classic, in Haydon, came home to us more warmly and humanly than in the masters commended as 'old', who, at the National Gallery, seemed to meet us so little half-way, to hold out the hand of fellowship or to suggest something that *we* could do, or

> could at least want to. The beauty of Haydon was just that he was new, shiningly new, and if he hinted that we might perhaps in some happy future emulate his big bravery there was nothing so impossible about it.[64]

Vernon Lee penned an essay in 1881 on the challenges posed to and by juvenile connoisseurs: 'The Child in the Vatican'. She describes youngsters' bemusement before the intimidating old paintings, saying 'to the people in pictures, the splendid people in strange colours, and holding strange things, "Who are you? Why are you doing that?"'[65] But as Lee stresses, at least this acknowledged some curiosity, which in her experience children did not show for statues, which all seemed blandly identical to them.

What of pictures for the nursery, pictures that children were invited to live alongside? According to Henry Mayhew, mid-Victorian chronicler of *London Labour and the London Poor*, street vendors of cheap pictures would target children with images of cats, which they would implore their fathers to buy for them (not their mothers, explained one such merchant, because 'Women knows the value of money better than men, for men never understand what housekeeping is').[66] This appeal to children's own taste contrasts sharply with the various theories propounded over the years regarding the role of images in early education. In the seventeenth century John Evelyn undertook a learned apology for the art of printmaking – prompted by the invention of the mezzotint – under the aegis of the Royal Society. In *Sculptura* Evelyn advocates the use of prints, and images more generally,

> to insinuate all sorts of *Notions* and things into *Children*, and be made an Instrument of Education superiour to all those *Abstracted termes*, and *secondary intentions* wherewith *Masters* commonly torment and weary their tender and weak Capacities.[67]

Evelyn's reference to formal logic is typical of his ostentatiously scholarly text, in which he praises the ambition of the recently published *Orbis sensualium pictus*, the first children's iconographic encyclopaedia, and speaks of pictures constituting 'a kind of *Universal Language*' along the lines of those being developed across Europe by philosophers including John Wilkins of the Royal Society (his *Essay Towards a Real Character, and a Philosophical Language* appeared in the same decade as Evelyn's book). Yet this exciting way of thinking about domestic imagery for children – although maintained within the covers of books – retained little presence within discussions of pictures on the nursery wall. In place of the pictorial parsing of the world, Gerard de Lairesse at the beginning of the eighteenth century blandly proposes precisely the 'abstracted terms' that Evelyn had abjured:

> In the *Nursery* agree [painted allegorical] Bass-reliefs, and painted Emblems or Morals; whereby the Children may learn good Manners, and inure their tender Years to virtuous Actions: To these may be added, some Flowers, Fruit, Birds, and such like.[68]

Often in our period, the nineteenth and early twentieth centuries, writers recommend an even more spartan pictorial regime for children, more or less giving up on the question of which, or even whether, pictures would suit a nursery. A basic question to start with was, as already noted, height: pictures belonged out of the reach of children for good reasons. Ask your architect (advises a 1908 guide to designing a house) whether a dado will be installed tall enough to push any wall decorations up to their appropriate level, 'or will it invite baby to lick the pictures?'[69] Masculinity too was at issue. Many clearly felt that encouraging attachment between pictures and boys might be unhelpful to the task of breeding true men duty-bound to confront reality, not its reimagined representation. At Wellington College, a Victorian institution with a military ethos suiting its namesake, the boys' rooms early in the twentieth century were 'hung with pictures that had long been in the dormitory and were handed down from one generation to another'.[70] Boys at home were expected to take more interest in 'their collections of eggs, butterflies, beetles, and miscellaneous rubbish', but if they must have pictures, then they should be given no frames for them – these a boy 'should be encouraged to make with his own hands'.[71] Progressive educationalists now saw the nursery, after all, as a place for learning through doing, not for being preached at, no matter how well intentioned the pictorial lesson. Homiletic pictures rather suggested the kinds of things found in reformatory institutions, the gifts of clergymen or charitable print publishers passing on the ends of editions, or the hygienic imagery associated with the chromos contained within *Pears' Annual*, published by the soap manufacturer each Christmas from 1891 ('A Complete Picture Gallery for *One Shilling*'). Pears had famously acquired Millais's *A Child's World* (rechristened *Bubbles*) in 1887 after its success as a colour reproduction in the *Illustrated London News*, and their own print of it formed part of their 1897 *Annual*. An example can be seen in this photograph of the nursery at Holloway women's prison, taken about 1909, the year suffrage campaigners began the first hunger strikes there and when public interest in their treatment generated widespread press coverage (illus. 65).

Mrs Panton saw that moralizing pictures were of little appeal to the residents of nurseries, and was with the mainstream in decrying the spoiled child with their 'constant supply of mechanical and expensive toys' vitiating their imagination and self-reliance. But she still continued her vigorous promotion of the autotype: 'The walls of the nursery must either be picture-less or embellished by really good autotypes, sufficient of which can be procured for about £5 for quite a large room.' Down, she says,

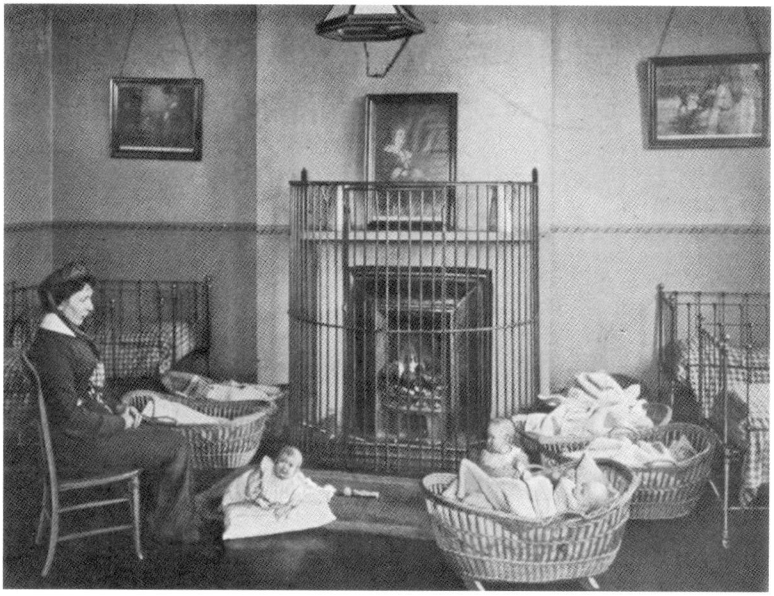

65 The nursery at Holloway women's prison in the early twentieth century. There was a tradition of charitable donation of prints to hospitals, prisons and asylums. Over the fire here is a chromo of Millais's *A Child's World* (i.e., *Bubbles*), which through its use as an advertisement by Pears soap became associated with infant hygiene.

with 'the glaring vulgar nursery pictures' which only give children 'bad and false ideas of art from their earliest days'.[72] She picks out in particular, as suitable nursery autotypes, child portraits by Reynolds and British landscapes by Millais and Benjamin Williams Leader. Rather less austere is her perhaps surprising recommendation for the nursery of prints after Charles Burton Barber, who specialized in pictures of golden-haired little girls enjoying the companionship of fluffy dogs (illus. 66). She also considered suitable *The Day of Reckoning* after the 1883 painting by S. E. Waller, showing a ruined young man on the steps of his ancestral home in the aftermath of the auction of his property.[73]

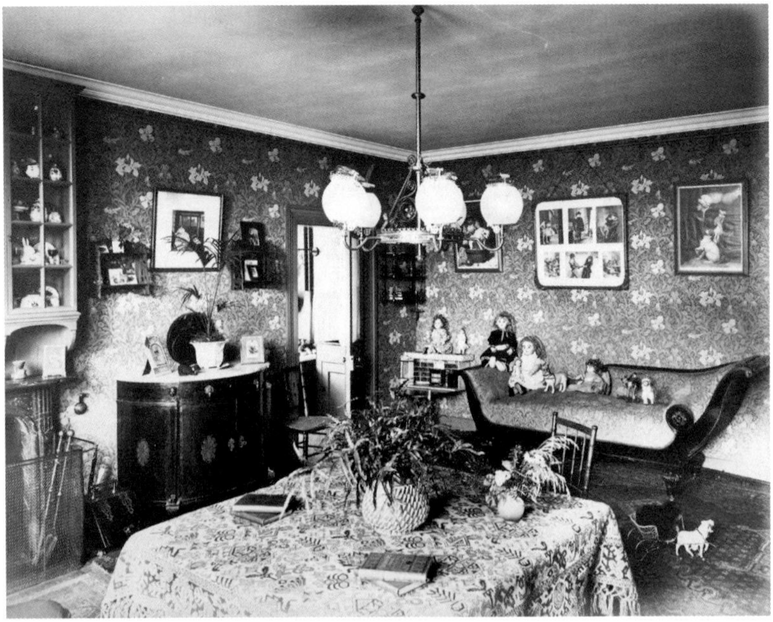

66 No. 1 Holland Park in Kensington was turned by the Ionides family into one of the great treasure-houses of late nineteenth-century London, with modern and ancient masterpieces set within interiors designed by William Morris and Walter Crane. In the nursery, the pictures (hung relatively high, out of reach) were primarily of women and girls with dogs. Obscured by the gasolier is *The Order of the Bath* by Charles Burton Barber.

This was one of the more subtle 'problem pictures' of the age, requiring more worldly knowledge of the rise and fall of fortunes than the average child could have been expected to show. Yet it was clearly a favourite purchase at the end of the nineteenth century, and was indeed used as a kind of archetype of the domestic picture by Mary Clive in her 1964 memoir, which so well blends the social history of the privileged classes of the early twentieth century with the prints they showed on their walls.[74] Clive evokes the evanescent reputation of particular images, ubiquitous for a generation and then utterly vanished, like Estella Canziani's fairy watercolour *The Piper of Dreams*, colour reproductions of which had such a massive reach during the First World War, 'hung over many a child's bed as a sort of honorary guardian angel'.[75]

The years around 1900 were indeed a golden age for children's art and book illustration, an energy some designers longed to harness for the improvement of the home. In a plea that was entirely typical among the Arts and Crafts generation for more decorative and fresco painting and fewer easel pictures, the architects Barry Parker and Raymond Unwin wrote in their 1901 book *The Art of Building a Home*:

> Let us call in the artist, bid him leave his easel pictures, and paint on our walls and over the chimney corner landscapes and scenes which shall bring light and life into the room; which shall speak of nature, purity, and truth; shall become part of the room, of the walls on which they are painted, and of the lives of us who live beside them; paintings which our children shall grow up to love, and always connect with scenes of home with that vividness of a memory from childhood which no time can efface.[76]

All very well to declare in favour of a return to decorative painting, says Clarence Cook in his earlier *The House Beautiful* (1878), but most of us cannot simply call in a muralist as we might a plumber. He proposes instead taking apart Walter Crane's children's books with their charming and well-composed illustrations, which are frankly 'altogether too good to be confined to the delighting of children', and somehow embed them in the furniture or panelling of a room.[77] This was a sophisticated upgrade from the practice, possible since the 1840s, of cutting out wood-engravings from the new illustrated journals to generate cheap and topical pictures for the nursery or bedroom wall (in contrast to the longer tradition of compiling print screens and the like, a hobby restricted to those with access to quantities of cast-off single-sheet engravings[78]). On one of the rare occasions when Mrs Panton leaves off her brisk tone of practical domesticity to indulge in earnest nostalgia, she writes of the pain of an empty-nester: 'I know of nothing sadder than an empty nursery . . . The most melancholy part of middle age is this being left behind by our children.' She recalls an emotional visit to the former nursery of out-of-town friends of her childhood in the 1860s, where the walls had been 'papered by ourselves with pictures from the "Illustrated News"', every one of which she claims to remember, 'from the marriage of the Princess Royal in one corner to pictures of the American War in the other'.[79] (Regrettable perhaps that she did not think to recommend such a DIY approach to her readers instead of yet more autotypes.) A writer born in 1893, in the time of Mrs Panton's celebrity, the poet Frank Kendon, wrote movingly in his memoirs of this same wrench of leaving behind a self-made environment of pictures:

> From wainscot to ceiling the walls of our nursery were papered with pictures. Most of these were those large lithographs in many colours which used to be given away with *Pears' Annual*. They were stuck to the wall itself and varnished there, so that they were as much a part of the room as the walls and floor and window, and more permanent than the chairs and table, the toys and other movables. All of our pictures were peaceful and genial, domestic or quietly humorous scenes. If they did not tell a story to grown-ups we soon made them do so for us, for we took them into our lives with unquestioning frankness, accepting them as things not less permanent and objective than trees and roads and real people. . . . They were poor art, but we cared little for that. When we first knew them,

> because we had come to them and found them there already, we treated them as things established, beyond criticism, needing no justification, and likely to be there for ever. When the old nursery was abandoned and made into a bedroom, we tried with water and a knife to remove the pictures from the walls to save them, but the paste and varnish were too strong for us. At length they were covered over by wall-paper, and yet, among the stirring excitements of such changes, it was impossible not to feel regret and not by any means out of a sentimental regard for our old pictures, but because this change . . . struck hard at our natural belief in the permanence of the world. The tremor struck deep which began in such an insignificant way, the walls of our nursery were going now, and we felt, though still dimly, the shadow of the gnomon, our whispered mortality.[80]

Vernon Lee, in her essay 'The Child in the Vatican', also refers to the way children accept their pictures as reality. From all the pictures of every kind that we experience in early life,

> out of all this, confused with haunting impressions, of things seen or heard of (the strange, deeply significant sights and words of our childhood), do we get our original, never really alterable ideas and feelings about art; for much as we may clip, trim, and bedizen our minds with borrowed things, we can never change, never even recast its solid material.[81]

Ruskin's initiation into the world of watercolour landscape painting is an example of this, a passion embedded in his relationship with his father, himself a collector and amateur painter. 'I was particularly fond of watching him shave,' remembered Ruskin:

> Over his dressing-table hung one of his own watercolour drawings, made under the teaching of the elder Nasmyth . . . It represented Conway Castle, with its Frith, and, in the foreground, a cottage, a fisherman, and a boat at the water's edge. When my father had finished shaving, he always told me a story about this picture.

Gradually 'the plot of the drama afterwards thickened' and even became involved with those of gothic plays in which the elder Ruskin had appeared in domestic theatricals in his youth.[82] This endlessly generative picture remained a treasured possession of Ruskin's and can be seen in the bedroom of his last home, Brantwood, on Coniston Water, over the fireplace above a still life by his favourite William Henry Hunt and surrounded by Turner watercolours (illus. 67).

A twentieth-century picture lover, Osbert Sitwell, recounted a similar story of his connecting with his aloof father through an old picture of the notorious moment in the 1784 Westminster election when the radical Duchess of Devonshire was said to have kissed a butcher in the hope of securing his vote for Charles James Fox. For the infant Osbert a visit to this picture 'became a regular turn, a treat' and for the adult writer, in retrospect, an admirable lesson in how to introduce children to art:

> Its story was easy to explain, and it was precisely the painting to arouse a child's interest and hold his attention at an age when the greatest work of Titian or Raphael or Michelangelo would to him signify nothing. Thus it would ensure an early inclination towards noticing pictures, and looking at them.[83]

A single picture was enough for Ruskin, Sitwell and their fathers, a unique image, just theirs, through which to go on a

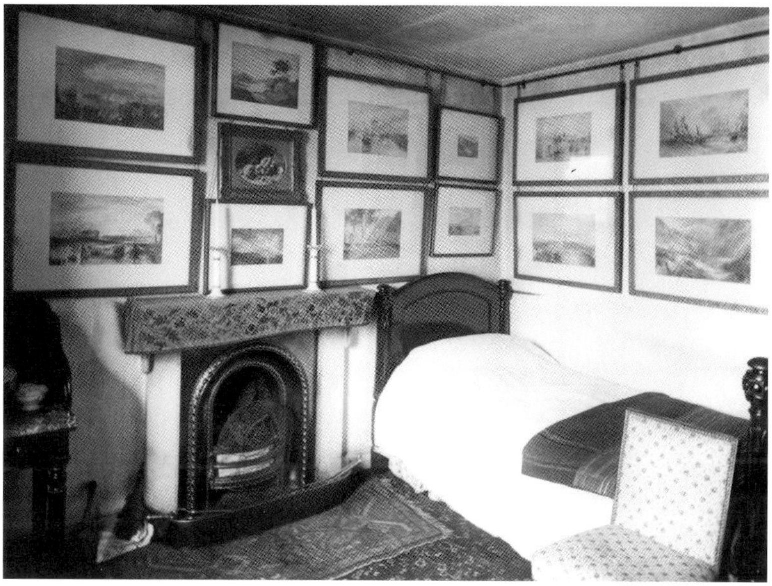

67 Ruskin's bedroom at Brantwood on Coniston Water, shown in the 1890s towards the end of his life. A grid of Turner watercolours makes way, over the fireplace, for a fruit piece by William Henry Hunt and, above it, the view of Conwy Castle around which Ruskin's father had woven stories for his son many decades earlier (photograph by John McClelland).

journey together. In both these cases the picture was a unique painting, but for others who bonded closely with a print there was a further lesson to be learned through encountering the same image outside of their own home. We noted Mary Clive's sensitivity to the fashions that blew certain images throughout well-to-do homes and then mercilessly swept them out again, a cycle less obvious in the case of much more expensive paintings. She was unusual in paying the phenomenon such careful attention, but there were certain especially dramatic shifts that everyone noticed: above all, the rise and fall of the animal painter Edwin Landseer. This one-time pupil of Haydon, with the help of royal favour, lived to see engravings of his pictures become so ubiquitous as to help define the mid-Victorian interior. These pictures were rarely commented on in their heyday, but there are countless references to their disappearance, and to the headlong collapse of the once gargantuan prices for Landseer's original paintings. The artist's work became an emblem of how the madness of speculative markets careered its way in and then out of the home. W. J. Loftie, writing a few years after Landseer's death in 1873, described both how an instinctive investor made a mint through collecting the artist's work early in his career, and how another young man later lost a great deal of money through buying Landseer engravings at the top of the market.[84] Landseer dog engravings could still, just, be considered suitable for a new Edwardian country house – they can be seen dominating the staircase of the newly completed Crathorne Hall in Yorkshire in 1906 – but this was now a sign of a commitment to Victorian values.[85] When the Futurist artist C.R.W. Nevinson was invited to dinner by the poet John Masefield during the First World War, he had to find his way in the dark due to an air-raid blackout. Having been shown into the drawing room, he was 'astonished to see [Landseer's masterpiece] "The Monarch of the Glen" over the mantelpiece', but simply refused to believe his eyes: 'such pictures could not be', at least not in the home of a poet. Indeed, Nevinson had come to the wrong house. Why, he reflected, did 'some people damn themselves by their pictures'? Many had a skeleton in their cupboard, but 'The Englishman hangs his on the wall.'[86]

Nevinson was able to congratulate himself on finding his moral world-view confirmed by pictures: the bourgeoisie liked Landseer, and intellectuals liked more modern pictures – his own, for instance (see illus. 53). Different kinds of people had different kinds of picture. How much less comfortable, especially for a child, to find that different people had the *same* cherished picture as the special image around which he or she had woven their imagination at home. Marcel Proust composed his essay 'On Reading' in 1905 as a preface to his translation of Ruskin's *Sesame and Lilies*.[87] Here, among his reflections on his childhood culture, the novelist remembers his negligence of good taste in interior design in favour of a single picture in his room, a print of the Habsburg military commander Prince Eugene of Savoy, 'terrible et beau dans son dolman'. The youthful owner was astonished one day to find, in a hailstorm at a busy railway station, the very same picture now serving, at the entrance to the buffet, as an advertisement for a brand of biscuits. Later Proust surmised that his grandfather had been given the print and had put it up in the child's room. But once there, the boy had no care for its origins and accepted the figure as a real person, a permanent co-habitant of his room, 'historique et mystérieuse', of whom it was impossible for him to imagine that there might exist multiple versions.

The experience leads the adult writer to reflect on interiors in terms that reflect the broader Proustian aesthetic as explored in *À la recherche du temps perdu*. He will leave it to others, 'les gens de goût', he says, to decorate their rooms with photographs after Botticelli (there was an example elsewhere in the Proust family home), and indeed to them too to create in those rooms a facsimile of their good taste, full of things of which they did not disapprove. What he needed, on the contrary, was 'a room in which everything is the creation and the language of lives profoundly different from my own, of a taste opposed to mine, where I can discover nothing of my conscious thought, where my imagination exalts in feeling itself plunged into the heart of not-me'.[88] For Proust, the authentic experience of an artwork, or of another person, must involve a separation requiring perception through layers of distancing – the '"épaisseurs" d'art' that we cited in Chapter One when considering Proust's later co-habitant, Carlyle. The worst possible form of interior, for Proust, was a period ensemble in which everything matches in a false unity, featuring pictures

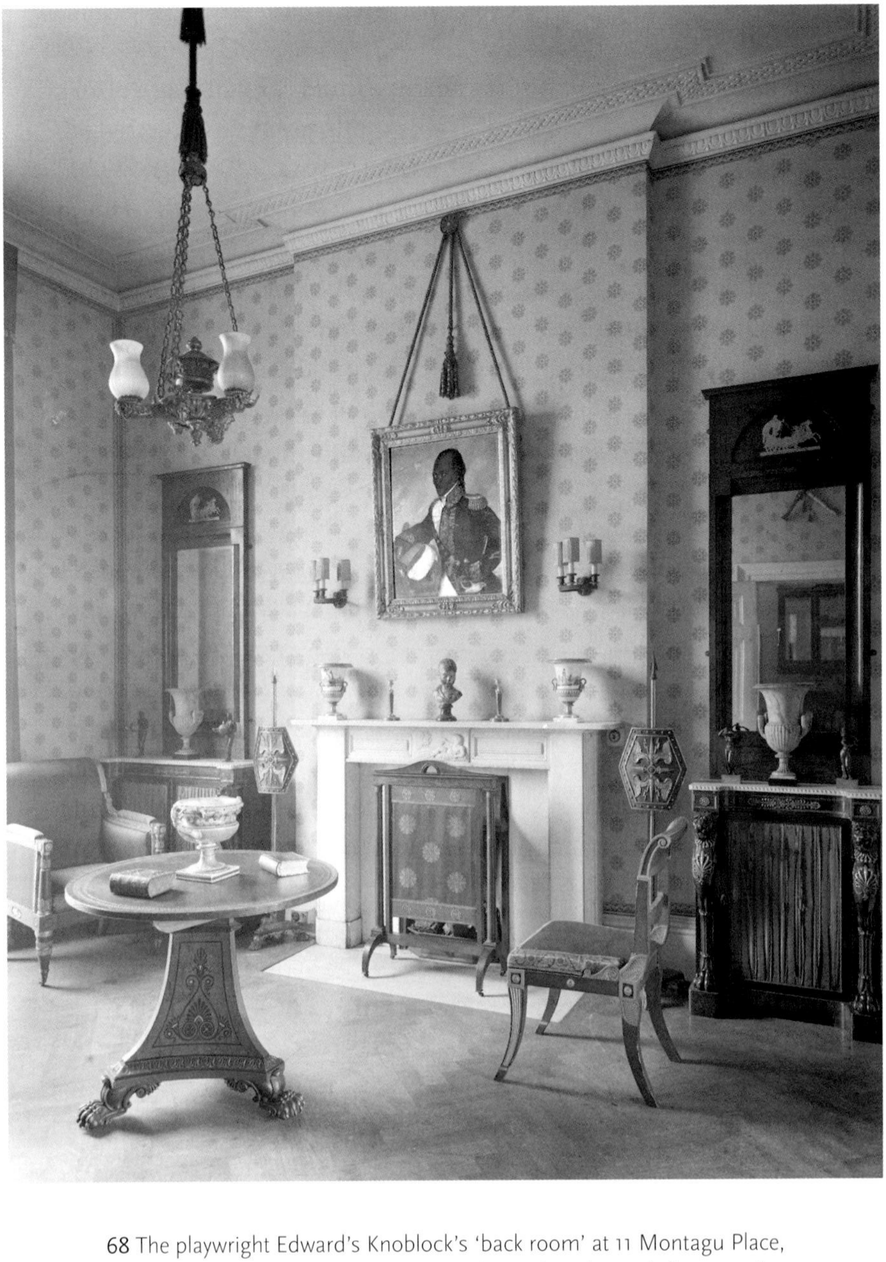

68 The playwright Edward's Knoblock's 'back room' at 11 Montagu Place, showing some of his famous collection of French and British furniture from around 1800. This scholarly ensemble includes – as period-appropriate and with tasselled cord – the striking presence over the fireplace of Toussaint Louverture, leader of the Haitian Revolution of the 1790s (photographed in 1931).

'amid furniture, knick-knacks or hangings from the same period . . . depriving them [the pictures] of the essential, that act of mind which isolated them from reality in the first place'.[89]

Certainly a picture in a period room seems in some sense a lesser, more deferential thing, and yet that modest role of simply complying with a period look must have brought onto walls pictures that would otherwise not have been hung. An example can be seen in this room assembled by the playwright Edward Knoblock in his London house in the 1920s (illus. 68). Knoblock was a pioneer scholar of the furniture of Thomas Hope (see illus. 3) and curated a series of rooms recreating interiors of around 1800. Here, over the fire, suspended with fussy cords, we can identify a portrait of Toussaint Louverture, leader of the 1791 slave uprising against French rule in Haiti. The picture was included, of course, for its period fit, but it nevertheless smuggled in to this refabricated time capsule something of the otherwise tastefully obscured political urgency of that period.

To return to Proust, his entire aesthetic turned on the isolation of the artwork from time and context, not its reintegration. It was indeed only when one was letting go of an object, selling it or giving it away, that one finally saw it for what it really was. This was ultimately a particular instance of the larger truth that any experience only became real through memory, once it had been isolated from the vague context in which it had first taken place. Precious things worthy of being so retrieved – memories of love, artworks – do not exist in the same space-time as the rest of the world. Thus Proust thinks of special objects having a provenance not through successive collectors but through the history of emotional states of a single owner. To place a picture in a prominent position in a domestic hang, to integrate it into a fixed environment, is – paradoxically – to hide it from view.[90] Soon after completing 'On Reading', Proust was faced with the challenge of inheriting paintings from his recently deceased parents. Resentful at having to take any of them, and vowing to place those he could not evade in shadow, Proust remonstrated: 'But for my part, any picture that one has not *desired*, bought with suffering and love, is atrocious in an apartment.'[91] He reminds us how often paintings and other valuable furniture were effectively imposed through inheritance, with the interior having to accommodate them as best it could.

Proust's philosophy, whereby memory eventually produces the truth, was acutely vulnerable to being undermined by pictures simulating memories. It was a cliché of popular accounts of memory that this faculty functioned like today's selfies, special moments captured and stored in a virtual picture gallery. 'There is no man so poor', the Revd F. A. Malleson (a Lake District neighbour and devotee of Ruskin) assured his readers in 1895, 'but he possesses the endowment of a picture-gallery treasured up in the unseen recesses of his memory.'[92] Mrs Panton boasted of her own memory, which 'seems to me like a room hung round with paintings', and stressed how her mother had taken an active role in fixing her earliest memories, ensuring these were turned into pictures for her mental gallery: she advises her readers to do similarly with their own children.[93] This model of the memory gallery suggests a highly structured archive of personal history not easily dismantled into its components, as the Proustian version of memory required, to sift the precious kernel from its surroundings. The notion of the architectural arrangement of pictures as a mnemonic technique is familiar from intellectual history, such as the Renaissance examples described in Frances Yates's classic 1966 book *The Art of Memory*. Later the collector or connoisseur was imagined to possess both an extensive repertoire of paper prints cumulatively representing the world of knowledge and 'a fine Collection of Mental Pictures' derived from nature, art and literature.[94] Yet there was a long-standing counter-tradition which imagined the memory bank not as an inert picture gallery but as something active, alive. As one seventeenth-century Italian writer put it (his words are paraphrased here), 'memory is not a gallery decorated with mute and immobile paintings; behind it there is a seraglio, a harem, full of living images' likely to take it upon themselves to dictate the meaning of things, whatever the will of their nominal possessor.[95] Such an unruly room of mental pictures was especially apt to come into uncomfortable tension with the actual physical pictures they superficially resembled: each might go masquerading as the other.

For Hazlitt, as we saw in Chapter One, the ideal connoisseur had no possessions but distilled the pictures they had seen into 'a gallery in the mind' – the ethereal alternative to the Duke of Wellington, of whom it was said, possibly unfairly, that he could only remember the names of all the famous pictures in his gallery at Apsley House in London so long as he was able to tell them off in memorized sequence from a certain point in the room.[96] Yet before we start congratulating Hazlitt on having democratically prised painting from the clutches of the titled owners of private galleries to release it into virtual collections possessed by an aristocracy of talent, we must bear in mind the nostalgic regret with which the painter-turned-critic always contemplated the original paintings he loved best.[97] We saw that Hazlitt had a rather tortured relationship with the copies after Titian he made in Paris in 1802. When he was able to return to the Louvre in the 1820s, he could not resist returning also to the challenge of trying to capture the colours of the most beautiful pictures in the world. But of course, after so many years without a brush in his hand, the exercise proved to be 'a piece of presumption or affectation in me', ending in 'an inexcusable daub' which risked

> blotting from my memory, covering with a dark veil, all that I remembered of those pictures formerly, my hopes when young, my regrets since; it was wresting

> from me one of the consolations of my life and of my declining years.

His only comfort lay in 'the excess of pain I felt; this was at least some distinction' – an emotion foreshadowing Proust's conclusion that the only aesthetic certainty was the pain of *not* possessing the artwork.[98]

In Paris in 1824 Hazlitt had met the novelist Stendhal – they were admirers of one another's writings. Stendhal too had an unsettling story about the capacity of real pictures to override precious memories. As a teenage soldier he had been with Napoleon's Grande Armée when it crossed the Alps into Italy in 1800 (already story enough). The memory he retained of the view on the descent from the Hospice St-Bernard was fixed in his memory such that it was a shock to find, years later, that this mental image matched exactly an engraving he had forgotten he owned: 'mon souvenir *n'est plus* que la gravure.'[99] The revelation of this pictorial subterfuge has been given a new currency by the writer W. G. Sebald, who refers to it in his novel *Vertigo* (1990). Sebald recounts elsewhere his own startling moment in the tradition of Proust's Prince Eugene, finding, 'leaning against the plinth of an altar in a dark corner of one of the side aisles' in an obscure Corsican church, the very same religious print that had hung over his parents' bed, since disappeared. The disruption to his memory, and so to his sense of self, was acutely disturbing: 'Such is the dark backward and abysm of time' (quoting Prospero in *The Tempest*). 'Everything lies all jumbled up in it, and when you look down you feel dizzy and afraid.'[100] This giddy balancing act between picture and memory can be shown up especially starkly when memory believes itself to have stored a specific composition. It is remarkable how often such a mental picture of a picture goes wrong. Henry James claimed, when writing his memoirs, that 'every attitude and figure' in Haydon's *Aristides* 'stares out at me still'. Yet a foreshortened boy stooping to pick up stones to shy at the hero, whom James 'especially' remembers, is in fact an old man: the boy in the picture is Aristides' son, and he walks innocently and loyally alongside his father.

BEDROOM

If we wish to complete our tour of the house with a look through the bedrooms, we cannot expect to be made welcome there by the pictures. This was no place for the showing off of artworks, although the bedroom offered plenty of scope for intense engagement for the nightly occupant with those pictures that had some special meaning for them. To hang pictures in a bedroom was almost automatically a guilty pleasure, an arrangement that suited the person in the bed and no other. The view from the bed is not one that features strongly in official histories of art, but it clearly had great potential for some picture lovers. Shown here (illus. 69) is the prospect from 'My Bed' given in a drawing by George Scharf, the indefatigable founding curator of the National Portrait Gallery. The room was within his family apartment over the Gallery's first premises on Great George Street, in the heart of Westminster. The many artworks – mainly prints and casts – are arranged to the view of the reclining solipsistic connoisseur. Scharf's annotations even point out the reflection of Raphael's *Madonna of Foligno* in the mirror on the dressing table (the print itself is suspended from a cast of a Gothic saint's head). To the right is Rembrandt's *Anatomy Lesson of Dr Tulp*, which must occasionally have given even the phlegmatic Scharf some pause for morbid reflection with its image of the flayed recumbent figure echoing his own posture.

In her classic book of 1913, the American interior designer Elsie de Wolfe wrote:

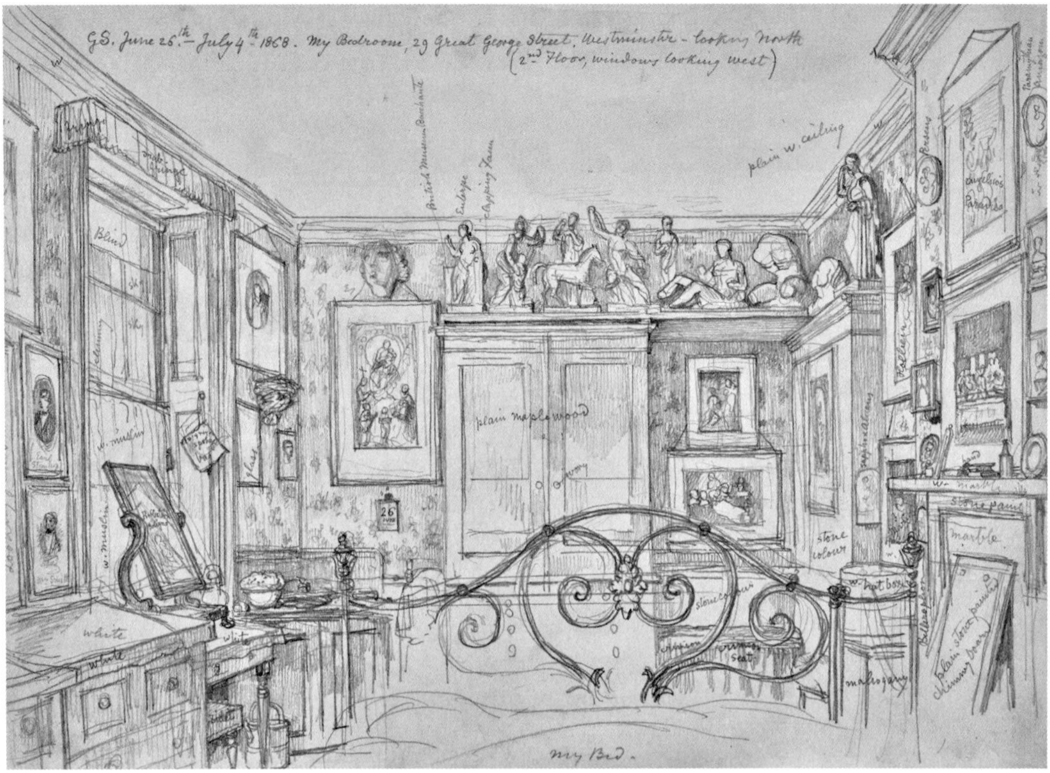

69 George Scharf was the dynamic founding director of the National Portrait Gallery. He made countless careful pencil studies of old pictures and buildings. Here Scharf turns his eye to the view from his own bed in his apartment over the Gallery in Great George Street (1868).

> Be wary of hanging many pictures in your bedroom. I give this advice cheerfully, because I know you will hang them anyway (I do) but I warn you you will spoil your room if you aren't very stern with yourself. Somehow the pictures we most love, small prints and photographs and things, look spotty on our walls. We must group them to get a pleasant effect.[101]

The photographs should be placed on horizontal surfaces, says de Wolfe, so they might be picked up, while an earlier British writer suggested for the bedroom, 'to keep photographs or prints

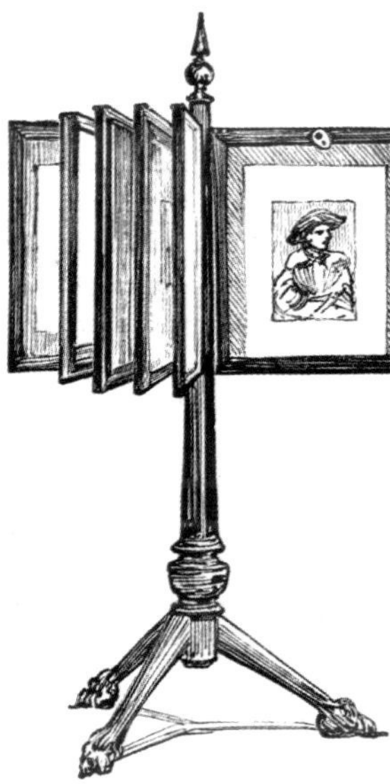

70 The 'radiating pillar stand', with turning leaves to display small pictures, photographs or medals, was introduced at the V&A by Henry Cole in the 1860s. An example was illustrated in Clarence Cook's *The House Beautiful* (1878) as suiting too the domestic drawing room. Cook's engraving was borrowed in turn by Mary Anne Barker for her *Bedroom and Boudoir* (in Macmillan's *Art at Home* series, also 1878).

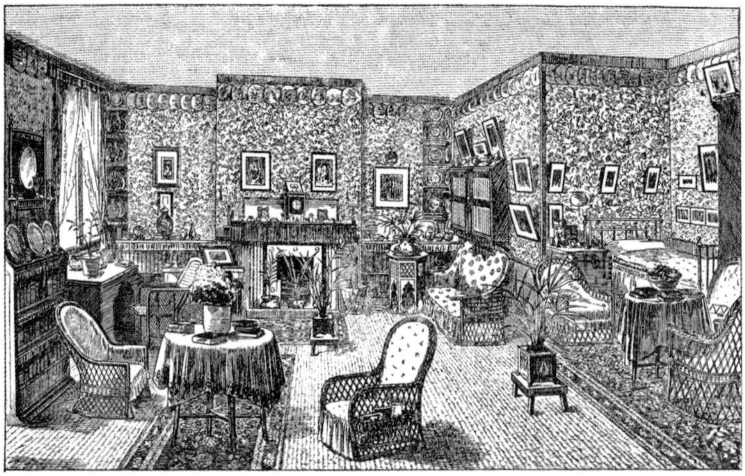

71 This boudoir-bedroom allowed an elder daughter her own room to which to withdraw and where she might entertain. The bed on the right, which could be screened off to create a separate room, has smaller pictures placed within intimate touching distance, as recommended by advice writers (Jane Ellen Panton, *Nooks and Corners*, 1889).

at hand', one of the turnstile-type stands adopted at the V&A (illus. 70).[102] The spottiness warned of by de Wolfe can be seen in this plate from another of Mrs Panton's volumes, *Nooks and Corners* (illus. 71). She calls the room a 'Boudoir-Bedroom' and describes it as suiting an elder daughter, who has outgrown the nursery but requires some space apart from the main drawing room 'that she can call her own, and where she can in some measure do much as she likes' (that measure did not extend to entertaining guests unknown to her mother).[103] The idea is that the alcove with the bed on the right can easily be screened off to separate the boudoir, or private sitting room, with its more conventionally proportioned pictures, from the almost-room with the bed and little pictures within touching distance. Henry Havard, describing an ideal home in the 1880s, felt that a very intimate, female space required a different kind of art from that which suited the drawing room. In such a room, 'where everything is in reach of the eye and the hand', pictures should be highly finished, complete little works of art – no loose sketches or broadly handled paintings but rather things suited to inspection from inches away from the face. Havard frankly addresses the 'légende pornographique' of the boudoir, its role in literary scenes of seduction, betrayal and moral compromise. In modern times, however, 'The voluptuous Graces have deserted this sanctuary. They have fled to cede place to more reasonable spirits.' Today one will find there a woman needing a room apart in order to write, to hold private (but unimpeachable) conversations or to take some sick leave from her rounds of duties. The boudoir is now the female equivalent of the man's 'cabinet de travail'.[104]

All very well, and Mrs Panton, who offered up her own daughter's boudoir for public inspection, was evidently not squeamish about the term's past history. Yet the author of the volume on *The Bedroom and Boudoir* in Macmillan's *Art at Home* series, the multifarious journalist Mary Anne Barker, surely had her title imposed on her, for she openly objects within the book that while a woman needed 'one's own little den', she personally 'should *never* myself dignify [it] by the name of boudoir, a word signifying a place to idle and sulk in, instead of a retreat in which to be busy and comfortable'.[105] So the kinds of pictures considered appropriate for women's bedrooms and boudoirs, in addition to religious imagery, were those of the bureau – family, friends and special places in tangible miniature: nothing ambiguous or open to alternative interpretations. The irreproachably high-minded imagery of Watts, with its motifs of sublimated passion, seems to have been a late Victorian exception, welcome in the rooms of even very young women (illus. 72).

Were the voluptuous Graces entirely banished from the Victorian house? There were precious few justifications for erotic

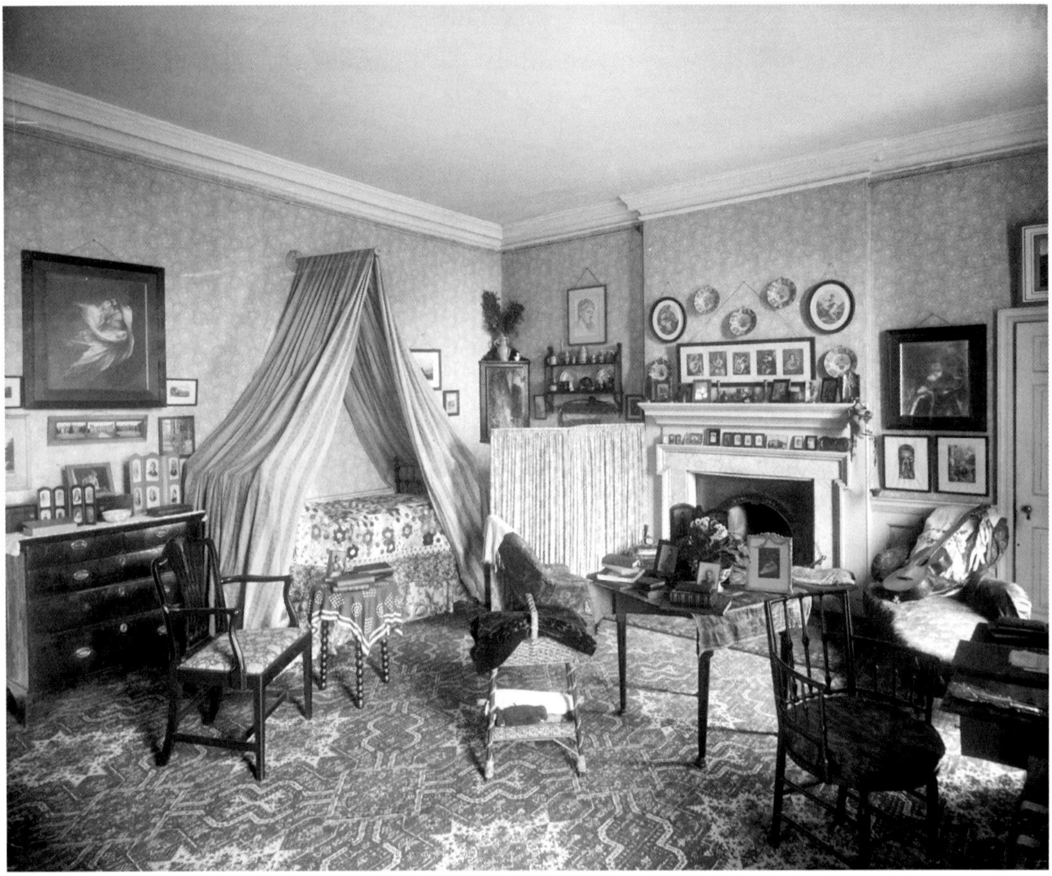

72 The bedroom of Norah Quilter in her wealthy politician father's house in Suffolk, photographed in 1893 when she would have been in her early twenties. Small portrait photographs proliferate, with dainty eighteenth-century decorative prints over the fire. But adding passion are two heavily framed reproductions of G. F. Watts's imagery of ecstasy-in-death: *Paolo and Francesca* (on the left) and *The Happy Warrior* (to the right).

imagery left, such as the old idea that gazing on beautiful naked bodies would help in the conception of lovely babies, now only available as a joke.[106] Few men in our period still made use of what had been known as a picture cabinet, the kind of room that in eighteenth-century literature was likely to witness someone's honour being risked. The imaginary Soames Forsyte maintained such a space, but met with no one there. Only a few male aristocrats followed Lord Chesterfield in having his own boudoir. The Earl's boudoir at Chesterfield House in London boasted, he reported to a French friend in 1748, 'une très belle femme' by the pastel specialist Rosalba Carriera.[107] As a traditionally masculine space with some clear function, the library or study was the nearest nineteenth-century equivalent, and there was some acceptance that images of naked women were appropriate here, just as it was accepted that somewhere in that same library were probably, should one care to look, books or portfolios not suitable for the whole family.[108] John Morritt of Rokeby Park (near Barnard Castle in County Durham), the owner of Velázquez's *Venus and Cupid*, boasted to Walter Scott in 1820:

> I have been all morning pulling about my pictures and hanging them in new positions to make more room for [my] fine picture of Venus's backside by Velasquez, [which] I have at length exalted over my chimney piece in the library. It is an admirable light for the painting, and shows it in perfection, whilst by raising the said backside to a considerable height the ladies may avert their downcast eyes without difficulty, and connoisseurs steal a glance without drawing in the said posteriors as a part of the company.[109]

Parts, at least, of this letter have often been cited, and well known too is the eventual response of the suffrage campaigner Mary

Richardson, who in 1914 made some serious insertions into the painting, by then in the National Gallery, with a small axe, complaining later of 'the way men visitors gaped at it all day long'.[110] But it is worth thinking about the idea of a gendered and doubled audience proposed by Morritt, each component of which was expected to respond differently, a split effected by raising the picture up high ('exalted'), a practice disapproved of, as we saw in Chapter Two, by anyone who expressed a public opinion on the subject of picture hanging. Morritt indeed suggests his great picture is not really to be looked at at all, only glanced at by the men and ignored by the women. It was an interesting solution to an old problem, namely how to integrate an erotic picture into family life, a response – the removal from direct sight – which, as we have seen throughout this book, often seemed necessary to resolve tensions around the domestic picture. At the National Gallery no such gender division in looking was acknowledged – the pictures there were, after all, publicly owned lessons in art history – at least not until Richardson made her point so forcibly. In Morritt's scheme women, expected to lower their eyes, were put in an inferior position, clearly not welcome as equals in the room where the Venus hung. So when the nude left the gentleman's cabinet to venture into the nominally shared spaces of the house, it carried its gender exclusivity with it. Dorothea in *Middlemarch* prefers the facts of the maps and architectural views displayed in her adopted home to the 'classical nudities and smirking Renaissance-Correggiosities': 'she had never been taught how she could bring them into any sort of relevance with her life.'[111]

To take a cruder, later case, Stanmore Hall, north of London, was extended around 1890 for the industrialist William Knox D'Arcy with contributions to the decoration by Morris & Co., including the famous set of Holy Grail tapestries after designs by Burne-Jones. The Business Room, however, sported a very different kind of image, a brash and entirely uncharacteristic

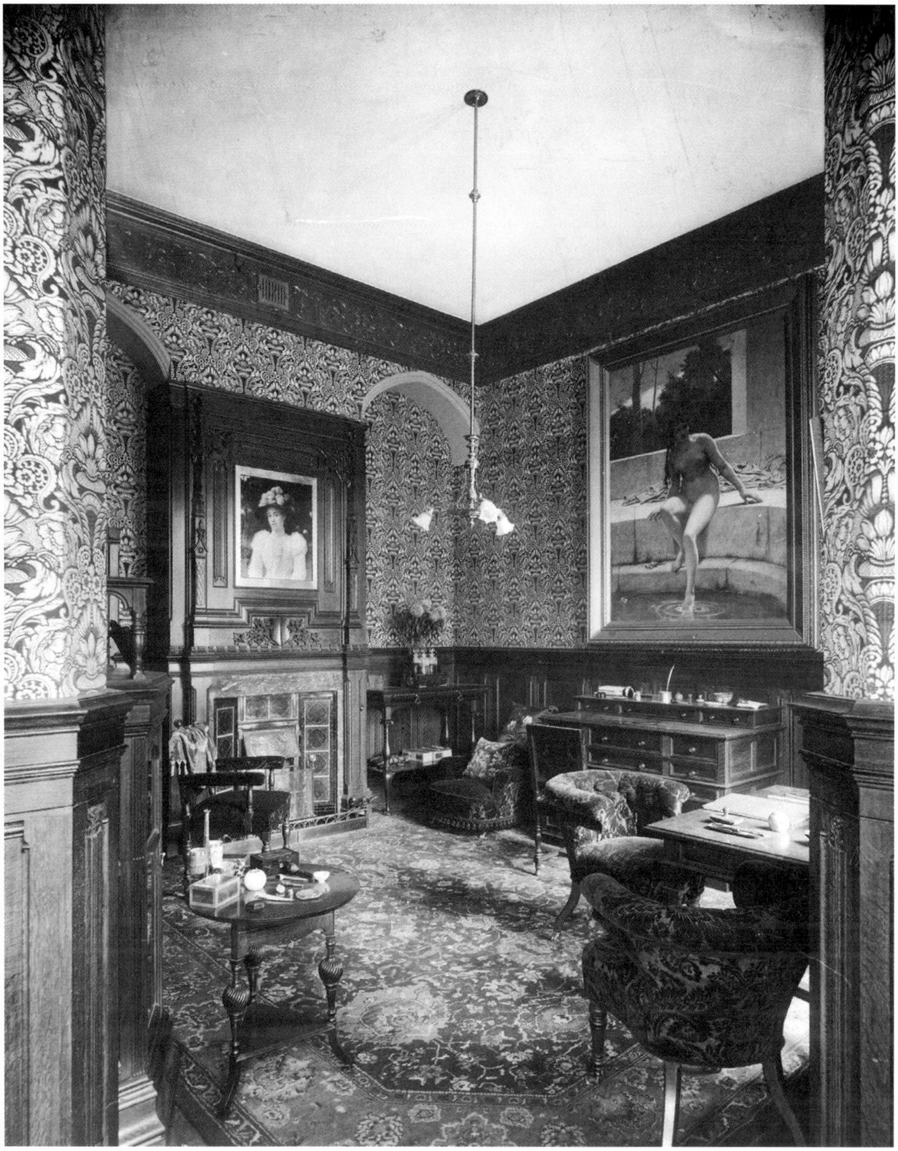

73 Stanmore Hall was remade around 1890 as London home to William Knox D'Arcy, founder of what became British Petroleum. The interiors are usually cited as among the most sumptuous designed by Morris & Co., but the Business Room was dominated by a large nude of *Susannah in Her Bath* by Frederick Goodall. The Old Testament heroine was typically shown surveyed by lecherous elders; D'Arcy himself was, in their absence, cast in their role.

life-size nude – *Susannah* – by the specialist in Egyptian subjects Frederick Goodall, showing a woman apparently climbing down onto the desk in this inner sanctum of power, which the picture surely discouraged women from entering (illus. 73).[112]

It became a truism of the Victorian art scene that nudes did not sell because people were not sure what to do with them in their homes. In 1875 it was written of the nude specialist William Etty that his naked figures were signs of his dedication to his art in the face of the restricted market he necessarily faced on account of pictures being 'a part of domestic life in England, being hung in rooms that are commonly inhabited', so that 'there is a dislike to nude figures amongst English purchasers generally'.[113] Yet few owned up to such a dislike. Burne-Jones said of the Pre-Raphaelite patron William Graham, 'When I first knew him I used to hide some pictures from him – pictures where people were naked – but I soon found he liked them best of all.' Nevertheless, Graham declined Rossetti's nude *Ligeia Siren*, not because he himself believed 'in all that nonsense' about enjoying nudity in pictures being a sign of 'delinquency' but because he could not ignore the mutterings of 'wellmeaning respectable donkeys'.[114] Even the resolutely bourgeois *Art Journal* hinted that the suburban classes were the prudes: 'Nude figures are not those that are elected into the quiet and modest circles, into which the taste for art has descended.'[115] So the artists blamed the collectors, who blamed the middle classes, who themselves ultimately blamed women. In 1851 a campaigner against the nude in art claimed to know a drawing room in which a picture was 'entirely covered with gauze' owing to the image being one 'which the daughters of the family cannot look upon'.[116] To display a nude prominently in your home became therefore a sign that one was above such structures of policing behaviour, either through sheer arrogance of social rank, as in the case of Morritt, or as a sign of belonging to a different, better kind of social structure altogether. So in artistic Chelsea the

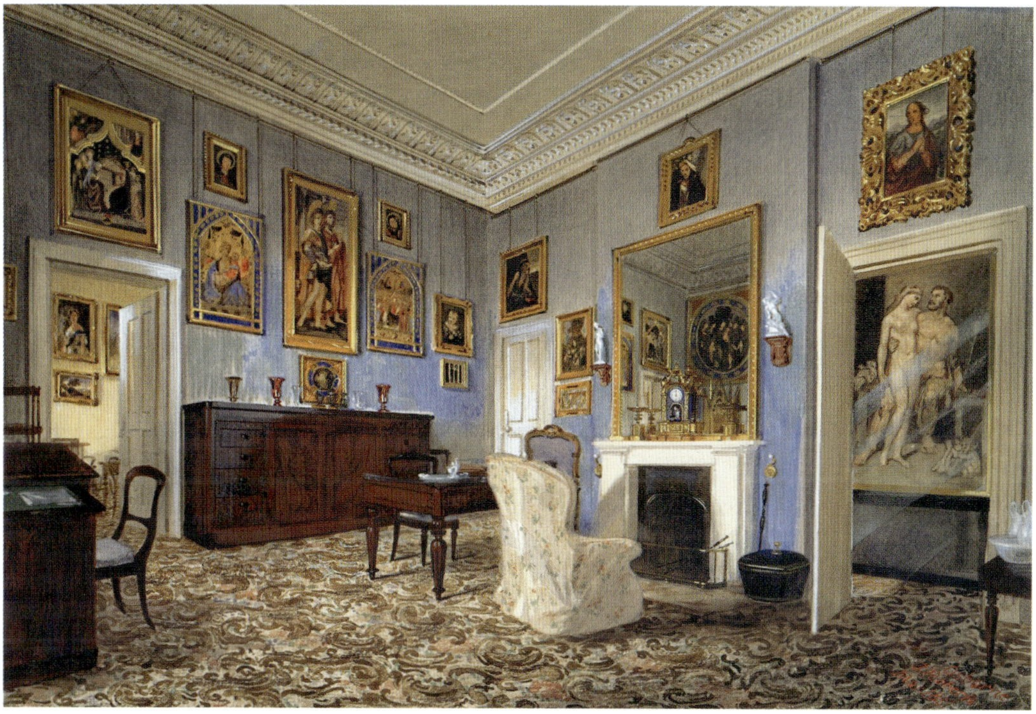

74 An 1851 view of Prince Albert's dressing room in the recently completed Pavilion at Osborne, dominated by some of his collection of early Italian paintings, also only acquired in the last few years. The door into the bathroom at right has been left open to allow sight of the fresco of *Omphale and Hercules* by Josef von Gegenbaur (watercolour by James Roberts).

painter William Bell Scott, a neighbour of Rossetti's, had a large picture of his own, a nude *Eve*, over his drawing-room fireplace, and, whether accurately or not, in illustrated press reports of the sale of the contents of Wilde's Tite Street house in 1895, the disgraced aesthete was revealed to be the owner of a comparable full-length female nude.[117]

To return to bedrooms, while there are suggestions of erotic pictures being relegated to guest rooms, any man willing to have

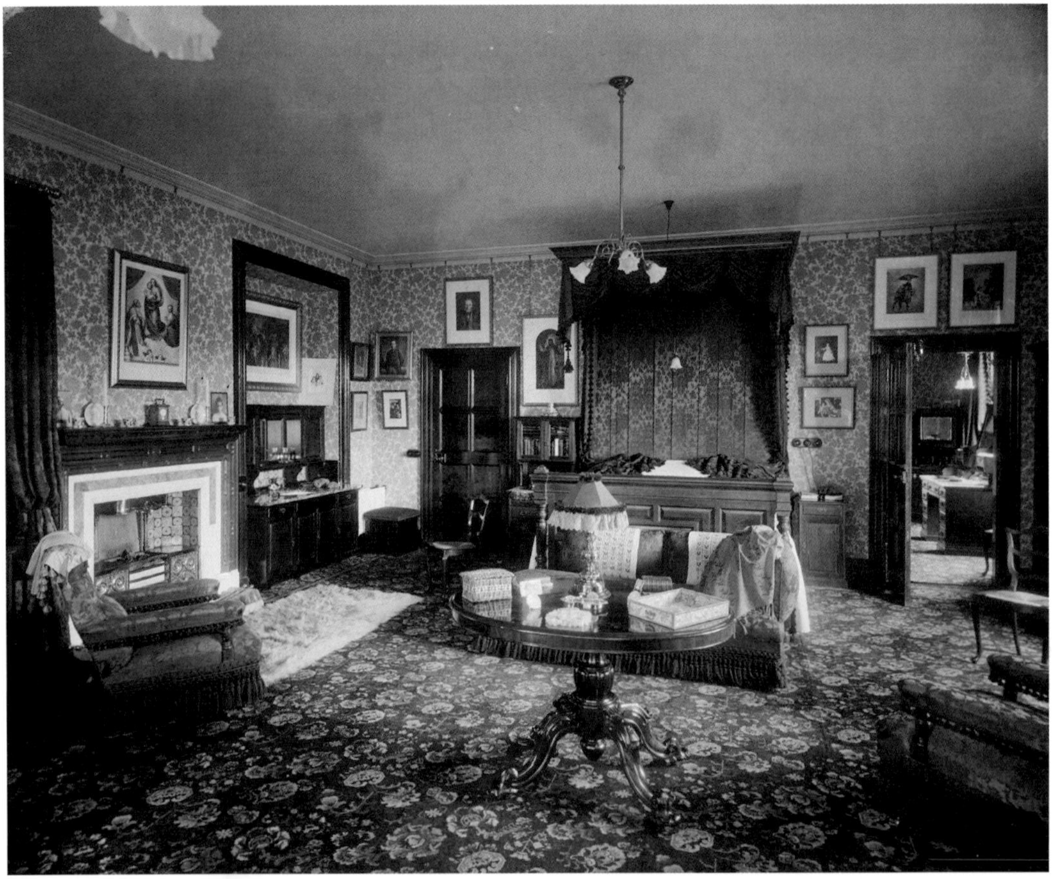

75 Edward Brown-Lees, an Oldham cotton magnate, restored Thurland Castle in Lancashire in the 1890s. The iconography of his bedroom is primarily religious, with engravings after Holman Hunt and – over the fireplace – Raphael's *Sistine* (or *Dresden*) *Madonna*, the single most popular Christian image of the nineteenth century. Over the door to the left is a reproduction of Herkomer's portrait of Ruskin, who lived not far distant at Coniston.

his bedroom painted or photographed, at least, was not likely to advertise anything lascivious.[118] Prince Albert's dressing room at Osborne House on the Isle of Wight displayed some of his collection of chaste early Italian pictures, so that the modern fresco of Hercules in thrall to Omphale, seen in the view into the bathroom, was, in this company, beyond suspicion (illus. 74).[119] We may, however, feel that Colonel Edward Brown-Lees, of Thurland Castle in Lancashire, whose bedroom in the 1890s had engravings of *The Light of the World, The Triumph of the Innocents* (both after Holman Hunt), the *Sistine Madonna* and even a portrait of Ruskin over the door, risked overdoing the chaste aesthetic (illus. 75). At the other end of the spectrum lies, albeit in fiction, the adoption by Leopold and Molly Bloom in *Ulysses* of a cheap chromo of a bathing nymph.[120] 'Given away with the Easter number of *Photo Bits*', a 'Splendid masterpiece in art colours', the nymph was placed over the couple's bed, but descends from her 'oak and tinsel' frame in the hallucinatory Circe episode of Joyce's novel to confront Bloom with her own perspective on life as a bedroom picture. While relieved to have been rescued from the vulgar magazine in which Bloom found her ('in evil company, highkickers, coster picnic makers, pugilists, popular generals, immoral panto boys'), hers has not been an easy role: 'Unseen, one summer eve, you kissed me in four places. And with loving pencil you shaded my eyes, my bosom and my shame.' She has had to put up with observing Bloom's snoring, masturbating and administration of enemas, as well as his soiled linen and Molly's cracked commode. Now a tragic classical heroine, disgusted, she flees.

THE END

The idealists among picture lovers, those for whom the mental image of the picture was as valuable as the object itself, or more so, were ostensibly liberated from the care of the framed canvas.

Woolf's *To the Lighthouse* ends with Lily Briscoe finally, after a decade, completing her painting showing Mrs Ramsay and her house on Skye. Adding one last stroke into her composition, she realizes that 'I have had my vision'. The painting itself 'would be hung in the attics . . . it would be destroyed. But what did that matter?'[121] This was also D. H. Lawrence's uncompromising solution to the materiality of pictures – love the image, lose the commodity. But a century earlier Hazlitt had realized that the renunciation of the original was not so straightforward. Could the mind be trusted as an alternative repository of pictorial treasures? The arts 'have their seat in the heart of man and in his imagination', he wrote; 'it is there they labour, have their triumphs there, and, unseen and unthought of, perform their ceaseless task.'[122] This is art as the unconscious, churning away out of sight, discernible in what Freud called the 'picture language of dreams and visions'. But what horrible dreams might ensue from the sense of losing those mental pictures, as when Hazlitt returned again to write of his struggle to make painted and mental copies of the masterpieces of Paris in 1802:

> It is now seventeen years since I was studying in the Louvre . . . but long after I returned, and even still, I sometimes dream of being there again – of asking for the old pictures – and not finding them, or finding them changed or faded from what they were, I cry myself awake![123]

Here, in this need to know that those original youthful impressions were retained somewhere, we feel an echo of what the Surrealist generation later took to be the ancient foundation of our modern sense of the apartness of art: that it was not intended to be seen, only preserved. In the 1930s Walter Benjamin suggested of cave paintings that 'Artistic production begins with images that serve cultic purposes. With such images, presumably, their presence is more important than the fact that they are seen.'[124] Benjamin also references, in Christian tradition, pictures kept out of sight in crypts or *cellas*. Very similar language equating such hidden pictures with the unconscious was used by Henri Lefebvre in his later *The Production of Space*:

> What is the *raison d'être* of Lascaux's frescoes, or of those in the crypt of St-Savin? The answer is that these paintings were made not to be seen, but merely to 'be' – and so that they might be known to 'be' there. They are magical images, condensing subterranean qualities, signs of death and traces of the struggle against death, whose aim is to turn death's forces against death itself.[125]

Individual memory-pictures are not enough: we must believe that they are backed up *somewhere*, even if that somewhere is never visited.

Those who sought to help define the economy of the bedroom in the nineteenth century always recalled its purpose as the refuge of the poorly (illus. 76). When confined to a bedroom, the decoration of the walls became paramount to the patient's mental health as the images there, the only ones left to them for interminable hours and days, took on a distressingly real presence. 'A room intended for repose ought to contain nothing which can fatigue the eye by complexity,' states the younger Eastlake in *Hints on Household Taste*.

> How many an unfortunate invalid has lain helpless on his bed, condemned to puzzle out the pattern of the hangings over his head, or stare at a wall which he feels instinctively obliged to map out into grass plots, gravel paths, and summer houses, like an involuntary gardener?[126]

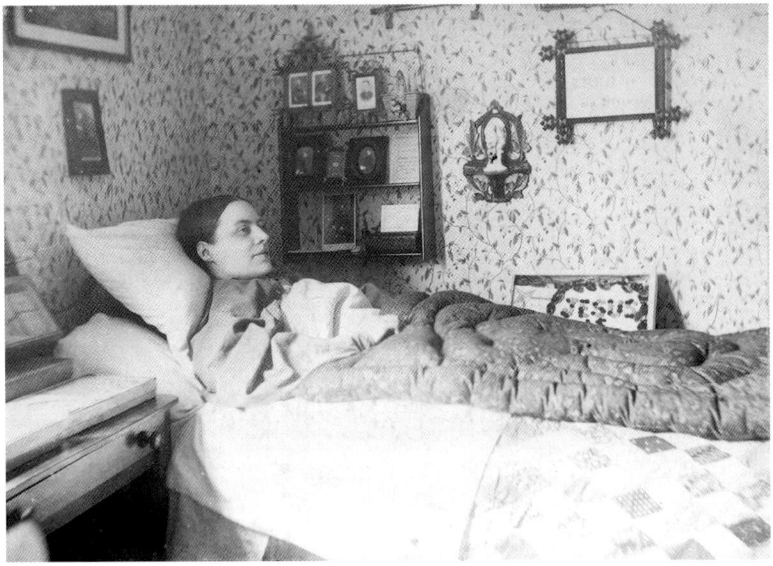

76 Portrait of an unknown woman in her sickbed, a cabinet photograph by Ebenezer Pannell of Brighton, *c.* 1900. The subject has around her emblems of the consolations of religion (note the text-work in an 'Oxford' frame) and a set of hanging shelves allowing portrait photographs to be kept within touching distance. Prints hang over her head.

Here was medical support for the argument against any attempt to replicate real forms in decoration, especially wallpapers. A contributor to an 1890s volume edited by Candace Wheeler on *Household Art* praised Eastlake's influence in America in this regard, reiterating the dangers of representational papers, which

> kill the effect of the best pictures, and to many a nervous invalid render his hours intolerable, as he counts and combines over and over again the meaningless recurrence of a marked angle or curve, or the ever-repeated big, awkward rose or tiresome convolvulus.[127]

Julia Stephen, Virginia Woolf's mother, in her *Notes from Sick Rooms*, again acknowledged images as a real barrier to convalescence:

> When an illness has gone on for some time the sick person becomes very weary of the things which surround her. She has looked at all the pictures which hang on the walls, and at the patterns which ornament or disfigure the paper, till she can bear them no longer.[128]

Clearly Oscar Wilde was not alone in feeling, when direly ill in Paris, that he was engaged in mortal combat with the hideous wallpaper that enveloped him. At least pictures could be changed or moved. Pictures in the bedroom of a sick person must be placed flat against the wall, advised Florence Caddy, because 'the effect of them hanging much forward makes many people giddy, and in an invalid will sometimes produce a feeling akin to sea-sickness.'[129] Panton for once did not recommend autotypes for the sickroom, but instead, on hygienic grounds, proposed cheap glazed prints given away with the illustrated press, 'as the frames could be disinfected, the glass washed, and the pictures themselves destroyed'.[130]

No advice author presumed to recommend specific images to comfort the sick and dying, although others wrote of their own experiences, such as the economist Harriet Martineau, who was one of the very many devotees of Ary Scheffer's *Christus Consolator* (1837). This composition has Christ at the centre of a varied assembly of suffering humanity, including an enslaved African man, a dramatic feature that helped propel the image around the world and into the sick room of the abolitionist Martineau, who, although later a brave early public atheist, turned her anthropological eye on this image to find in its idea something almost magical:

> If such a picture as the CHRISTUS CONSOLATOR of Scheffer be within view of the sick-couch, it may well be a cause of wonder, almost amounting to alarm, to those who, not having needed [solace in suffering], have never felt its power. If there were now burnings or drownings for sorcery, that picture, and some who possess it, would soon be in the fire, or at the bottom of a pond. No mute operation of witchcraft, or its dread, could exceed the silent power of that picture over sufferers.[131]

Samuel Rogers, the banker, poet and collector, had a print of Scheffer's picture which in late life he kept next to his bed. He also planned to have one of his most precious paintings, a small panel by Raphael, in the room with him when he died, suggesting a carefully curated deathbed scene, fitting given Rogers's own description, in his long poem *Italy*, of the deathbed of Raphael himself, at which the artist's friends are moved to find the great painter beneath his last work, the *Transfiguration*.[132] A picture could help with a good, or at least a better, death: one prepared for, with thoughts focused on the only future remaining. The passionately religious Christina Rossetti, in her last months, liked to keep near to an autotype of Christ as *The Good Shepherd* by her friend Frederic Shields (see illus. 58). When a few intimates were allowed into the house to pay their respects after her death in December 1894, the 'small, narrow, curtainless bed was standing immediately below' it.[133]

There were always those, often pleasure-loving aristocrats, who are recorded as having been repelled by pictures – who felt in them a pull away from society and from life itself. The easy-going third Lord Holland 'persisted in saying that pictures gave him more pain than pleasure', according to Samuel Rogers, while the vivacious Empress Eugénie was 'bored to death' by them.[134] Others suspected that an excessive attachment to pictures was unhealthy, as is the case with Soames Forsyte's sister Winifred, who, recovering from her own disastrous marriage, is 'depressed' by the pictures hoarded by her brother.[135] But just how dangerous could pictures be? There were Renaissance traditions of the risks around exceedingly lifelike pictures. One of Raphael's portraits is said to have done to death a rival artist who was overcome with jealousy on seeing it, while there were fears, akin to those in Islamic tradition, of divine displeasure at an artist's effort to create their own lifelike human forms: who would be responsible for these people?[136] In Early Modern English drama a poisoned portrait may become a murderer's instrument of choice when the victim kisses it, as in Webster's *The White Devil* (1612). For our period the risk was in preferring pictures to people. Towards the end of Galsworthy's *Forsyte Saga*, Soames's house catches fire, and in the process of trying to rescue his pictures ('Save the Courbet!') he is dealt a mortal blow to the head by a falling Goya – in fact only a copy after Goya but a picture that had great sentimental value as his daughter had attended a fancy-dress ball as one of the characters in it. By this point in the story many readers may however have headed for the gooseberry bushes, where, according to Woolf in *A Room of One's Own*, we will wish to run for cover from such a clunky and portentously hyper-masculine plotline with its 'symbolical' conclusion visible from afar.[137] Soames Forsyte had sought to fix his affections to his walls in concrete form, and paid the penalty that Woolf's Lily Briscoe in *To the Lighthouse*, content with her vision alone, did not risk incurring. It was safer not to try to pin down a vision of beauty.

Proust, as we saw, consistently emphasized the suppression of aesthetic feeling in the home, the invisibility induced by domesticity, which at least allowed daily life to be carried on. When his character Bergotte, an elderly writer, confronts an exquisite Vermeer at a loan exhibition – his unique opportunity to see the masterpiece and in ideally focused, unfiltered circumstances – the experience is so intense that, famously, it kills him. To move from the sublime to the ridiculous, the most telling case of a killing picture in fiction or drama, for our interest in the distribution of pictures through the home, comes from rather beyond our time frame. In Mike Leigh's suburban satire *Abigail's Party* (1976), Beverly and Laurence display in their living room colour prints after Van Gogh and Lowry, which by now would be read as the equivalent of the tasteful old autotypes after soulful Renaissance museum paintings. But the tipsy Beverly has never really liked them, and instead insists on bringing down from the bedroom a print of a recent erotic high-street classic, *The Wings of Love* by Stephen Pearson, which has been well described as showing 'a naked couple on a lurid patio stretching out into a fantastical ocean and sheltered by a majestic oversized swan with a welcoming wingspan'.[138] 'Cheap pornographic trash,' says Laurence: 'don't bring that picture down!' But off goes Beverly, only to find as she returns embracing the picture, that Laurence has collapsed with a heart attack. The old chromo versus autotype battle has been joined again, now with a merciless winner.

Following a death, a picture may yet have a role to play in the mourning process. The custom of covering over mirrors when a body is laid out has been observed in many cultures, and seems to have been observed in some Victorian households: certainly the tradition remained strong in Jewish homes. The reasons for doing so are, necessarily for something defined as a custom rather than a practicality, lost in time but are said to relate to the need to focus only on the departed person, and to prevent their migrating soul being in any way waylaid or absorbed by a replica image of itself. Pictures are sometimes said to have been treated similarly, covered or turned during mourning, and yet explicit evidence for this is scarce. W. G. Sebald started an elusive hare in the very last lines of his *Rings of Saturn*, where he cites Sir Thomas Browne's seventeenth-century account of the Dutch custom of draping both mirrors and naturalistic pictures, 'so that the soul, as it left the body, would not be distracted on its final journey, either by a reflection of itself or by a last glimpse of the land now being lost for ever'. But too few of Sebald's readers took the hint, in his reference to 'a passage of the *Pseudodoxia Epidemica* [by Browne] that I can no longer find', of a fiction: Browne does not appear ever to have recounted such a practice.[139] The mournful turning away, or taking down, of pictures is also said to have been practised in Britain at the same period, but again with few if any precise accounts.[140] One exception appears in Celia Fiennes's journal of the 1690s, in which she describes the Yorkshire seat of Sir Edward Blackett, the recently completed Newby Hall: 'there was Severall pictures but not Set up the house being in mourning for his Lady, and her mother the Lady Yorke, wch dyed a month or two of Each other.'[141]

To turn a picture against the wall in later times was more likely to suggest the cancelling of its subject, to use the social media term – in effect the turning of one's own back against a picture which one cannot actually evict or destroy. Jean-Paul Sartre opened his autobiography with the disgrace of an ancestor, a priest whose abandonment of his calling caused the family to turn his portrait to the wall.[142] The writer Jeanette Winterson tells an extraordinary story of her severely fundamentalist mother, who inherited some pictures from an uncle but felt unable to display them. 'What she did was hang them in the living room for all to see, but back to front. For sixteen years I thought art was stained damp canvas, steel tacks, brown paper and string' – strangely avant-garde, as Winterson notes. Once, she turned over one of the pictures to find nothing worse than 'a sylvan scene – woods, cottage, stream – the kind that came into vogue as talismanic against the collective nervous breakdown that was the Industrial Revolution'.[143] Superstition, Winterson implies, was involved whichever side of the picture was shown.

This book has emphasized the self-conscious rationalism with which the nineteenth century looked at pictures, and the unpredictable displacements and disturbances that followed from this. Most old picture legends survived only to be smiled at. Yet the twentieth century invented new superstitions. 'The pictures of an ostrich or peacock are considered unlucky,' warns a 1918 guide to signs and omens (who knew?), while the old protecting image – say, of the Madonna – found new secular analogues in portraits of absolute rulers, the removal of which would bring misfortune.[144] The opposite idea, of the picture that invites disaster, in the gothic tradition, was given new life as recently as the 1980s with the discovery of the Curse of the Crying Boy – the phenomenon of house fires being associated with prints of certain kitsch paintings of lachrymose infants. It seems some of these were sprayed with a varnish that acted as a fire retardant, leaving the pictures still in place, tearfully surveying burned-out rooms.[145]

Prints of all sorts ended up in the rubbish over the years. As Leigh Hunt had advised, surely it was better to enjoy such expendable items and then replace them than store them somewhere unobserved. Images printed on paper would evaporate in a moment when thrown into the fire (evidently with the exception of the *Crying Boy*), but oil paintings were a different matter – they are not easily destroyed other than in an outright conflagration such as that suffered by Soames Forsyte. Fumes from gas lighting and other chemicals might cause some damage, as experienced by the writer and chemist Primo Levi, whose youthful home experiments were disturbed by the occasional thumps of pictures collapsing to the floor as their nails were eaten through by the fumes released by the aspiring scientist.[146] But they would be all right, albeit with cracked frames. Even stabbed or hacked pictures could survive, as witness the scars of the Rokeby *Venus*, today not easily visible to the naked eye. At the end of *The Picture of Dorian Gray*, Dorian grows disgusted by his ageing portrait and its recriminating expression, and determines to destroy it. In the text, when published as a book, the resolution is, truth be told, rather lame: Dorian 'stabbed the picture', and falls down dead. Yet the original serialized version has Dorian thrusting the knife into the canvas and then 'ripping the thing right up from top to bottom', a phrase which, as the editor of the original typescript notes, would have brought to readers' minds the recent horrific deeds of Jack the Ripper.[147] Equally Wilde may have been recalling the passage in *Melmoth the Wanderer* in which John Melmoth does away with the portrait of his cursed ancestor, adopting no half-measures. Tearing the canvas from its frame, he 'tore, cut, and hacked it in every direction, and eagerly watched the fragments that burned like tinder in the turf-fire'.[148] This gothic treatment deliberately echoes much earlier traditions of punishing individuals vicariously through attacks on images of them. But the threat of the flames remained a regular motif for anyone in our period wishing to stress how urgently the pictorial economy needed reformation. We cited in Chapter Two D. H. Lawrence's fiery solution to the oversupply of pictures, while Ruskin regularly proposed burning art of which he did not approve on moral grounds, much like those who threatened to persecute to destruction, as a religious duty, overtly erotic paintings.[149]

Paintings tended, in fact, to come to slower, cooler ends. As was often pointed out, they were likely to 'outlast all the other belongings of the house', an idea that forms the basis of Thomas Hardy's poem 'The Enemy's Portrait'.[150] Here the narrator finds in an auction the portrait of one who had done him a terrible wrong. After he has bought it with the intention of burning the canvas and reusing the frame, the picture is laid against a wall pending its destruction, but, being a trip hazard, it is hung by a servant on the wall, where it is forgotten, eventually outliving the embittered owner. Portraits of loved ones were less likely to be marked for execution but therefore all the more likely to suffer a humiliating series of evictions from room to room. Horace Walpole, reflecting on the glut of portrait painters offering their products to his generation, concluded that it was

> almost as necessary that the representations of men should perish and quit the scene to their successors, as it is that the human race should give place to rising generations. And indeed the mortality is almost as rapid. Portraits that cost twenty, thirty, sixty guineas, and that proudly take possession of the drawing-room, give way in the next generation to those of the newly married couple, descending into the parlour, where they are slightly mentioned as 'my father's and mother's pictures'. When they become 'my grandfather and grandmother', they mount to the two pair of stairs; and then, unless despatched to the mansion-house in the country, or crowded into the housekeeper's room, they perish among the lumber of garrets, or flutter into rags before a broker's shop at the Seven Dials.[151]

There may have been some half-hearted attempts at repurposing canvases. We read of paintings being recycled 'to stop windows' or to make up a waistcoat for an impoverished artist or even a burial shroud, which is what Turner liked to say was the fate he intended for his *Dido Building Carthage*.[152] By the early twentieth century, those writing for more superior homeowners might recommend giving pictures away to local municipal art galleries, as one might redistribute old clothes to poorer neighbours.[153] The extreme example of such nationalization of private pictures took place after the Russian Revolution, which resulted in this scene, described by a British visitor, at the Hermitage in St Petersburg, where the confiscated pictures of the aristocracy were gathered:

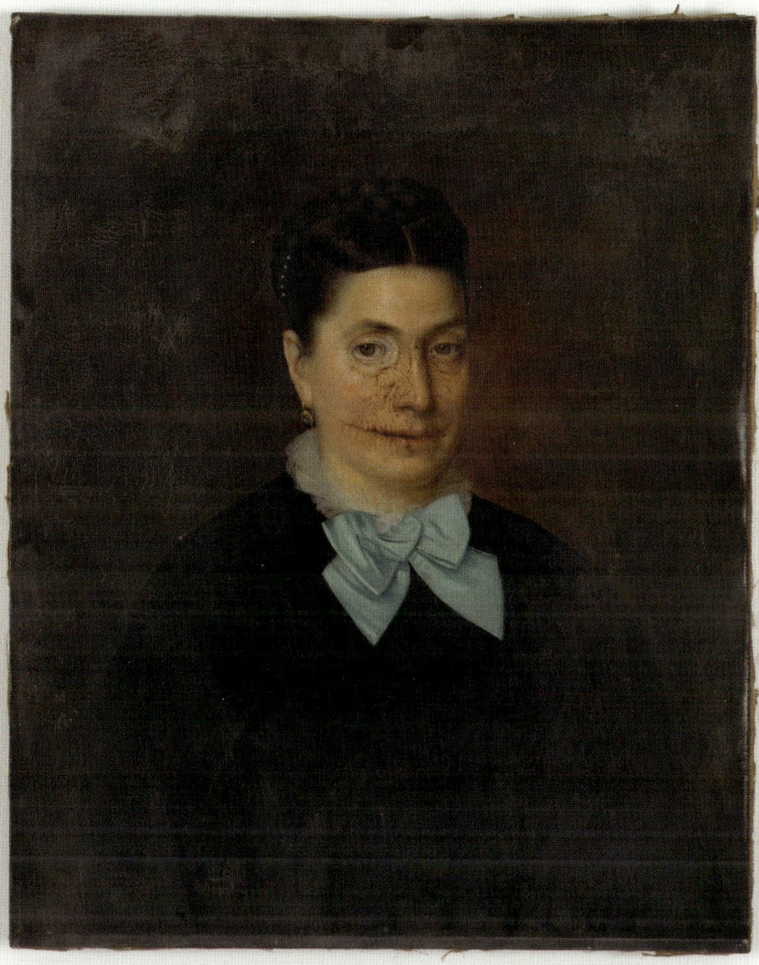

77 Jake and Dinos Chapman, ever alive to the gothic tradition, have seized on the horror to be found in the gap between people and representations of them. Their series *One Day You Will no Longer be Loved (that it should come to this ...)*, begun around 2008, involves giving a zombie twist to old portraits found in antique shops, now nameless and separated from the homes where they had once been cherished.

> The whole place seemed peopled by ghosts. A deadly silence reigned. No one came there; no one had any business there except the curators who were studying the pictures. It was a sort of Hades into which one might imagine the dead pictures passed in some after-life of unbroken sleep.[154]

For a portrait, the loss of a home meant often the loss of a name, the face moving on anonymously to the kind of fate described by Walpole or even, for the unlucky few, eventually to be picked up by the Chapman brothers to be given a few additional ghoulish deformities and added to their gallery of old portraits cruelly titled *One Day You Will no Longer be Loved (that it should come to this . . .)* (illus. 77).

References

Introduction

1 See Didier Maleuvre, *Museum Memories: History, Technology, Art* (Stanford, CA, 1999), pp. 100–104.

2 Although just as I write (March 2021), Christie's has sold a digital file by the artist Beeple for $69 million – a non-fungible token dependent on a blockchain, capturing the entirety of the artist's recent back-catalogue of work.

3 James Bloom sets out to ask this of the Early Modern period in 'Why Painting?', in *Mapping Markets for Paintings in Early Modern Europe, 1450–1750*, ed. Neil De Marchi and Hans van Miegroet (Turnhout, 2006), pp. 17–31.

4 Walter Crane, *The Claims of Decorative Art* (London, 1892), p. 109.

5 Percy Fitzgerald, 'Picture Frames', *Art Journal*, XLVIII (1886), p. 324.

6 Edward Gladstone-Lingham, *The Science of Taste: Being a Treatise on Its Principles* (London, 1879), p. 105.

7 Henry Mayhew, *London Labour and the London Poor* (London, 1861), vol. I, p. 447.

8 Edmund Gosse, 'The Place of Sculpture in Daily Life. II. – Sculpture in the House', *Magazine of Art*, XVIII (1895), p. 372. For an overview of scholarship on the display of sculpture – which is not addressed in this book – see Malcolm Baker, 'Writing about Displays of Sculpture: Historiography and Some Current Questions', *Cahiers de l'École du Louvre*, VIII (2016), http://journals.openedition.org/cel/332.

9 Henry Mogford, *Hand-Book for the Preservation of Pictures*, 3rd edn (London, 1851), p. 9, plagiarized by Charles Henry Savory, *The Practical Carver and Gilder's Guide*, 4th edn (London, n.d. [1876?]), p. 166.

10 Claude Lévi-Strauss, *La pensée sauvage* (Paris, 1962), p. 34.
11 David Freedberg, *The Power of Images: Studies in the History and Theory of Response* [1989] (Chicago, IL, and London, 1991), p. 436; cf. Caroline van Eck, *Art, Agency and Living Presence: From the Animated Image to the Excessive Object* (Munich and Leiden, 2015), p. 72.
12 John Lucas Tupper, 'The Subject in Art. No. II', *The Germ* (March 1850), p. 118.
13 Like anyone else writing about domestic spaces, I have been inspired by Gaston Bachelard, *The Poetics of Space* [1958], trans. Maria Jolas (Boston, MA, 1994). More recently Judith Flanders has used a house-tour structure to excellent effect in her *The Victorian House: Domestic Life from Childbirth to Deathbed* (London, 2004).
14 Walter Benjamin, *One-Way Street and Other Writings*, trans. J. A. Underwood (London, 2009), p. 180. The mention of photographs prompts a confession of some of the other types of image not given any special treatment here. These include illustrations in books and newspapers; framed embroidery, and any kind of text-picture; shellwork or imagery worked in straw, flowers, etc.; standing screens decorated with images such as fire screens, print screens and room dividers.
15 Van Eck, *Art, Agency and Living Presence*, p. 60.
16 Horace Walpole, *Anecdotes of Painting in England* [1762–80] (London, 1879), p. 4.
17 See Freedberg, *The Power of Images*, chap. 5; Van Eck, *Art, Agency and Living Presence*; Elsje van Kessel, *The Lives of Paintings: Presence, Agency and Likeness in Venetian Art of the Sixteenth Century* (Munich and Leiden, 2017).
18 On Early Modern British picture curtains see J. O. Halliwell, commentary on *Twelfth Night*, I, iii, in *The Works of William Shakespeare* (London, 1853–65), vol. VII, and Bruce R. Smith, *The Key of Green: Passion and Perception in Renaissance Culture* (Chicago, IL, 2008), pp. 18–19.
19 See Margaret A. Morse, 'Creating Sacred Space: The Religious Visual Culture of the Renaissance *casa*', in *Approaching the Italian Renaissance Interior*, ed. Marta Ajmar-Wollheim, Flora Dennis and Ann Matchette (Oxford, 2007), figs 7 and 8; and Abigail Brundin, Deborah Howard and Mary Laven, *The Sacred Home in Renaissance Italy* (Oxford, 2018), pp. 87–9.
20 For an imagined account of a Catholic woman hiding her crucifixes behind curtains, see Daniel Defoe, *Religious Courtship* (London, 1729), pp. 227–8. In the second picture of Hogarth's *Marriage à la Mode* series, 'The Tête à Tête', can be seen a painting from behind whose curtain a naked foot pokes out. On the decline of picture curtains in Britain see

Jacob Simon, *The Art of the Picture Frame: Artists, Patrons and the Framing of Portraits in Britain*, exh. cat., National Portrait Gallery, London (1996), pp. 14, 49–50.

21 John Ruskin, *Works*, ed. E. T. Cook and Alexander Wedderburn (London, 1903–12), vol. XIII, p. lii.

22 Quoted in Giles Waterfield, 'The Town House as Gallery of Art', *London Journal*, XX/1 (1995), p. 55.

23 By 1815 it was claimed some thirty private collections of art in London were to some degree 'open': see Anne Nellis Richter, 'Improving Taste in the Private Interior: Gentlemen's Galleries in Post-Napoleonic London', in *Architectural Space in Eighteenth-Century Europe*, ed. Denise Amy Baxter and Meredith Martin (Farnham, 2010), p. 172.

24 William Hazlitt, *Table-Talk* (London, 1821–2), vol. II, p. 15.

25 Quoted in Nicholas Tromans, 'Museum or Market? The British Institution', in *Governing Cultures: Institutions of Art in Victorian London*, ed. Colin Trodd and Paul Barlow (Aldershot, 2000), p. 51.

26 *Art Journal* article of 1851, quoted in Giles Waterfield, 'Picture Hanging and Gallery Decoration', in *Palaces of Art: Art Galleries in Britain, 1790–1990*, ed. Giles Waterfield, exh. cat., Dulwich Picture Gallery, London (1991), p. 55.

27 Charles Lock Eastlake, *The National Gallery: Observations on the Unfitness of the Present Building for Its Purpose* (London, 1845), pp. 11–13. On Eastlake's hanging systems see Charlotte Klonk, *Spaces of Experience: Art Gallery Interiors from 1800 to 2000* (New Haven, CT, and London, 2009), pp. 28 ff.

28 Ruskin, *Works*, vols XII, pp. 412–14, and XIII, pp. xxviii, 176–9.

29 E. M. Forster, 'Not Looking at Pictures' [1939], in *Two Cheers for Democracy* (London, 1951), p. 126.

30 'The Adornment of Houses with Works of Art', *Art Journal*, IX (1847), p. 297. On the massive expansion of the London secondary market for pictures *c.* 1820–40 see Mark Westgarth, '"Florid-Looking Speculators in Art and Virtu": The London Picture Trade *c.* 1850', in *The Rise of the Modern Art Market in London 1850–1939*, ed. Pamela Fletcher and Anne Helmreich (Manchester, 2011), p. 28.

31 Gustav Waagen, *Treasures of Art in Great Britain* (London, 1854), vol. III, pp. 7–8.

32 The sense of movement that Sheraton gives in this plate reflects the new fashion for allowing furniture to wander out into the room from its traditional position up against the walls: Peter Thornton, *Authentic Décor: The Domestic Interior, 1620–1920* [1984] (London, 2000), pp. 145–7.

33 Katie Scott, *The Rococo Interior: Decoration and Social Spaces in Early Eighteenth-Century Paris* (New Haven, CT, and London, 1995), pp. 255, 263.
34 Sabine Melchior-Bonnet, *The Mirror: A History* [1994] (New York and London, 2002), p. 152.
35 See Suga Yasuko, 'Designing the Morality of Consumption: "Chamber of Horrors" at the Museum of Ornamental Art, 1852–53', *Design Issues*, XX/4 (2004), pp. 43–56.
36 See George Godwin, *London Shadows* (London, 1854), pp. 5–6, and Mayhew, *London Labour and the London Poor*, vol. II, p. 110.
37 David Halle, *Inside Culture: Art and Class in the American Home* (Chicago, IL, and London, 1993). See also the similar approach taken in Mihaly Csikszentmihalyi and Eugene Rochberg-Halton, *The Meaning of Things: Domestic Symbols and the Self* (Cambridge, 1981), pp. 65 ff.
38 Painter went on to publish several important and intriguing studies relating to our theme but without the comprehensive approach taken in the PhD. See, for example, Colin Painter, *At Home with Constable's Cornfield*, exh. cat., National Gallery, London (1996).
39 See Nicholas Cooper, *The Photography of Bedford Lemere & Co.* (London, 2011). The Bedford Lemere archive is now maintained by Historic England.
40 On the nomenclature of domestic rooms see Ben Highmore, *The Great Indoors: At Home in the Modern British House* (London, 2014), pp. 40–41.
41 Ruskin, *Works*, vol. XVI, pp. 320–21.
42 John Loughman and John Michael Montias, *Public and Private Spaces: Works of Art in Seventeenth-Century Dutch Houses* (Zwolle, 2000), p. 69. Similar findings were reported by Jeffrey M. Muller, 'Private Collections in the Spanish Netherlands: Ownership and Display of Paintings in Domestic Interiors', in *The Age of Rubens*, ed. Peter C. Sutton, exh. cat., Museum of Fine Arts, Boston, MA (1993), p. 200.
43 William Sanderson, *Graphice* (London, 1658), pp. 26–7, a passage plagiarized in the following generation by William Salmon in his *Polygraphice*. Sanderson's precedents include G. P. Lomazzo's *Trattato dell'arte della pittura, scoltura, et architettura* (1584; translated into English 1598), which was so thorough as to recommend pictures for rooms given over to torture and executions.
44 Eastlake in *The Country House*, ed. Mary Fox (London, 1843), p. 57.
45 Francis Russell claims that several conventions of matching pictures to rooms were established during the eighteenth century, including portraits or sporting pictures in the hall; still lifes and fowl pieces in the dining room; subject paintings in large apartments; drawings and prints in bedrooms; family portraits in the galleries of older houses:

'The Hanging and Display of Pictures, 1700–1850', in *The Fashioning and Functioning of the British Country House*, ed. Gervase Jackson-Stops et al. (Washington, DC, 1989), p. 135. The tourist John Byng, writing in 1792, gives an intriguing list of his ideal pairings of rooms with types of picture, but one couched as an exasperated response to the 'filthy, naked, or dying pictures' he actually encounters on his travels – a tidy fantasy representing a great cleaning-up operation: *The Torrington Diaries*, ed. C. Bruyn Andrews (London, 1934–8), vol. III, p. 157.

1 Put Up a Picture in Your Room

1 Ray Monk, *Ludwig Wittgenstein: The Duty of Genius* (London, 1991), p. 317.
2 Leigh Hunt, *Correspondence* (London, 1862), vol. I, p. 73.
3 *Examiner* (22 March 1812), p. 179.
4 Benjamin Robert Haydon, *Diary*, ed. W. B. Pope (Cambridge, MA, 1960–63), vol. II, p. 423 (entry for 27 July 1823).
5 Nicholas Roe, *Fiery Heart: The First Life of Leigh Hunt* (London, 2005), p. 187; Leigh Hunt, *Autobiography* (London, 1850), vol. II, p. 148; Hunt, *Correspondence*, vol. I, p. 89.
6 Clarence Cook, *The House Beautiful: Essays on Beds and Tables, Stools and Candlesticks* (New York, 1878), p. 315.
7 Hunt, *Correspondence*, vol. I, p. 289.
8 Charles Cowden Clarke and Mary Cowden Clarke, *Recollections of Writers* (London, 1878), p. 134.
9 The prints have not been identified, but some plausible suggestions were made by Sidney Colvin, *John Keats* [1887] (New York, 1917), p. 54.
10 William Hazlitt, *Criticisms on Art* (London, 1843), p. 63 (essay written 1823).
11 William Hazlitt, *Table-Talk* (London, 1821–2), vol. I, pp. 10–13.
12 Peter George Patmore, *My Friends and Acquaintance* (London, 1854), vol. III, pp. 103–6.
13 Samuel Smiles, *Thrift* (London, 1875), pp. 375–8. Hunt's text is referenced also, for example, by Lucy Orrinsmith, *The Drawing-Room* (London, 1878), p. 123, although the passage quoted here has been mistakenly attributed by one modern scholar to Smiles: Thad Logan, *The Victorian Parlour: A Cultural Study* (Cambridge, 2001), pp. 136–7 and 250–51 n. 80. Smiles's borrowed phrases had in fact already taken on a life of their own, being quoted, for instance, in a biography of a late Victorian art collector: Dianne Sachko Mcleod, *Art and the Victorian Middle Class: Money and the Making of Cultural Identity* (Cambridge, 1996), p. 212.

14 There was a Neapolitan tradition of preventing pictures observing nefarious business deals, according to Abigail Brundin, Deborah Howard and Mary Laven, *The Sacred Home in Renaissance Italy* (Oxford, 2018), p. 88.

15 *New Monthly Magazine*, XII (1819), p. 520.

16 J. R. Oldfield, *Popular Politics and British Anti-Slavery* (Manchester, 1995), pp. 156–63.

17 Gertrude, 'The Memory of the Dead – A Mother's Picture', *Edinburgh Literary Journal* (14 January 1832), p. 26.

18 L. Forbes Winslow, *Mad Humanity: Its Forms Apparent and Obscure* (London, 1898), p. 274.

19 'The Picture on My Wall', *Sixpenny Magazine* (October 1863), pp. 289–90.

20 *Aeneid*, I, line 462, discussed by Van Eck, *Art, Agency and Living Presence*, pp. 74–5.

21 Nicholas Tromans, *David Wilkie: The People's Painter* (Edinburgh, 2007), p. 133.

22 Charles Robert Leslie, *Life and Letters of John Constable, R.A.*, new edn (London, 1896), p. 397.

23 From a memoir by the artist George Jones in J.M.W. Turner, *Collected Correspondence*, ed. John Gage (Oxford, 1980), p. 4.

24 Adrian Tinniswood, *The Polite Tourist: Four Centuries of Country House Visiting* [1989] (London, 1998), p. 77. However, the landscape gardener Humphry Repton dissented, writing that a picture only ever showed a narrow segment of an actual view on a landscape and so to base an improvement on paintings would result in something resembling 'five or six pictures of Claude in one long frame': *Observations on the Theory and Practice of Landscape Gardening* (London, 1805), p. 117.

25 John Knowles, *The Life and Writings of Henry Fuseli* (London, 1831), vol. II, p. 217.

26 Alfred Herbert Palmer, *The Life and Letters of Samuel Palmer* (London, 1892), p. 353.

27 Stanley Jones, *Hazlitt: A Life. From Winterslow to Frith Street* (Oxford, 1989), p. 368.

28 William Hazlitt, *Sketches of the Principal Picture-Galleries in England* (London, 1824), p. 5; Hazlitt, *Sketches and Essays* (London, 1839), pp. 284–5.

29 Hazlitt, *Sketches of the Principal Picture-Galleries*, p. 112.

30 John Barrell, *The Political Theory of Painting from Reynolds to Hazlitt* (New Haven, CT, and London, 1986), pp. 309, 337; Paul Hamilton, 'Critical Dilation: How William Hazlitt Judged Paintings', *Tate Papers*, XXIV (2015), www.tate.org.uk/research/publications/tate-papers/24.

31 Brundin et al., *The Sacred Home*, pp. 193–4, and see David Freedberg, *The Power of Images: Studies in the History and Theory of Response* [1989] (Chicago, IL, and London, 1991), pp. 179, 192.

32 Hazlitt, *Table-Talk*, vol. II, p. 13.

33 Samuel Taylor Coleridge, *Table-Talk and Omniana* (Oxford, 1917), p. 141.

34 Robert Kemp Philp, *The Lady's Every-Day Book* (London, 1875), p. 6.

35 David H. Solkin, ed., *Art on the Line: The Royal Academy Exhibitions at Somerset House, 1780–1836* (New Haven, CT, and London, 2001), pp. 17, 23–4.

36 A list of reasons not to tilt is given, for example, in 'Hanging Pictures', *The Decorator and Furnisher*, VIII/2 (May 1886), p. 48.

37 Edgar Allan Poe, 'The Philosophy of Furniture', *Burton's Gentleman's Magazine*, VI/5 (May 1840), pp. 243–5.

38 Henry Mogford, *Hand-Book for the Preservation of Pictures*, 3rd edn (London, 1851), p. 13. On Mogford see his entry in www.npg.org.uk/research/programmes/directory-of-british-picture-restorers.

39 Mogford, *Hand-Book*, p. 12. On the pre-nineteenth-century decoration of the picture fittings themselves, see Peter Thornton, *Seventeenth-Century Interior Decoration in England, France and Holland* (New Haven, CT, and London, 1978), pp. 252–3. Especially elaborate lion-headed nail-heads were in use at Sir John Leicester's gallery in London, while in Naples there seems to have been a penchant for using outsized heads resembling saucers: Mario Praz, *An Illustrated History of Interior Decoration* [1964] (London, 1982), figs 189, 191, 192.

40 The literature on picture frames is now extensive. Especially helpful for our place and period are Jacob Simon, *The Art of the Picture Frame: Artists, Patrons and the Framing of Portraits in Britain*, exh. cat., National Portrait Gallery, London (1996), and the same authority's online dictionary of framemakers: www.npg.org.uk/research/conservation/directory-of-british-framemakers. See also Victoria Rosner, *Modernism and the Architecture of Private Life* (New York, 2005), chap. 2.

41 Charles Locke Eastlake, *Hints on Household Taste*, 2nd edn (London, 1869), p. 174.

42 Mogford, *Hand-Book*, p. 11.

43 Lewis Foreman Day, *Every-Day Art: Short Essays on the Arts Not Fine* (London, 1882), p. 242.

44 Catharine E. Beecher and Harriet Beecher Stowe, *The American Woman's Home* (New York, 1869), p. 98. Very similar advice appears in Philp, *Every-Day Book*, p. 275. Mrs C. S. Jones and Henry T. Williams, in their *Household Elegancies* (New York, 1876), p. 101, illustrate bindweed twined around an Oxford frame (one with its four members crossing at the

corners, especially popular for religious imagery from the 1870s: see illus. 76). For the larger history of plants indoors, see Penny Sparke, *Nature Inside: Plants and Flowers in the Modern Interior* (New Haven, CT, and London, 2021).

45 Shirley Hibberd, *Rustic Adornments for Homes of Taste*, new edn (London, 1870), p. 135.

46 Charles Heathcote Tatham, *The Gallery at Brocklesby, in Lincolnshire: The Seat of the Right Honourable Lord Yarborough* (London, 1811), and *The Gallery at Castle Howard, in Yorkshire: The Seat of the Earl of Carlisle, K.G.* (London, 1811). That there was some squeamishness about the visibility of picture poles is suggested by their omission from the early depiction of the Castle Howard gallery reproduced by John Cornforth, *English Interiors 1790–1848: The Quest for Comfort* (London, 1978), figs 26–7. Rods might be painted so as to minimize their presence, as in the Pall Mall house of the collector Robert Vernon: *Art-Union*, I (1839), p. 19.

47 It was claimed in the *Mirror of Literature* (20 March 1841, p. 187) that Potts's idea had been anticipated by the famous chef and inventor William Kitchiner, who used such a mechanism throughout his own Warren Street house.

48 Hermann Muthesius, *The English House* [2nd edn, 1908–11], trans. Janet Seligman (Oxford, 1987), pp. 201–2.

49 Caroline Powys, *Passages from the Diaries of Mrs. Philip Lybbe Powys*, ed. Emily J. Climenson (London, 1899), p. 172.

50 Sophie v. La Roche, *Sophie in London 1786*, trans. Clare Williams (London, 1933), p. 238.

51 John Feltham, *The Picture of London for 1802* (London, 1802), p. 226.

52 Charles Molloy Westmacott, *British Galleries of Painting and Sculpture* (London, 1824), pp. 230 ff. There is a watercolour view of the gallery by Robert Billings in the Metropolitan Museum in New York. Dwarf bookcases of this type were recommended for galleries by George Smith, *A Collection of Designs for Household Furniture and Interior Decoration* (London, 1808), p. 19.

53 John Soane, *Description of the House and Museum . . . The Residence of Sir John Soane* (London, 1835), pp. 15 ff.

54 George Redford, *Art Sales* (London, 1888), vol. I, p. 151; Dorothy Nevill, *Reminiscences* (London, 1906), p. 47. The collector and National Gallery benefactor Wynn Ellis had a similar set-up, according to William John Loftie, *A Plea for Art in the House* (London, 1876), p. 69, and indeed Mogford (*Hand-Book*, p. 14) implies the practice was not limited to a handful of eccentrics.

55 For two anecdotes of grandee picture-glass key-holders see Cyrus Redding, *Memoirs of William Beckford of Fonthill* (London, 1859), vol. II, p. 312, and Haydon, *Diary*, vol. IV, p. 643 (Duke of Wellington).

56 *Cassell's Household Guide* (London, 1869), vol. II, p. 128.

57 Alison Yarrington, 'Marble, Memory and Theatre: Portraiture and the Sculpture Gallery at Chatsworth', in *Placing Faces: The Portrait and the English Country House in the Long Eighteenth Century*, ed. Gill Perry, Kate Retford and Jordan Vibert (Manchester, 2013), p. 106; Haydon, *Diary*, vol. V, p. 406. Haydon created many versions of this pair of adversaries: one was in the dining room of Robert Peel's country seat, Drayon Manor (*Art-Union*, VIII [1846], p. 304).

58 Janis A. Tomlinson, 'Burn It, Hide It, Flaunt It: Goya's Majas and the Censorial Mind', *Art Journal*, L/4 (1991), pp. 59–64.

59 John Claudius Loudon, *An Encyclopaedia of Cottage, Farm, and Villa Architecture and Furniture* [1833], new edn (London, 1842), p. 911.

60 Ruskin, *Works*, vol. XIII, pp. 83–4, 180.

61 Quoted by Mcleod, *Art and the Victorian Middle Class*, p. 105.

62 John Hervey, *Memoirs of the Reign of George the Second* (London, 1848), vol. II, p. 33.

63 Jerome K. Jerome, *Three Men in a Boat* (Bristol, 1889), chap. 3.

64 Muthesius, *The English House*, p. 57; W. S. Rogers, 'Picture-Hanging', in *Every Woman's Encyclopaedia* (London, n.d. [1910–12]), vol. II, pp. 1181–5.

65 Isabella Beeton, *The Book of Household Management* (London, 1861), p. 990; Florence Caddy, *Household Organization* (London, 1877), p. 64; *Common Sense for Housemaids*, 2nd edn (London, 1853), p. 24.

66 Mogford, *Hand-Book*, p. 23; *Home Truths for Home Peace, or 'Muddle' Defeated* (London, 1852), p. 77.

67 Florence Nightingale, *Notes on Nursing* (Boston, 1860), p. 67. Another writer advised that pictures be covered in fabric before sweeping the room: Maria Parloa, *Home Economics* (New York, 1898), p. 339.

68 Shirley Forster Murphy, ed., *Our Homes, and How to Make Them Healthy* (London, 1883), p. 879.

69 R. Randal Phillips, *The Servantless House* (London, 1920), p. 30.

70 E. P. Hughes, 'Labour-Saving Contrivances', *Journal of the Royal Sanitary Institute*, XXXIV (1913–14), pp. 514–15. Regarding sanitation, several writers suggested that pictures might be used to cover ventilation flues.

71 The elder Eastlake, in his scholarly history of the materials of oil painting, had described the traditional benefits of sunlight but also its deleterious potential: Charles Lock Eastlake, *Materials for a History of Oil Painting* (London, 1869), vol. II, p. 76 n. For the current science see Joyce Townsend et al., 'The Yellowing / Bleaching Behaviour of Oil Paint.

Further Investigations into Significant Colour Change in Response to Dark Storage Followed by Light Exposure', *ICOM–CC, 16th Triennial Conference*, Lisbon, 19–23 September 2011, www.icom-cc-publications-online.org.

72 *Cassell's Household Guide*, vol. II, p. 52; cf. Mogford, *Hand-Book*, p. 60.

73 Thomas Webster and Frances Parkes, *An Encyclopaedia of Domestic Economy* (London, 1861), p. 221.

74 Charles Henry Savory, *The Practical Carver and Gilder's Guide*, 4th edn (London, n.d. [1876?]), pp. 108–9.

75 *Cassell's Household Guide*, vol. II, p. 128; 'Hanging and Framing Pictures', *Art Amateur*, VI/2 (January 1882), p. 39.

76 Henry Nevinson, *Neighbours of Ours: Slum Stories of London* (Bristol, 1895), p. 26.

77 Jonathan Crary, *Techniques of the Observer* (Cambridge, MA, 1992), p. 70.

78 The debates within psychology and aesthetics around the relation of the visual to the haptic are beyond me here, but good starting-points are the work of Robert Hopkins and Dominic Lopes. See also the papers given at the 2013 Birkbeck conference on 'The Victorian Tactile Imagination': https://19.bbk.ac.uk/issue/125/info.

79 See Eileen Cleere, *The Sanitary Arts: Aesthetic Culture and the Victorian Cleanliness Campaigns* (Columbus, OH, 2014).

80 *Report from the Select Committee on the British Museum* (London, 1860), p. 188.

81 Smith, *A Collection of Designs*, p. 12. The French tourist Louis Simond felt that a 'moveable balustrade' should be installed in front of the pictures in the galleries of great London houses when these were open to the public: *Journal of a Tour and Residence in Great Britain during the years 1810 and 1811* (Edinburgh, 1815), vol. I, p. 180.

82 Eamon Duffy, *The Stripping of the Altars: Traditional Religion in England c.1400–c.1580* (New Haven, CT, and London, 1992), p. 407.

83 See Susanna Avery-Quash, 'Sir Charles Eastlake and Conservation at the National Gallery, London', *Burlington Magazine*, CLVII (December 2015), pp. 846–54.

84 *Art Journal*, XIX (1857), p. 239; cf. Fiona Candlin, *Art, Museums and Touch* (Manchester, 2010), p. 62.

85 Candlin, *Art, Museums and Touch*, chap. 1.

86 Thomas De Quincey, *Confessions of an English Opium-Eater* [1821] (London, 2003), p. 13.

87 Haydon, *Diary*, vol. IV, p. 493.

88 Georgiana Burne-Jones, *Memorials of Edward Burne-Jones* (London, 1904), vol. I, p. 296.

89 Richard Jefferies, 'The Squire's "Round Robin"', in *Hodge and His Masters*, new edn (London, 1890), pp. 180–81.
90 Hilda Orchardson Gray, *The Life of Sir William Quiller Orchardson* (London, 1930), p. 278.
91 On art and smell in our period see, however, Christina Bradstreet, 'Scented Visions: The Nineteenth-Century Olfactory Imagination', PhD thesis, Birkbeck, University of London, 2008.
92 Horace Walpole lamented 'the Cant of the Virtuosi' in the mid-eighteenth century (*Ædes Walpolianæ: Or, A Description of the Collection of Pictures at Houghton-Hall in Norfolk*, 2nd edn [London, 1752], p. x), while Thomas Carlyle prided himself on being 'mute and deaf' on the subject of pictures, which he suggested improved his understanding of them: *Reminiscences*, ed. J. A. Froude (New York, 1881), p. 133. Etiquette books warned readers off art talk: 'When visiting picture galleries do not make criticisms or comments on the pictures to attract attention or display your knowledge,' says Julia M. Bradley, *Modern Manners and Social Forms* (Chicago, IL, 1889), p. 284.
93 Edmond and Jules de Goncourt, *Idées et sensations* (Paris, 1866), p. 96.
94 Eileen Cleere, 'Dirty Pictures: John Ruskin, Modern Painters, and the Victorian Sanitation of Fine Art', *Representations*, LXXVIII/1 (2002), p. 129.
95 Old Bailey Proceedings Online, www.oldbaileyonline: October 1717, trial of John Wood and John Murth, alias Mason; November 1907, trial of Henry Stapleton and George Hawkins.
96 Old Bailey Proceedings Online, www.oldbaileyonline: September 1906, trial of Henry Furnell; April 1908, trial of John Flint; October 1843, trial of Edward Thurgood (who was acquitted of other more serious crimes on account of insanity).
97 Hazlitt, *Criticisms on Art*, p. 78 (the quotation is from Wordsworth's 'Laodamia').
98 John Nichols, *Biographical Anecdotes of William Hogarth*, 3rd edn (London, 1785), pp. 450–51.
99 *General Evening Post* (20–21 October 1761), p. 4.
100 Varnish was, of course, also used on oil paintings, as a protective layer, but also to present a smooth finish bringing the surface into coherence with broader understandings of tactile beauty in decorative objects. So varnish on a picture – print or painting – acknowledged a suppressed haptic urge but also vicariously satisfied it: see Grant Allen, *Physiological Aesthetics* (New York, 1877), p. 94. Various writers gave recipes for home-made picture varnish – William Kitchiner's was designed to wash off easily to allow a proper clean of the picture surface when necessary: *The Cook's Oracle*, new edn (London, 1831), p. 396.

101 Greg Smith, 'Watercolourists and Watercolours at the Royal Academy, 1780–1836', in *Art on the Line*, ed. Solkin, pp. 194–5. Smith notes that when, in 1788, Thomas Hearne sent in to the Academy a watercolour landscape that he did not glaze but had varnished, it was treated as if it were an oil painting.
102 Hunt, *Correspondence*, vol. II, pp. 35–6 (1844).
103 Eastlake, *Hints on Household Taste*, p. 178.
104 See Lynn Roberts, 'The Framemaker James Wyatt: Turner, Millais & Grinling Gibbons' (2019), https://theframeblog.com.
105 It was in fact the narrator's grandmother in *Du côté de chez Swann* who expressed this preference for 'layers': see Thomas Baldwin, 'The Thickness of Art: Paintings and Photographs in Proust's *À la Recherche du Temps Perdu*', *Modern Language Review*, CVI/1 (2011), pp. 86–98. On Proust's rooms see Diana Fuss, *The Sense of an Interior: Four Writers and the Rooms that Shaped Them* (New York and London, 2004), pp. 182 ff.
106 Photograph in *Studio International*, LVII (1893), p. 202.
107 Francis Russell, 'The Hanging and Display of Pictures, 1700–1850', in *The Fashioning and Functioning of the British Country House*, ed. Gervase Jackson-Stops et al. (Washington, DC, 1989), p. 144.
108 Flora Thompson, *Lark Rise to Candleford* [1939] (London, 1973), p. 99.
109 Nikolaus Pevsner, *An Enquiry into Industrial Art in England* (Cambridge, 1937), p. 212.
110 Revd Samuel and Henrietta Barnett, *Practicable Socialism* (London, 1888), chap. 7. Picture galleries for the poor were controversially opened on Sundays to keep people from the pubs on their day off, although in Elizabeth Gaskell's *North and South* (London, 1855, vol. I, p. 211) a character suggests that one reason the poor went to pubs was 'to see things they never see at no other time – pictures, and looking-glass, and such like'.
111 T. C. Horsfall, *The Study of Beauty, and Art in Large Towns* (London, 1883), p. 32. It was on this principle of equivalence of response that Horsfall proposed to exclude nudes from the pictures he provided for the poor.
112 Emilie Barrington, *The Life, Letters and Work of Frederic Leighton* (London, 1906), vol. II, p. 277.
113 *British Architect* (21 November 1884), p. 246.
114 J. Beavington Atkinson, 'The Arts in the Household; or, Decorative Art Applied to Domestic Uses', *Blackwood's Edinburgh Magazine*, CV (1869), p. 376.
115 W. T. Stead, 'Put Up a Picture in Your Room', *Review of Reviews* (June 1900), p. 535.
116 Ibid.

117 George Acorn, *One of the Multitude* (London, 1911), p. 277; cf. Deborah Cohen, *Household Gods: The British and Their Possessions* (New Haven, CT, and London, 2006), p. 70 and fig. 60. Another similar enterprise was *The World's Greatest Pictures: The 'Daily Mail' Art Gallery of 100 Masterpieces Suitable for Framing* (London, 1902).

118 There are several other examples: for instance, in the novels of Somerset Maugham. Domestic advice columns explained how to frame up prints from magazines: for example, Carrie May Ashton, 'Pictures and Their Frames', *Decorator and Furnisher*, XVIII (1891), p. 65. Many companies ran schemes involving collecting coupons that could be exchanged for prints, of which cigarette cards are the best known: see T. T., 'Pictures on the Wall: The Working-Class Home', *Manchester Guardian* (12 April 1932), p. 6, and B.W.E. Alford, *W. D. and H. O. Wills and the Development of the UK Tobacco Industry, 1786–1965* [1973] (Abingdon, 2006), p. 345.

119 See, for example, George Gissing, *Our Friend the Charlatan* (London, 1901), p. 221. On Gissing in this context see Diana Maltz, *British Aestheticism and the Urban Working Classes, 1870–1900: Beauty for the People* (Basingstoke, 2006), chap. 6.

120 *Letters of George Gissing to Members of His Family* (London, 1926), p. 269; Maltz, *British Aestheticism*, p. 175; Mary Augusta Ward, *A Writer's Recollections* (London, 1918), pp. 123–4 (on Pater).

121 In France the print connoisseur Henri Béraldi described with witty irony the bourgeois taste for respectable imagery of torture, execution and suicide: see Pierre-Lin Renié, 'The Image on the Wall: Prints as Decoration in Nineteenth-Century Interiors', *Nineteenth-Century Art Worldwide*, V/2 (2006), www.19thc-artworldwide.org. In England, Mogford (*Hand-Book*, p. 17) was strict in saying such pictures had a place only in public galleries as evidence of the artists' skill, while in America the advice to remove anything of the 'death-bed-of-Washington style' was standard: for example, Almon C. Varney, *Our Homes and Their Adornments* (Detroit, MI, 1883), p. 299.

122 Gwen Raverat, *Period Piece: A Cambridge Childhood* [1952] (London, 1987), p. 194. The print can indeed be seen in many photographs of interiors of the last years of the century.

123 To hang a print of a Watts allegory was to declare a commitment to the cause of humanity – *Mammon*, for example, was adopted by Morris's Hammersmith Socialist Society, and D. H. Lawrence used the same image as an emblem of a radical home in *The White Peacock* (London, 1911, p. 444). There is a tradition of aesthetes, in search of formal values, finding Watts literally painful: for example, Horace Hutchinson, *Portraits of the Eighties* (New York, 1920), p. 222.

124 Fiona MacCarthy, *Anarchy & Beauty: William Morris and His Legacy, 1860–1960*, exh. cat., National Portrait Gallery, London (2014).
125 Arthur Warren, *London Days: A Book of Reminiscences* (Boston, MA, 1920), p. 112.
126 Sandra Gilbert and Susan Gubar, *The Madwoman in the Attic*, 2nd edn (New Haven, CT, and London, 2000), p. 559.
127 William Howitt, *Homes and Haunts of the Most Eminent British Poets*, 3rd edn (London, 1857), p. 425.
128 Warren, *London Days*, pp. 88–9.
129 'Art in the Shop-Windows', *Athenaeum* (4 February 1854), p. 155.
130 Mary Augusta Ward, *Lady Rose's Daughter* (London, 1903), p. 23.
131 Thomas Sheraton, *The Cabinet Dictionary* (London, 1803), p. 216. Beyond the realm of portraits on walls was the tradition of the 'grangerized' book of biographies into which portrait heads would be glued, a fashion that died away early in the nineteenth century: Marcia Pointon, *Hanging the Head: Portraiture and Social Formation in Eighteenth-Century England* (New Haven, CT, and London, 1993), pp. 56 ff.
132 Jack London, *The People of the Abyss* (London, 1903), p. 161.
133 Virginia Woolf, *Moments of Being* [1976] (London, 1989), p. 130.
134 Ibid., pp. 201, 212.
135 See Matthew Yde, *Bernard Shaw and Totalitarianism: Longing for Utopia* (New York, 2013).

2 The Picture and the Interior

1 M. H. Baillie Scott, *Houses and Gardens* (London, 1906), p. 70.
2 For a compelling study of the front room from a twentieth-century migrant perspective, see Michael McMillan, *The Front Room: Migrant Aesthetics in the Home* (London, 2009).
3 See Karen Halttunen, 'From Parlor to Living Room: Domestic Space, Interior Decoration, and the Culture of Personality', in *Consuming Visions: Accumulation and Display in America, 1880–1920*, ed. S. J. Bronner (New York, 1989), pp. 157–89.
4 Mass-Observation, *An Enquiry into People's Homes* (London, 1943), p. 104.
5 W. Somerset Maugham, *On a Chinese Screen* (London, 1922), p. 47. The original pictures were shown at the Royal Academy in 1888 and 1891 respectively. On *The Soul's Awakening* see Mary Clive, *The Day of Reckoning* (London, 1964), pp. 75–6. Harold Donaldson Eberlein et al. explicitly forbid 'the harrowingly sentimental of such pictures as "The Doctor"' in *The Practical Book of Interior Decoration* (Philadelphia, PA, and London, 1919), p. 351.

6 Old Bailey Proceedings Online, www.oldbaileyonline: January 1863, trial of George Buncher, William Burnett, Richard Brewer and James Griffiths.
7 George Gissing, *Demos: A Story of English Socialism* [1886] (London, 1908), p. 42.
8 George Gissing, *The Nether World* (London, 1889), p. 36.
9 Ibid., p. 97.
10 Diana Fuss, *The Sense of an Interior: Four Writers and the Rooms That Shaped Them* (New York and London, 2004), pp. 44, 67.
11 See Rachel Rich, 'Designing the Dinner Party: Advice on Dining and Décor in London and Paris, 1860–1914', *Journal of Design History*, XVI/1 (2003), pp. 49–61, and Jane Hamlett, 'The Dining Room Should be the Man's Paradise, as the Drawing Room is the Woman's', *Gender & History*, XXI/3 (2009), pp. 576–91.
12 Jacob von Falke, *Art in the House: Historical, Critical, and Aesthetical Studies on the Decoration and Furnishing of the Dwelling* [1871], trans. Charles C. Perkins (Boston, MA, 1879), p. 273.
13 H. J. Jennings, *Our Homes, and How to Beautify Them* (London, 1902), p. 149.
14 J. H. Elder-Duncan in *The House Beautiful and Useful* (New York, 1907), p. 152, suggests that the entire Victorian mode of decorating the dining room had been dependent on deferring to the paintings hung there. Now paintings were less common, the decorative conception of the room could move on too.
15 Arnold Bennett, *The Matador of the Five Towns and Other Stories* (New York, 1912), pp. 308–9. Bennett specifies that the chandelier had Welsbach lights, which gave a white tone to gaslight, which was otherwise assumed to be more yellow than daylight.
16 Juliet Kinchin, 'Interiors: Nineteenth-Century Essays on the "Masculine" and the "Feminine" Room', in *The Gendered Object*, ed. Pat Kirkham (Manchester, 1996), p. 17.
17 Eastlake, *Hints on Household Taste*, p. 181.
18 Mary Augusta Ward, *The Marriage of William Ashe* (Leipzig, 1905), vol. I, p. 59.
19 Samuel Rogers, *Recollections of the Table-Talk of Samuel Rogers* (New York, 1856), p. 287. The reference is to Matthew 25:30.
20 Thomas Smith, *Recollections of the British Institution* (London, 1860), p. 214; Michael Compton, 'The Architecture of Daylight', in *Palaces of Art*, ed. Waterfield, p. 42.
21 *Journal of the Society of Arts*, VII/349 (29 July 1859), p. 605. Enthusiasts for electric lighting often claimed that the costs of switching from gas were more than justified by the savings made through preventing

the damage caused by gas to pictures, books and other valuables: for example, Robert Hammond, *The Electric Light in Our Homes* (London, 1884), pp. 52, 148.

22 Andrew Saint, *Richard Norman Shaw*, revd edn (New Haven, CT, and London, 2010), p. 82; Oliver Garnett, '"Sold Christie's. Bought Agnew": The Art Collection of Lord Armstrong at Cragside', *Apollo*, CXXXVII/374 (April 1993), pp. 253–8.

23 Such individual lighting at least made less likely damage to a picture being caused by a candle taken up close to its surface to show off its details to guests; it was said that George IV dripped wax over a Mulready in his collection in this way: F. M. Redgrave, *Richard Redgrave, C.B., R.A.: A Memoir* (London, 1891), pp. 169–70.

24 Russell, 'The Hanging and Display of Pictures, 1700–1850', pp. 135, 146; Sanderson, *Graphice*, p. 19.

25 Henry Havard, *L'Art dans la maison: Grammaire de l'ameublement* (Paris, 1884), p. 379.

26 Von Falke, *Art in the House*, p. 271.

27 The objection to storytelling pictures generally was, of course, also made by aesthetes such as Wilde: for example, in his 1883 lecture to Royal Academy students reprinted in Oscar Wilde, *Art and Decoration* (London, 1920), p. 51.

28 Rhoda and Agnes Garrett, *Suggestions for House Decoration*, 2nd edn (London, 1877), p. 49. For similar complaints in America see Kenneth L. Ames, *Death in the Dining Room and Other Tales of Victorian Culture* (Philadelphia, PA, 1992), p. 44.

29 Edith Wharton and Ogden Codman, *The Decoration of Houses* (New York, 1897), p. 160.

30 *The Letters of Disraeli to Lady Chesterfield and Lady Bradford* (New York, 1929), vol. I, p. 309.

31 See Lori E. Rotskoff, 'Decorating the Dining-Room: Still-Life Chromolithographs and Domestic Ideology in Nineteenth-Century America', *Journal of American Studies*, XXXI/1 (1997), pp. 19–42.

32 Eastlake, *Hints on Household Taste*, p. 167.

33 Anna Jameson, *Companion to the Most Celebrated Private Galleries of Art in London* (London, 1844), pp. 329–30.

34 Sanderson, *Graphice*, pp. 26–7.

35 For a full account of the Garretts see Elizabeth Crawford, *Enterprising Women: The Garretts and Their Circle* (London, 2002).

36 Garrett and Garrett, *Suggestions for House Decoration*, pp. 43–4.

37 Mary Augusta Ward, *Daphne, or, 'Marriage à la mode'* (London, 1909), pp. 106–9, 197.

38 Henry James, *Portrait of a Lady* [1881] (New York, 1908), vol. I, p. 197.

39 Benjamin Disraeli, *Coningsby* (London, 1844), vol. II, p. 42.

40 On Vernon see *Art-Union*, I (1839), p. 19; on Brunel see Hilarie Faberman and Philip McEvansoneya, 'Isambard Kingdom Brunel's Shakespeare Room', *Burlington Magazine*, CXXXVII (February 1995), pp. 108–18.

41 *Art-Union*, IX (1847), p. 297.

42 William John Loftie, *A Plea for Art in the House* (London, 1876), p. 67.

43 Henry Mogford, *Hand-Book for the Preservation of Pictures*, 3rd edn (London, 1851), pp. 16–17.

44 The reformers too, of course, objected to the social climbing that this implied: for example, Halsey Ricardo, 'Of the Room and Furniture', in *Arts and Crafts Essays* (London, 1893), pp. 282–3.

45 Clive, *The Day of Reckoning*, p. 61.

46 Clarence Cook, *The House Beautiful: Essays on Beds and Tables, Stools and Candlesticks* (New York, 1878), p. 145.

47 Lewis Foreman Day, *Every-Day Art: Short Essays on the Arts Not Fine* (London, 1882), p. 232.

48 Jane Ellen Panton, *Nooks and Corners* (London, 1889), pp. 19, 62.

49 Eberlein et al., *Practical Book of Interior Decoration*, p. 362.

50 E. H. Gombrich, 'Pictures for the Home' [1977], in *The Uses of Images: Studies in the Social Function of Art and Visual Communication* (London, 1999), pp. 119–21.

51 To be sure, there have always been exceptions, pictures proposing spaces that only fully open when seen from below. Scholars have identified several seventeenth-century Dutch examples (John Loughman and John Michael Montias, *Public and Private Spaces: Works of Art in Seventeenth-Century Dutch Houses* [Zwolle, 2000], p. 116), and exhibition culture was believed to encourage the practice: see the case of Thomas Lawrence's *Hamlet* mentioned below.

52 Solkin, ed., *Art on the Line*, p. 3.

53 *Art-Union*, III (1841), pp. 43, 61–2, 88, 135.

54 John Cornforth, *Early Georgian Interiors* (New Haven, CT, and London, 2004), p. 239.

55 James Ayres, *Domestic Interiors: The British Tradition 1500–1850* (New Haven, CT, and London, 2003), pp. 57, 203.

56 See Clare Latimer, 'The Division of the Wall: The Use of Wallpapers in Decorative Schemes, 1870–1910', *Journal of the Decorative Arts Society*, XII (1988), pp. 18–25.

57 Eastlake, *Hints on Household Taste*, p. 168.

58 Paul N. Hasluck, *Mounting and Framing Pictures* (London, 1899), chap. 9, gives an account of how to construct a picture rail.
59 *Builder* (24 December 1898), p. 576.
60 Baseden Butt, 'A Perfect Home in a Victorian House', *Woman's Magazine Annual* (London, 1935), pp. 760–62.
61 Emily Genauer, *Modern Interiors: Today and Tomorrow* (New York, 1939), p. 140.
62 T. R. Spence, 'Wall-Papers and Stencilling', *Journal of the Society of Arts*, XLI/2102 (3 March 1893), p. 370; Lewis Foreman Day, 'Wall-Paper Decoration', *Magazine of Art*, XV (1892), pp. 189–90; and Day, *Every-Day Art*, p. 235. A writer in 1887 spoke of 'the band space where the pictures are hung': J. Moyr Smith, *Ornamental Interiors, Ancient and Modern* (London, 1887), p. 123.
63 Oliver Garnett, 'The Letters and Collection of William Graham – Pre-Raphaelite Patron and Pre-Raphael Collector', *Volume of the Walpole Society*, LXII (2000), pp. 216–18. Rossetti's *Loving Cup* can be seen displayed on an easel in an 1884 photograph of the picture gallery at Dawpool, the Merseyside house built by Norman Shaw for Thomas Henry Ismay (RIBA photo. 7376).
64 Thomas Sheraton, *The Cabinet Dictionary* (London, 1803), p. 216; Mogford, *Hand-Book*, pp. 18–19. Havard (*L'Art dans la maison*, p. 451) gives as one reason to adopt top-lighting in galleries that this would not, as it were, take sides against the left-to-right or right-to-left direction of light in the different pictures.
65 Two landscape watercolours by Dadd are inscribed with the instructions 'Light from the left' and '*Luce al sinistro*'.
66 For example, H. Hudson Holly, *Modern Dwellings in Town and Country* (New York, 1878), p. 160.
67 Eastlake in *The Country House*, ed. Fox, p. 63.
68 Burne-Jones objected to all strong colours as backgrounds to his pictures, and to crimson above all: Georgiana Burne-Jones, *Memorials of Edward Burne-Jones* (London, 1904), vol. II, pp. 77–8.
69 Ronald Gower, *Bric à brac* (London, 1888), p. 8; Moncure Daniel Conway, *Travels in South Kensington* (London, 1882), p. 193.
70 Robert W. Edis, *Decoration and Furniture of Town Houses* (New York, 1881), p. 171.
71 Smith, *Ornamental Interiors*, p. 57 (disapproving of the received wisdom); Mabel Tuke Priestman, *Artistic Homes* (Chicago, IL, 1910), p. 83. Jennings, *Our Homes*, pp. 106–7, thought modern papers inspired by Morris were so wonderful as to be 'pictures in themselves' on which it would be a sin to hang anything.

72 John Ruskin, *Samuel Prout and William Hunt*, exh. cat., Fine Art Society, London (1879), pp. 5–6.
73 Martin Hardie, *Water-Colour Painting in Britain*, vol. II: *The Romantic Period* (London, 1967), p. 207.
74 David Blayney Brown in *Watercolour*, ed. Alison Smith, exh. cat., Tate Britain, London (2011), p. 106.
75 George Eliot, *Middlemarch* [1871–2] (Edinburgh and London, 1891), pp. 287–8.
76 Lucy Crane, *Art and the Formation of Taste* (London, 1882), p. 91.
77 William Morris, *Hopes and Fears for Art* (London, 1882), p. 100.
78 Walter Crane, *The Claims of Decorative Art* (London, 1892), p. 149.
79 Charles H. Caffin, 'How to Buy Pictures', *House and Garden* (USA) (March 1918), p. 32.
80 Loudon, *An Encyclopaedia of Cottage, Farm, and Villa Architecture and Furniture*, p. 797.
81 Eastlake in *The Country House*, p. 61.
82 Sheraton, *Cabinet Dictionary*, p. 218.
83 Florence Hartley, *The Ladies' Book of Etiquette* (Boston, MA, 1860), pp. 82, 98.
84 *Etiquette for Gentlemen* (Philadelphia, PA, 1847), pp. 173–4.
85 Lydia E. White, *Success in Society* (Boston, MA, 1889), p. 172.
86 Christopher Dresser, *Principles of Decorative Design* (London, 1873), p. 82. Even a severe Modernist such as Adolf Loos felt that 'A cultivated man does not look out of the window' and incorporated this principle into his domestic architecture: Beatriz Colomina, 'Intimacy and Spectacle: The Interiors of Adolf Loos', *AA Files*, XX (1990), p. 5.
87 John Ruskin, *Praeterita* [1885–9] (London, 1907), vol. I, pp. 128–9.
88 Virginia Woolf, *A Haunted House and Other Short Stories* (London, 1943), p. 53.
89 Henry James, *The Sacred Fount* (New York, 1901), p. 26; James, *The Awkward Age* [1899] (London, 1922), p. 150. In James this idea of the picture as an interruption of verbal engagement extends to the erotic: in *Portrait of a Lady*, Isabel Archer pretends to look at a picture in order to show off her 'charming back' (vol. I, p. 185).
90 Mogford, *Hand-Book*, p. 10; Von Falke, *Art in the House*, p. 205.
91 Edis, *Decoration and Furniture of Town Houses*, p. 201.
92 Gladstone-Lingham, *The Science of Taste*, pp. 112–13.
93 Day, *Every-Day Art*, p. 237.
94 Shirley Nicholson, *A Victorian Household* (Stroud, 1994), p. 25.
95 Charlotte Gere, with Lesley Hoskins, *The House Beautiful: Oscar Wilde and the Aesthetic Interior* (Aldershot, 2000), p. 99; Victoria Rosner,

Modernism and the Architecture of Private Life (New York, 2005), figs 5 and 6.

96 Oscar Wilde, *Reviews*, vol. 2 (Toronto, 1909), p. 328.

97 Harriet Beecher Stowe, *House and Home Papers* (Boston, MA, 1865), p. 92.

98 'Art in the House', *New York Times* (9 February 1879), p. 6.

99 Peter C. Marzio, *The Democratic Art: Chromolithography, 1840–1900. Pictures for a Nineteenth-Century America* (London, 1980), p. 207.

100 Harriet Beecher Stowe, 'What Pictures Shall I Hang on My Walls?', *Atlantic Almanac* (Boston, MA, 1869), pp. 41–4.

101 *Prang's Chromo: A Journal of Popular Art*, 1/4 (Christmas 1868), p. 6; Catharine E. Beecher and Harriet Beecher Stowe, *The American Woman's Home* (New York, 1869), p. 91.

102 Photograph by Emery Walker of the library at Kelmscott House in London (William Morris Gallery, P753).

103 David Ramsay Hay, *The Laws of Harmonious Colouring*, 3rd edn (Edinburgh, 1836), pp. 56–7.

104 Edward S. Prior, 'Furniture and the Room', in *Arts and Crafts Essays* (London, 1893), pp. 265–6.

105 Day, *Every-Day Art*, p. 221.

106 Walter Benjamin, 'Paris, Capital of the Nineteenth Century' and 'The Interior: The Trace', both in *The Arcades Project* (Cambridge, MA, 1999), pp. 3–26, 212–27.

107 For a typical example see Samuel Butler, *The Way of All Flesh* [1903] (London, 1947), pp. 110–11.

108 In Arnold Bennett's 1908 novel *The Old Wives' Tale* one of the main characters struggles to understand her artist son, who has only a single Japanese print on the walls of his studio-bedroom: this strikes her as 'entirely preposterous, considered as a picture' (New York, 1912, p. 269).

109 Day, *Every-Day Art*, p. 225.

110 Ibid., p. 221.

111 Mary Eliza Haweis, *The Art of Decoration* (London, 1881), pp. 379, 10. Haweis was the daughter of a picture artist and moved with her family into the painter Dante Gabriel Rossetti's former house in Chelsea after his death in 1882. She had herself exhibited at the Royal Academy, in 1866, as Miss M. E. Joy. On Haweis see Bea Howe, *Arbiter of Elegance* (London, 1967); Deborah Cohen, *Household Gods: The British and Their Possessions* (New Haven, CT, and London, 2006), chap. 3; and Judith A., Neiswander, *The Cosmopolitan Interior: Liberalism and the British Home, 1870–1914* (New Haven, CT, and London, 2008), pp. 102–7.

112 J. Beavington Atkinson, 'The Arts in the Household; or, Decorative Art Applied to Domestic Uses', *Blackwood's Edinburgh Magazine*, CV (1869),

p. 378. This passage is quoted approvingly by Edis, 'Internal Decoration', in *Our Homes, and How to Make Them Healthy*, ed. Forster Murphy, p. 344.

113 *Modern British Domestic Architecture and Decoration* [special summer number of *Studio*] (London, 1901), p. 28. Holme was the editor of this volume; presumably he was also the author of this otherwise unattributed contribution.

114 Richard Norman Shaw, 'The Home and Its Dwelling Rooms', in *The British Home of To-Day*, ed. W. Shaw Sparrow (London, 1904), p. cv.

115 Barry Parker and Raymond Unwin, *The Art of Building a Home* (London, 1901), pp. 72–3.

116 Muthesius, *The English House*, p. 51.

117 Scott, *Houses and Gardens*, p. 70.

118 S. E., 'The Modern House and the Modern Picture', *Burlington Magazine*, x (February 1907), pp. 293–6.

119 Arthur Clutton-Brock, 'The Modern House and the Modern Picture – A Reply', *Burlington Magazine*, xi (April 1907), pp. 13–16. A decade earlier another writer had complained that Impressionism was unique among painterly styles in being impossible to correlate with any kind of interior design: Rosamund Marriott Watson, *The Art of the House* (London, 1897), p. 60.

120 Crawford, *Enterprising Women*, p. 194; Neiswander, *The Cosmopolitan Interior*, p. 134.

121 Compare the illustration on p. 133 of Cook, *The House Beautiful*, and Lucy Orrinsmith, *The Drawing-Room* (London, 1878), p. 19.

122 Edmund Gosse, 'The Place of Sculpture in Daily Life. ii. – Sculpture in the House', *Magazine of Art*, xviii (1895), pp. 368–72.

123 Gere, *The House Beautiful*, p. 15.

124 Edmund Gosse, *Father and Son* [1907] (New York, 1916), p. 257; Garnett, 'The Letters and Collection of William Graham', p. 218.

125 E. Beresford Chancellor, *The Private Palaces of London* (London, 1908), p. 130.

126 Elizabeth Eastlake, *Journals and Correspondence* (London, 1895), vol. i, p. 155.

127 Edward S. Morse, *Japanese Homes and Their Surroundings* (Boston, MA, 1886), pp. 314–15.

128 Muthesius, *The English House*, pp. 201, 219.

129 Le Corbusier, *Towards a New Architecture* [1923], trans. Frederick Etchells (London, 1931), p. 120.

130 Tim Benton, 'La maison La Roche et les ateliers d'artistes de Le Corbusier', in *Le Corbusier mise au point*, ed. Jorge Torres Cueco

(Valencia, 2012), pp. 8–33. The episode uncannily realized a satire written by the young Loos in 1900 about a foolish client who allowed a domineering architect to design a home too perfect for him to live in and into which he was forbidden to introduce any pictures: translated in August Sarnitz, *Adolf Loos, 1870–1933: Architect, Cultural Critic, Dandy* (Cologne, 2003), pp. 18–21.

131 D. H. Lawrence, 'Pictures on the Wall' [first published as 'Dead Pictures on the Wall' in *Vanity Fair*, December 1929], in *Assorted Articles* (London, 1930), pp. 175–89.

132 Virginia Woolf, *Three Guineas* (New York, 1938), p. 49.

133 See, for example, Paul Nash, 'The Artist in the House' [*Listener*, 16 March 1932], in *Paul Nash: Writings on Art*, ed. Andrew Causey (Oxford, 2000), pp. 72–3.

134 Andrew Stephenson, '"Telling Decoratively": Ben Nicholson's "White Reliefs" and Debates around Abstraction and Modernism in the Home in the Late 1920s and 1930s', *Visual Culture in Britain*, IX/2 (2008), pp. 43–60.

135 As an example of the latter, see 'Pictures in the Home', *Fine Arts Journal* (USA), XXXV/1 (1917), pp. 72–4.

136 Osbert Sitwell, *Laughter in the Next Room* (London, 1949), p. 57.

137 See Christopher Reed, 'Taking Amusement Seriously: Modern Design in the Twenties', in *Designing the Modern Interior*, ed. Penny Sparke et al. (Oxford, 2009), pp. 79–94.

3 Picture Galleries of the Memory

1 From Stendhal's autobiography written in the 1830s: *Vie de Henri Brulard* (Paris, 1913), vol. II, p. 181.

2 See the recent cultural history of the corridor by Roger Luckhurst, *Corridors: Passages of Modernity* (London, 2019).

3 *The Illustrated Manners Book* (New York, 1855), p. 121.

4 Richard Colt Hoare, *Catalogue of the Paintings and Drawings at Stourhead* (London, 1840), p. 29.

5 Eastlake in *The Country House*, ed. Fox, p. 59.

6 Virginia Woolf, *Diary*, vol. I (1915–19), ed. Anne O. Bell (London, 1977), p. 245 (entry for 25 February 1919).

7 Katharine Tynan, *Twenty-Five Years: Reminiscences* (London, 1913), p. 107.

8 Candace Wheeler, *Principles of Home Decoration* (New York, 1903), p. 194.

9 *Cassell's Household Guide* (London, 1869), vol. I, p. 125.

10 Wharton and Codman, *The Decoration of Houses*, p. 120.

11 Stefan Muthesius, *The Poetic Home: Designing the Nineteenth-Century Domestic Interior* (London, 2009), pp. 181 ff.
12 Havard, *L'Art dans la maison*, p. 296.
13 See Junichiro Tanizaki, *In Praise of Shadows* [1933] (London, 2001).
14 On the autotype and its relatives such as the photogravure and collotype see Helene E. Roberts, ed., *Art History through the Camera's Lens* (Abingdon, 1995); Anthony Hamber, *'A Higher Branch of the Art': Photographing the Fine Arts in England, 1839–1880* (Amsterdam, 1996); and Gerry Beegan, *The Mass Image: A Social History of Photomechanical Reproduction in Victorian London* (London, 2008).
15 The company published its own account of its technical processes by the Director of the Autotype Works: J. R. Sawyer, *The 'A.B.C.' Guide to the Making of Autotype Prints in Permanent Pigments* (London, 1887).
16 Within the fine art world, the *Art Journal* was an early admirer of the autotype: see, for example, 'Autotype and Its Relation to Art', *Art Journal*, v (1879), p. 208. The critic P. G. Hamerton spelt out the reasons to prefer an autotype to a chromo in his survey of *The Graphic Arts* (London, 1882), p. 375.
17 George Gissing, *In the Year of Jubilee* (London, 1894), p. 2.
18 Jane Ellen Panton, *Nooks and Corners* (London, 1889), p. 93.
19 Jane Ellen Panton, *A Gentlewoman's Home* (London, 1896), pp. 107, 262, 298, 423.
20 Rosalys Coope, 'The "Long Gallery": Its Origins, Development, Use and Decoration', *Architectural History*, xxix (1986), pp. 43–84.
21 Quoted in Sarah Hyde, 'Printmakers and the Royal Academy Exhibitions, 1780–1836', in *Art on the Line*, ed. Solkin, p. 219 (1795).
22 J. H. Elder-Duncan, *The House Beautiful and Useful* (New York, 1907), p. 23.
23 Christopher Whitehead, *The Public Art Museum in Nineteenth-Century Britain: The Development of the National Gallery* (Aldershot, 2005), p. 59.
24 Loudon, *An Encyclopaedia of Cottage, Farm, and Villa Architecture and Furniture*, p. 795.
25 Robert Kerr, *The Gentleman's House*, 2nd edn (London, 1865), p. 451.
26 Ibid., p. 190 and plan facing page 452; Mark Girouard, *The Victorian Country House* (New Haven, CT, and London, 1979), p. 271.
27 Kerr, *The Gentleman's House*, pp. 58–9 and plate xix. For the architecture of picture galleries, both public and private, around 1850 see John W. Papworth and Wyatt Papworth, *Museums, Libraries, and Picture Galleries, Public and Private* (London, 1853).
28 Gustav Waagen, *Works of Art and Artists in England* (London, 1838), vol. i, p. 182.

29 Charles Lock Eastlake, *Contributions to the Literature of the Fine Arts*, 2nd series (London, 1870), pp. 173–4.

30 Raverat, *Period Piece*, p. 116.

31 Mary Seton Watts, *George Frederic Watts: The Annals of an Artist's Life* (London, 1912), vol. II, p. 230. In the early days of the National Gallery some, including Lord Liverpool, had encouraged the admission of small children, but primarily so as not to exclude poorer parents.

32 See Mark Ledbury, 'Art versus Life: A Dissenting Voice in the Grande Galerie', *Journal18*, 11 (Fall 2016), www.journal18.org/866.

33 Sanderson, *Graphice*, p. 27.

34 Celia Fiennes, *Through England on a Side Saddle in the Time of William and Mary* (London, 1888), p. 123.

35 [Joseph Addison and Richard Steele], *The Sir Roger de Coverley Papers from 'The Spectator'* (New York, 1900), p. 44.

36 Horace Walpole, *A Description of the Villa of Mr. Horace Walpole* (privately printed, 1784), pp. ii–iii. On the complex fluidity of family identities as expressed through portrait collections in the eighteenth century, see Kate Retford, *The Art of Domestic Life: Portraiture in Eighteenth-Century England* (New Haven, CT, and London, 2006).

37 Dorothy Nevill, *Reminiscences* (London, 1906), p. 10.

38 James, *Portrait of a Lady*, vol. I, pp. 188–9.

39 As recommended by the architect and geologist Thomas Webster in his eminently practical *Encyclopaedia of Domestic Economy* (with Frances Parkes, London, 1861, p. 259). He continues: 'Since it is almost impossible to find good situations for many pictures in a moderately-sized house, the best mode is to place them in a gallery built for the purpose.'

40 *Art-Union*, III (1841), p. 62.

41 Henry Treffry Dunn, *Recollections of Dante Gabriel Rossetti and His Circle* (London, 1904), p. 64; Nicholas Tromans, *The Art of G. F. Watts* (London, 2017), p. 67.

42 George Moore, 'Art for the Villa', *Magazine of Art*, XII (July 1889), pp. 296–300.

43 As early as the 1870s Burne-Jones had playfully declared that 'no private person ought to own pictures': *Burne-Jones Talking: His Conversations, 1895–98*, ed. Mary Lago (London, 1982), p. 29.

44 See Marguerite A. Tassi, *The Scandal of Images: Iconoclasm, Eroticism, and Painting in Early Modern English Drama* (Cranbury, NJ, 2005), and Emanuel Stelzer, *Portraits in Early Modern English Drama* (London, 2019). One important role of portraits of women on stage was to mitigate the absence of female actors from the Early Modern theatre.

45 *The Journal of Beatrix Potter, 1881–1897* (London, 1989), p. 174.
46 On the 'surplus value of images' see W.J.T. Mitchell, *What Do Pictures Want? The Lives and Loves of Images* (Chicago, IL, 2005), chap. 4.
47 Clare Haynes, *Pictures and Popery: Art and Religion in England, 1660–1760* (Aldershot, 2006), pp. 74 ff.
48 Horace Walpole, *The Castle of Otranto* [1764] (London, 1886), pp. 8–9.
49 For analysis of this episode and its literary repercussions, see Jakub Lipski, *Painting the Novel: Pictorial Discourse in Eighteenth-Century English Fiction* (New York, 2018), chap. 3.
50 Diana E. Bellonby emphasizes the use of the portrait to suggest the violence inherent in the romantic legend of the unfettered male artistic genius: 'A Secret History of Aestheticism: Magic-Portrait Fiction, 1829–1929', PhD thesis, Vanderbilt University, Nashville, TN, 2012. A classic example would be Poe's 'The Oval Portrait' (1842), which tells of an artist who kills his young bride through his selfish determination to paint her: 'he was a passionate, and wild, and moody man, who became lost in reveries; so that he *would* not see that the light which fell so ghastlily in that lone turret withered the health and the spirits of his bride, who pined visibly to all but him.' See also Kerry Powell, 'Tom, Dick, and Dorian Gray: Magic-Picture Mania in Late Victorian Fiction', *Philological Quarterly*, LXII/2 (Spring 1983), pp. 147–70.
51 But on the cruder rhetoric of some popular literature, see Diane Long Hoeveler, *The Gothic Ideology: Religious Hysteria and Anti-Catholicism in British Popular Fiction, 1780–1880* (Cardiff, 2014).
52 John Henry Newman, *Remarks on Certain Passages in the Thirty-Nine Articles* [*Tracts for the Times* no. 90] (London, 1841), pp. 23 ff. Edward Pusey reasserted the charges against Roman picture-superstition while defending Newman's general argument in *The Articles Treated on in Tract 90 Reconsidered and Their Interpretation Vindicated* (Oxford, 1841), pp. 160 ff.
53 Mcleod, *Art and the Victorian Middle Class*, p. 282.
54 Katharine Tynan, 'The Picture on the Wall', *English Illustrated Magazine*, CXLVII (December 1895), pp. 297–304. Lee's 'Oke of Okehurst' is collected in *Hauntings: Fantastic Stories* (New York, 1890).
55 Jasper Hopkins, *Nicholas of Cusa's Dialectical Mysticism* (Minneapolis, MN, 1988), pp. 680–81; cf. David Freedberg, *The Power of Images: Studies in the History and Theory of Response* [1989] (Chicago, IL, and London, 1991), pp. 52, 202.
56 Charles Maturin, *Melmoth the Wanderer* (Edinburgh, 1820), vol. I, p. 35.
57 Walter Scott, 'Introduction' to Horace Walpole, *The Castle of Otranto* [1764] (Edinburgh, 1811), p. xxix.

58 See G. D. Schott, 'Gombrich and "Pictures That Follow with Their Eyes"', *Journal of Art Historiography*, XIX (2018), pp. 1–11.

59 Neil Arnott, *Elements of Physics* (London, 1865), vol. I, p. 551 (the first edition of this standard work appeared as early as 1827). 'The Shadow of a Shade' (1869) is collected in *The Oxford Book of Victorian Ghost Stories*, ed. Michael Cox and R. A. Gilbert (Oxford, 1991).

60 Mezzotint is a form of tonal copperplate printmaking in which the creator works from dark to light, polishing highlights into a roughened plate, allowing richly atmospheric effects. For the baroque-period theorist Gerard de Lairesse it was 'the Black Art': *The Art of Painting* [1707], trans. J. F. Fritsch (London, 1738), p. 651. It was the technique used, for example, to create the image notorious during the first half of the nineteenth century as the *Miraculous Entombment* (after Leonello Spada), in which Christ's body, laid out feet-first towards the viewer, allegedly appeared to move as one walked past it: *New Monthly Magazine*, IV (1816), p. 535.

61 A precedent to this process was recorded by William Blake. He placed his delicate tempera of the *Canterbury Pilgrims* over a door in his sitting room, ignoring it until a rival, Stothard, produced his own version. On taking down his picture, Blake 'found it nearly effaced: the result of some malignant spell of Stothard's, he would, in telling the story, assure his friends': Alexander Gilchrist, *The Life of William Blake* [1863] (London, 1907), p. 246.

62 George Eliot, *The Mill on the Floss* (Edinburgh and London, 1860), vol. I, pp. 50–51.

63 Samuel Butler, *The Way of All Flesh* [1903] (London, 1947), p. 164.

64 Henry James, *A Small Boy and Others* (New York, 1913), p. 314.

65 Vernon Lee, *Belcaro, Being Essays on Sundry Aesthetical Questions* (London, 1883), p. 21.

66 Mayhew, *London Labour and the London Poor*, vol. I, p. 303.

67 John Evelyn, *Sculptura* [1662] (Oxford, 1906), p. 138.

68 De Lairesse, *Art of Painting*, p. 395.

69 Walter Shaw Sparrow, *The English House* (London, 1908), p. 313.

70 Jane Hamlett, *At Home in the Institution: Material Life in Asylums, Lodging Houses and Schools in Victorian and Edwardian England* (Basingstoke, 2014), p. 151.

71 Mary Anne Barker, *The Bedroom and Boudoir* (London, 1878), p. 13.

72 Jane Ellen Panton, *Suburban Residences and How to Circumvent Them* (London, 1896), pp. 206–7.

73 Jane Ellen Panton, *From Kitchen to Garret: Hints for Young Householders* (London, 1888), p. 193.

74 Clive, *The Day of Reckoning*, pp. 7–9.

75 Ibid., p. 41; Estella Canziani, *Round about Three Palace Green* (London, 1939), pp. 204–5.
76 Parker and Unwin, *The Art of Building a Home*, pp. v–vi.
77 Cook, *The House Beautiful*, p. 87.
78 Some grand eighteenth-century houses boasted 'print rooms' with wall decoration made up of pasted engravings: see Anna Frances O'Regan, 'Collection, Display, and Conservation: The Print Room at Castletown House', in *Women and the Art and Science of Collecting in Eighteenth-Century Europe*, ed. Arlene Leis and Kacie L. Wills (New York and Abingdon, 2021), chap. 13.
79 Panton, *Nooks and Corners*, p. 100.
80 Frank Kendon, *The Small Years* [1930] (Cambridge, 1950), pp. 56, 69–70.
81 Lee, *Belcaro*, p. 22.
82 John Ruskin, *Praeterita* [1885–9] (London, 1907), vol. I, pp. 41–2.
83 Osbert Sitwell, *Left Hand, Right Hand!* (London, 1945), pp. 184–5.
84 William John Loftie, *A Plea for Art in the House* (London, 1876), pp. 13, 47.
85 Historic England archives, photograph BL19630.
86 C.R.W. Nevinson, *Paint and Prejudice* (New York, 1938), pp. 121–2.
87 Marcel Proust, 'Sur la lecture', preface to John Ruskin, *Sésame et les Lys*, trans. Proust (Paris, 1906).
88 Ibid., pp. 17–18.
89 Marcel Proust, *In the Shadow of Young Girls in Flower* [1919], trans. James Grieve (London, 2003), pp. 223–4.
90 Marcel Proust, *Sodom and Gomorrah* [1921–2], trans. John Sturrock (London, 2003), pp. 303, 385.
91 Marcel Proust, *Letters*, trans. Mina Curtiss (New York, 1949), p. 161 (1906).
92 Revd F. A. Malleson, 'The Picture Galleries of the Memory', *Leisure Hour* (October 1895), p. 761.
93 Panton, *From Kitchen to Garret*, p. 179.
94 Roger de Piles, *The Art of Painting* (London, 1754), p. 54; Jonathan Richardson, *Two Discourses* (London, 1719), p. 191.
95 From Van Eck, *Art, Agency and Living Presence*, p. 73.
96 William Powell Frith, *My Autobiography and Reminiscences* (London, 1887–8), vol. I, p. 323. The painter Frith was the father of Mrs Panton.
97 On Hazlitt's mental pictures see Laurie Kane Lew, 'Collection and Recollection: William Hazlitt and the Poetics of Memory', *Studies in Romanticism*, XXXVI/3 (1997), pp. 349–89, and Luisa Calè, '"A Gallery in the Mind"? William Hazlitt, Edmund Spenser and the Old Masters', *Tate Papers*, XXIV (Autumn 2015), www.tate.org.uk/research/publications/tate-papers/24.

98 'On Means and Ends' (1827), in William Hazlitt, *Winterslow: Essays and Characters Written There* (London, 1850), pp. 153–5.

99 Stendhal, *Vie de Henri Brulard*, vol. II, p. 181.

100 Postscript to 'Air War and Literature', in W. G. Sebald, *On the Natural History of Destruction* [1999] (New York, 2004), pp. 73–4.

101 Elsie de Wolfe, *The House in Good Taste* (New York, 1913), p. 209. This famous book was in fact ghostwritten by Ruby Ross Wood.

102 Barker, *Bedroom and Boudoir*, p. 90. Barker's illustration was one of several examples of engravings from Clarence Cook's *The House Beautiful* (1878) being borrowed to illustrate volumes in Macmillan's *Art at Home* series: see Emma Ferry, '"The Other Miss Faulkner": Lucy Orrinsmith and the *Art at Home* Series', *Journal of William Morris Studies*, XIX/2 (2011), pp. 47–64, and the same author's '"Any Lady Can Do This Without Much Trouble . . .": Class and Gender in *The Dining Room* (1878)', *Interiors*, V/2 (2014), pp. 141–59.

103 Panton, *Nooks and Corners*, pp. 119–20.

104 Havard, *L'Art dans la maison*, pp. 418, 411, 416, 417.

105 Barker, *Bedroom and Boudoir*, pp. 83–4.

106 For example in Butler, *The Way of All Flesh*, p. 84.

107 Philip Dormer Stanhope, Earl of Chesterfield, *Letters* (London, 1845), vol. III, pp. 286–7. Pastels were more commonly associated at this time with women's dressing rooms, according to Ruth Kenny in *Placing Faces: The Portrait and the English Country House in the Long Eighteenth Century*, ed. Gill Perry, Kate Retford and Jordan Vibert (Manchester, 2013), pp. 144, 149.

108 However erotic a picture on a wall might be, its immediate temptation to sin was modest compared with the risks of people examining together prints in a portfolio, which required putting their heads close (hence 'come up and see my etchings'). In *Jane Eyre*, when Mr Rochester asks to see Jane's drawings, he directs her to pass them to him one at a time and not to press her face up to his.

109 *The Private Letter-Books of Sir Walter Scott: Selections from the Abbotsford Manuscripts*, ed. Wilfred Partington (London, 1930), p. 32.

110 Freedberg, *Power of Images*, p. 410.

111 Eliot, *Middlemarch*, pp. 51–2.

112 Frederick Goodall, *Reminiscences* (London, 1902), p. 387. The subject was clearly chosen with a show of knowing humour, as when, in *Psycho*, Hitchcock has Anthony Perkins spy on Janet Leigh through a hole hidden by a reproduction of a painting of the same story: see Katrina Powers, 'Marion, Venus, and Susanna in the Mirror: The Paintings in the Parlor of The Bates Motel', *Americana: The Journal of American Popular Culture*, XV/2 (2016), https://americanpopularculture.com/journal.

113 P. G. Hamerton, *Portfolio Papers* (London, 1889), p. 98.
114 Oliver Garnett, 'The Letters and Collection of William Graham – Pre-Raphaelite Patron and Pre-Raphael Collector', *Volume of the Walpole Society*, LXII (2000), p. 161.
115 Alison Smith, *The Victorian Nude* (Manchester, 1996), p. 69 (1862).
116 Ibid., p. 39.
117 Moncure Daniel Conway, *Travels in South Kensington* (London, 1882), pp. 188–9; *Illustrated Police Budget* (4 May 1895).
118 For an early nineteenth-century letter describing erotic pictures in a man's guest bedroom, see James Hamilton, *A Strange Business: Making Art and Money in Nineteenth-Century Britain* (London, 2014), pp. 298–9.
119 On Albert and the nude see Smith, *Victorian Nude*, pp. 60, 71–3.
120 James Joyce, *Ulysses* (Paris, 1922), pp. 509 ff.
121 Virginia Woolf, *To the Lighthouse* [1927] (London, 1930), p. 320.
122 Hazlitt, *Criticisms on Art*, p. 221.
123 'On the Pleasure of Painting', in William Hazlitt, *Table-Talk* (London, 1821–2), vol. I, p. 32.
124 Walter Benjamin, 'The Work of Art in the Age of Mechanical Reproduction' [1936], in *One-Way Street and Other Writings*, p. 237.
125 Henri Lefebvre, *The Production of Space* [1974], trans. Donald Nicholson-Smith (Oxford, 1991), p. 254.
126 Eastlake, *Hints on Household Taste*, p. 186.
127 Susan N. Carter in *Household Art*, ed. Candace Wheeler (New York, 1893), p. 80.
128 Julia Stephen, *Notes from Sick Rooms* (London, 1883), p. 32.
129 Caddy, *Household Organization*, p. 164.
130 Panton, *Nooks and Corners*, p. 212.
131 Harriet Martineau, *Life in the Sick-Room: Essays*, 2nd edn (London, 1844), p. 158. Patrick Noon writes that Scheffer's composition 'competed with Holman Hunt's *Light of the World* (1853–4) as the Protestant image most coveted throughout the Western world during the middle decades of the nineteenth century': 'A Reduced Version of Ary Scheffer's *Christ Consolator*', *Nineteenth-Century Art Worldwide*, VIII/2 (Autumn 2009), www.19thc-artworldwide.org/autumn09.
132 E. Beresford Chancellor, *Memorials of St James's Street* (New York, 1922), p. 111. Raphael's deathbed was illustrated by Stothard in the 1830 edition of *Italy* (p. 144).
133 Mackenzie Bell, *Christina Rossetti* (London, 1898), p. 175.
134 Samuel Rogers, *Recollections of the Table-Talk of Samuel Rogers* (New York, 1856), p. 276; Ethel Smyth, *Streaks of Life* (London, 1921), p. 10.
135 John Galsworthy, *The Forsyte Saga* (London, 1922), p. 872.

136 Van Eck, *Art, Agency and Living Presence*, p. 59; Van Kessel, *The Lives of Paintings*, p. 176.
137 John Galsworthy, *A Modern Comedy* [1923] (London, 1958), pp. 715 ff.; Virginia Woolf, *A Room of One's Own* (London, 1935), p. 154.
138 Jeremy Allen, 'Swan Songs: Baxter Dury Interviewed', https://thequietus.com (2014).
139 W. G. Sebald, *The Rings of Saturn* [1995], trans. Michael Hulse (London, 2002), p. 296. It has recently been proposed that Sebald took the idea of a picture in mourning instead from the last line of a 1993 book by the Polish writer Zbigniew Herbert: Terry Pitts, 'So that the Soul Would Not Be Distracted', https://sebald.wordpress.com (29 April 2020).
140 See Nigel Llewellyn, *The Art of Death: Visual Culture in the English Death Ritual c.1500–c.1800* (London, 1991), p. 90.
141 Fiennes, *Through England on a Side Saddle*, p. 67.
142 Jean-Paul Sartre, *Les Mots* (Paris, 1964), p. 11.
143 Jeanette Winterson, preface to *Eileen Cooper: Showing Off*, exh. cat., Art First, London (2011), n.p.
144 Astra Cielo (pseud. of Milton Goldsmith), *Signs, Omens and Superstitions* (New York, 1918), p. 136; Jane Portal, *Art under Control in North Korea* (London, 2005), p. 87.
145 David Clarke, 'The Curse of the Crying Boy', *Fortean Times*, no. 234 (2008), pp. 32–8: Clarke traces the legend to the *Sun* newspaper.
146 Primo Levi, *The Periodic Table* [1975] (London, 2000), p. 156.
147 Victoria Rosner, *Modernism and the Architecture of Private Life* (New York, 2005), p. 184 n. 60; Nicholas Frankel in Oscar Wilde, *The Picture of Dorian Gray: An Annotated, Uncensored Edition* (Cambridge, MA, 2011), p. 252.
148 Maturin, *Melmoth the Wanderer*, vol. I, p. 146.
149 The monarchs of Spain in the eighteenth century had threatened to destroy erotic works in the royal collection, a notion often referenced later: Tomlinson, 'Burn It, Hide It, Flaunt It', pp. 59–64. Ruskin famously suggested he had made a bonfire of Turner's explicit drawings: for further comparable threats see his *Works*, vol. XV, p. 226, and Ruth Bernard Yeazell, *Art of the Everyday: Dutch Painting and the Realist Novel* (Princeton, NJ, 2008), p. 24. Somerset Maugham, in his novel *Of Human Bondage* (1915), imagines a group of young artists in Paris around 1900 fantasizing about making a fire of all the works of the great Victorians, including Ruskin and Watts. Most such conflagrations were surely restricted to the imaginary, as must have been the Quaker who, according to Heinrich Heine, sacrificed his entire fortune 'in buying up and burning Giulio Romano's most beautiful mythological paintings':

The Romantic School [1833], trans. S. L. Fleishman (New York, 1882), p. 54.

150 Estelle May Hurll, 'Selecting Pictures for the Home', *Decorator and Furnisher*, XXIII/4 (January 1894), p. 133; Thomas Hardy, *Selected Poems* (Harmondsworth, 1978), pp. 164–5.

151 Walpole, *Anecdotes of Painting in England*, pp. 323–4.

152 The makeshift curtains were made up from the paintings of the seventeenth-century poet Samuel Butler when a youthful amateur artist: William Howitt, *Homes and Haunts of the Most Eminent British Poets*, 3rd edn (London, 1857), p. 70; the waistcoat belonged to the eighteenth-century artist John Astley: James Northcote, *The Life of Sir Joshua Reynolds*, 2nd edn (London, 1818), vol. I, p. 44. For Turner see Charles Robert Leslie, *Autobiographical Recollections* (London, 1860), vol. I, p. 207.

153 John Cash in *The British Home of To-Day*, ed. Walter Shaw Sparrow (London, 1904), p. GVii.

154 Martin Conway, *Art Treasures in Soviet Russia* (London, 1925), p. 35.

Acknowledgements

I am very grateful to David Blayney Brown and Alison Smith for comments on a first draft, and also to the anonymous publisher's reader, whose report was so encouraging and full of constructive criticism. Thanks too to Joanna Banham, Elizabeth Crawford, Margaret Macdonald and Holly Trusted for help with specific enquiries, and to the staff at the museums and archives from which the illustrations were sourced. A special thanks to Martha Tromans for the diagram of picture hangs.

Photo Acknowledgements

The author and publishers wish to thank the organizations and individuals listed below for authorizing reproduction of their work.

Mary Ann Beinecke Decorative Art Collection, Sterling and Francine Clark Art Institute Library, Massachusetts: 1; The British Library, London: 3, 5, 11, 17, 20, 21, 22, 30, 40, 46, 49, 50, 58, 60, 63, 64, 70, 71; The British Museum, London: 29, 69; Cartwright Hall, Bradford/Bridgeman Images: 51; Cheadle Civic Society, Greater Manchester: 39; Cheltenham Borough Council and The Cheltenham Trust: 48, 77 (photo © Jake and Dinos Chapman. All Rights Reserved, DACS/Artimage 2022); Columbia University Libraries, New York: 32; © F.L.C./ADAGP, Paris and DACS, London 2022: 52; Richard Fox collection: 76; © Garden City Collection (Letchworth Garden City Heritage Foundation): 42; © the copyright holder. Photo courtesy: Grundy Art Gallery, Blackpool: 57; Harold B. Lee Library, Brigham Young University, Utah: 7; Harvard Art Museums/ Fogg Museum, Gift of William Gray from the collection of Francis Calley Gray, © President and Fellows of Harvard College: 15; Alfred E. Henson/*Country Life* Picture Library: 68; Historic England Archive: 34, 36, 37, 38, 41, 43, 53, 54, 55, 56, 61, 66, 72, 73, 75; The Hospitalfield Trust, Arbroath: 16; Howard League for Penal Reform Archive, Modern Records Centre, University of Warwick: 65; © Leeds Museums and Galleries/Bridgeman Images: 26; Library of Congress, Washington, DC: 47; Maidstone Museum and Art Gallery/Bridgeman Images: 13; National Gallery of Ireland: 2; © National Portrait Gallery, London: 12, 27, 31, 67; © National Trust: 33, 59; Private Collection: 52; Rare Book & Manuscript Library, University of Illinois at Urbana-Champaign: 62; RIBA Collections, London: 9, 35, 44, 45; Rijksmuseum, Amsterdam: 14; Royal Collection Trust/© Her Majesty Queen Elizabeth II 2022: 74; Tate, London: 6, 24, 28; Tullie House Museum & Art Gallery, Carlisle/Bridgeman Images: 19; Victoria & Albert Museum,

London: 4, 18; Walker Art Gallery, National Museums Liverpool/Bridgeman Images: 10; The Wellcome Collection, London: 23; World History Archive/Alamy Stock Photo: 8; Yale Center for British Art, Paul Mellon Collection, Connecticut: 25.

Drawings by Martha Tromans: pp. 132–4.

Index

Illustration numbers are indicated in *italics*.